W9-AQV-978

LEADERSHIP
IS
OVERRATED

HOW THE NAVY SEALs
(and Successful Businesses)
CREATE SELF-LEADING
TEAMS THAT WIN

CHRIS MEFFORD AND KYLE BUCKETT

HarperOne
An Imprint of HarperCollins*Publishers*

LEADERSHIP IS OVERRATED. Copyright © 2023 by Culture Force. All rights reserved. Printed in the United States of America. No part of this book may be used or reproduced in any manner whatsoever without written permission except in the case of brief quotations embodied in critical articles and reviews. For information, address HarperCollins Publishers, 195 Broadway, New York, NY 10007.

HarperCollins books may be purchased for educational, business, or sales promotional use. For information, please email the Special Markets Department at SPsales@harpercollins.com.

FIRST EDITION

Library of Congress Cataloging-in-Publication Data has been applied for.

ISBN 978-0-06-320990-9

23 24 25 26 27 LBC 5 4 3 2 1

CHRIS

To my amazing wife, Mindy. Through every page of this book and every chapter of our lives, you have been my constant companion and biggest supporter.

KYLE

To my amazing wife, Candice. You have always been my greatest source of inspiration and support. Your love, patience, and encouragement have made all the difference. Thank you for always being there for me.

CHRIS AND KYLE

To all those who have struggled with leadership and have doubted themselves yet risen above their doubts. We honor your struggles and efforts, and we hope this book will serve as a source of inspiration and guidance on your leadership journey.

Authors' Note

———

This is a coauthored book. We have pulled together our backgrounds in both corporate America and the Navy SEALs, coupling those experiences with stories from around the world and throughout history—all with the intention of helping organizations build and sustain teams that win.

Some of these anecdotes and case studies come directly from our consulting and coaching work as part of the organization we founded, Culture Force. Culture Force helps organizations create a positive and engaging workplace culture by providing expert guidance, tools, and resources so that leaders can build self-led teams (which is a term we will unpack shortly). We do this by empowering companies to attract and retain top talent, increase productivity, and foster innovation through workplace cultures employees love. With a comprehensive and counterintuitive approach to leadership development, businesses are able to cultivate cohesive and supportive environments where team members feel valued, respected, and motivated to achieve their best work. Our solutions are tailored to the unique needs of each organization, and we work closely with clients to ensure they see measurable results and a positive impact on the bottom line. You can learn more about our work at cultureforce.team, but that's where we're coming from.

The stories and examples in this book are a mix of personal experiences in our own lives; recollections from friends, peers, and guests of our podcast; and accounts from books we've read and research we've done over the years. Because we thought it would be confusing to jump back and forth between voices, and given the collaborative subject matter, it seemed most appropriate to write the book in the first person, plural—that is, to use "we" and "us" instead of "I" and "me." In other words, whenever one of us had an insight or observation to share, we chose to present it from the both of us. The exception to that rule is when we tell a story about one of us, in which case we put it in the third person to avoid confusion. For example, when we tell a story about Kyle, we say "Kyle" instead of "we."

We hope this is the clearest way to get our message across to you. The fact of the matter is that this book, like most significant projects, took a whole team to create, and it would be dishonest for either of us to take more than our fair share of credit. This really is a book written by and for all of us. We hope you enjoy it.

—*Chris Mefford and Kyle Buckett*

Contents

——

Introduction

—

LEADERSHIP IS OVERRATED

How did a group of nineteenth-century explorers survive a deadly winter in Antarctica on a ship trapped in ice, with no working instruments to guide them and in a sunless environment that turned men mad? It might have had something to do with the penguins.

In 1896, the Belgian naval officer Adrien Victor Joseph de Gerlache de Gomery bought a whaling ship from Norway called the *Patria*. He renamed it the *Belgica* and set sail for Antarctica the following year on the first scientific mission to explore the continent.[*]

Carrying a crew of scientists and officers from Norway, Romania, and Poland, the *Belgica* set sail from Antwerp in August 1897. On board were more than twenty men, including the Norwegian Roald Amundsen, who would later lead the first successful expedition to the South Pole. On the way to Antarctica, the *Belgica* stopped in Rio de Janeiro, where the crew was joined by Frederick Cook, an American who be-

---

[*] Sancton, *Madhouse at the End of the Earth*.

came the ship's doctor and would later lead an expedition to the North Pole. Both he and Amundsen would keep detailed journals of the trip, making notes and observations to be used for future adventures.

The group was far from prepared for what was to come. Many of the men lacked basic seamanship skills, and others did not possess the discipline necessary to survive such a harrowing journey. Some quit, others were dismissed, and those who remained were not any better off.

In January 1898, the crew reached the coast of the Antarctic Peninsula, the northernmost part of Antarctica; over the next month, they sailed through a string of islands, charting and naming several of them, then crossing the Antarctic Circle in February.

By March, the ship had gotten trapped in the ice of the Bellingshausen Sea. Despite the crew's attempts to break free, they soon realized their predicament would not be easily overcome. Cook wrote: "We are imprisoned in an endless sea of ice. . . . We have told all the tales, real and imaginative, to which we are equal. Time weighs heavily upon us as the darkness slowly advances."*

In May, the sun set, and it did not rise for months. The crew, deprived of sunlight and enough winter clothing for every man on board, grew sick and demoralized. There was not enough food, so they hunted to stay alive. In spite of the only doctor on board—Cook—recommending a diet of high protein (which included raw penguin and seal meat) to avoid the effects of scurvy, the ship's commander forbade the diet because he didn't like the strange taste of the meat. Both he and the captain grew so sick that they wrote their wills and confined themselves to bed, expecting to die. Some men did die; others became deathly ill or went insane. The crew was filled with despair, and death loomed over the darkened horizon of each day.

In June, Émile Danco, a Belgian geophysicist, died of a previously existing heart condition worsened by the lack of proper food and the extreme conditions. The Polish geologist Henryk Arctowski, who was also on board, wrote of his burial, "In the obscurity of the midday twilight we carried Lieutenant Danco's body to a hole which had been cut in the ice,

---

* Cook, *Through the First Antarctic Night*, 231.

and committed it to the deep. A bitter wind was blowing as, with bared heads, each of us silent, we left him there. . . . And the floe drifted on."*

With both commander and captain now ill, the first mate, Amundsen, and the ship's doctor, Cook, took charge and ordered the men to eat high rations of the stored penguin and seal meat. Soon the crew members were eating seven meals per day, which restored them to relatively good health, improving their mental faculties and physical strength. As the men improved, Cook encouraged them to sit in front of the fire each night and play card games, gambling with imaginary sums of money. This helped the crew focus on something other than the imminence of their own extinction, and soon they drummed up enough courage and motivation to break out of their ice tomb.

After a series of experiments based on ideas from various crewmates and officers, they used a combination of saws, explosives, and pure luck to break through the ice. It took the ship a month to get out. This effort was directed by Cook with the help of Amundsen and the rest of the crewmates who were still healthy. Commander de Gerlache eventually was converted to the diet of raw meat and was slowly nursed back to health, as was the captain, Georges Lecointe. By this time, they had joined the other two men now in command of the ship; together, the foursome led the crew out of the icy quagmire.

When the *Belgica* returned to Antwerp in November 1899, de Gerlache was praised and awarded high honors, the mission considered a success. They had spent thirteen months trapped in ice, their crew nearly perished, and the man who became so sick he could no longer lead his poorly prepared crew was made a hero.

The Old Guard Is Gone

This is a familiar story, like many we are told when it comes to accounts of heroism and bold action. It is a tale that makes for great movies and

---

* Cool Antarctica, "Adrien de Gerlache—Belgica Belgian Antarctic Expedition 1897–1899."

inspiring feats of bravery, the sort of thing old men tell their grandchildren. It is the kind of leadership and courage men and women hope to expect of themselves in the worst of circumstances.

And it is a complete lie.

What saved the *Belgica* during its two-year voyage to the end of the earth and back was not one man put in charge of a crew of unruly explorers, scientists, and seafarers. It wasn't even just the copious amounts of penguin meat they consumed. It was, in fact, leadership, but not the kind we are taught about in business school or Scouts. What allowed these men to succeed was not the efforts of a single leader but the will of an entire team. In spite of being ill prepared and poorly led, a group of inexperienced explorers found it in themselves to step up, take control while lacking any real authority, and save the mission. They led themselves to victory.

In this book, we make a simple argument: small but dedicated teams of empowered individuals can and do outperform large organizations driven by top-down leadership. We share this from our unique perspectives in both the Navy SEALs and corporate America, trading stories and opportunities to offer our unique views on this important topic. None of this is news, of course, as many entrenched in the world of organizational development have known this fact for years. Human beings have always organized themselves into bands of families, tribes, and teams that allow them to move through the world more efficiently and effectively. Leadership, in a sense, has always been a bit overblown in our view, as it has always taken a group to make any success possible. With the rise of the factory system over the past two hundred years, however, we've especially lost what makes each of us extraordinary, exchanging the cumulative contributions of individuals for conformity to the masses. It's time for a change, to step up and reclaim our right to lead from within. What makes organizations great—truly great and not temporarily successful—is not a single leader but a culture of self-leadership. Thirty years of organizational research demonstrates that the more autonomy individuals have, the greater a group's capacity for output. When done right, a self-led team will always be superior to the antiquated methods of a hierarchical organization.

If we want to do more in the world, we must change the culture of our organizations. More and more, we see all kinds of change happening in the world that supports this argument. Technology and communication have made the top-down approach to running just about any organization nearly obsolete. With the rise of automation, artificial intelligence, and other advancements, the obsolescence of one person bossing everyone around will be a reality in our lifetime. Leadership, as we've conventionally understood it, is overrated and failing us entirely. The way forward will require a completely different approach to organizational development and management than we've ever known.

Of course, old habits die hard. Conventional patterns for leadership live on in our culture and in our history books, so it's hard to conceive of a radical transformation in how organizations are structured, including the one you may be in right now. Changing the culture of a team, an organization, or even an entire nation sounds daunting; but as we will soon see, this sort of change is happening around us every day. Cultures can and do change quickly, especially when it's a matter of life and death. And for some of us, it actually is—at least when it comes to the survival of our organization.

The Rise of Self-Led Teams

In 2011, British bookseller Waterstones faced a number of significant challenges when James Daunt took over as CEO. One of the biggest was the rise of online retailers, which had clearly made it difficult for brick-and-mortar bookstores to compete with online juggernauts such as Amazon. In response to this increasing business threat, Daunt implemented a strategy that focused on creating a personalized, exceptional customer experience at the local level. Instead of trying to compete with a larger company, the retailer leveraged its smallness.

Part of this strategy involved empowering local store managers to make decisions and feel that they were running independent businesses. Staff were encouraged to speak with customers, ask about their reading preferences, and make recommendations. Team members didn't have to consult some list on a computer screen; they were free to work independently and without corporate bureaucracy, an approach that helped

Waterstones build trust with customers and gave its staff a sense of ownership of their work.

Unlike the officers of the *Belgica*, the leadership of Waterstones listened to the company's managers and made conscious efforts to hire employees who were passionate about books and could demonstrate their knowledge and understanding of them. This helped the company maintain its reputation as a destination for booklovers and set it apart from online retailers, which carried the same inventory but lacked that level of expertise and personalization.

This strategy has been successful in helping Waterstones stand out in a competitive retail market and create an unparalleled customer experience in the United Kingdom. "Staff are now in control of their own shops," Daunt explained. "Hopefully they're enjoying their work more. They're creating something very different in each store."* The success of this somewhat unconventional approach was evident in the almost zero returns collected—a remarkable 97 percent of books placed on the shelves were purchased by customers during this campaign. This is an unbelievable achievement in an industry in which most bookstores buy their product on consignment, assuming they'll be returning a good portion of the books that don't sell. When top-down leadership pivots from what we call a "command-and-control" approach to a more self-led one, anything is possible. As teams learn to lead themselves, they can move more nimbly, accomplishing far more than anyone ever considered or expected.

And just exactly what happened to Waterstones's CEO, James Daunt? Not surprisingly, he was hired by Barnes & Noble in 2019 to step in as CEO. And what was the first thing he did to turn around an even larger company struggling with the same industrywide challenges? He went small, focusing on the local level and empowering teams to make the necessary decisions to help stores thrive. James Daunt's superpower is that he wants teams and stores to lead themselves. Again, this is a far cry from what we think of as the traditional approach of a command-and-control leader, which may be just why it worked.

---

* Eyre, "James Daunt."

Much to the surprise of many, Barnes & Noble experienced a resurgence in book sales in spite of their many attempts to chase one fad after another—all to utter failure. In 2021, B&N's sales returned to pre-pandemic levels and continue to increase, a change due in part to customers regaining trust in the company and increased motivation among store employees, who began acting like true booksellers and not mere employees. At a time when many retailers were closing down storefronts or experimenting with one sales gimmick after another, Barnes & Noble ditched the tchotchkes and went back to the basics: books. In 2022, the company opened sixteen new stores and, at the time of this writing, is on track to double that number in 2023. Despite the decline of digital platforms, a 136-year-old print media provider is somehow, surprisingly, thriving.

All, allegedly, thanks to one man. How, exactly, did he do it? He didn't. Instead, Daunt listened to and trusted his teams, empowering them to make the right choices that allowed them to succeed. He treated his employees as the core component to a companywide turnaround plan, and it worked. Of course it worked. He did what the leaders of the *Belgica* lacked the courage, empathy, and humility to do. Daunt respected his teammates, trusting they knew how to steer the "ship" better than he ever could from his corporate ivory tower. He listened to his employees, treating them more as partners than subordinates, setting them up to win and getting out of their way so they could get to work.

This is what every leader must do if he or she wants to survive the next evolution of leadership. Self-led teams can turn around any organization, or any ship, for that matter, even when it seems that all hope is lost.

What Really Saved the *Belgica*

The culture of self-leadership that was formed during those dark days on the *Belgica* became instrumental during what was later known as the Heroic Age of Antarctic Exploration. Out of necessity, the crewmates became what we call a self-led team—a truly independent group of individuals who are each empowered to act with full authority and autonomy to carry out the mission. Granted, this was not a formal shift in organizational structure; it was a matter of survival. They *had* to step up—their leaders were lying in bed, waiting to die.

What saved those men was not a captain or commander or even a doctor but their own ability to come together during a difficult time, strengthen themselves as a unit, and achieve the seemingly impossible. The discipline they learned, the activities they used to boost morale, and the necessary but unpleasant diet they adopted were all essential factors in their survival.

Thirteen years later, Roald Amundsen would lead his own expedition and safely return from the first successful mission to the South Pole. His competitor, Robert Falcon Scott, would attempt the same feat at the same time and not return. Often, such contrasts are meant to prize the efforts of one man over another's, but that's not the whole story. Certainly, individual skill can be a factor in extraordinary success, but Amundsen was not alone in the Antarctic wilderness. What allowed his team to succeed when others just as daring failed was what he had learned on the *Belgica* and during subsequent voyages, all of which prepared him for his ultimate challenge. He didn't do it alone. He couldn't have.

The same diet of penguin and seal meat Amundsen learned about from Cook became instrumental in his own mission more than a decade later. He and his crew wore Inuit-style fur clothing when it was considered unfashionable and savage to do so (not to mention hard to come by and expensive). In contrast to the other team of explorers, who traveled using horses, Amundsen's crew used dogs to pull sleds, something he had learned from his previous journeys to the coldest places on Earth.[*†] When it came time to eat, Amundsen's men disciplined themselves in eating incredible amounts of meat and would occasionally kill sled dogs to get enough protein. He had seen the alternative, and it wasn't pleasant.

These were not strategies devised by a lone genius; they were, in fact, proven tactics learned in the company of other men. They were

---

[*] Sancton, *Madhouse at the End of the Earth.*
[†] Ferguson, "The Secret of How Amundsen Beat Scott in Race to South Pole?"

cultural norms from previous organizations, you could say, borrowed and applied to a new team of intrepid explorers. Amundsen had been on a team in which the leadership had failed and the rest of the crewmates were forced to rely on one another. He knew what it took because he had been to hell and back, and he wasn't going to relive such horror again, if he could help it.

The *Belgica* team faced intense volatility, uncertainty, complexity, and ambiguity—the same factors describing our global business landscape today. Because of the speed of innovation and the ever-changing nature of today's technology, organizational models that once were the modi operandi are now being rebuilt from the ground up. In short, the old ways don't work anymore. The former organizational mold—a pyramidal structure with one person at the top with all the authority—is no longer tenable. The command-and-control model of leadership is defunct, replaced by networks of small teams that communicate with one another to carry out a clear mission.

We will spend the rest of this book explaining how such teams operate and what it takes to create one. To be sure, the old days are not entirely gone, but they are fading fast. According to one Deloitte study, only 38 percent of all companies are "functionally organized."* That is, individuals with a certain skill are placed in departments focused on a particular function of an organization (e.g., marketing, accounting). The other 62 percent are organizing themselves around product- and customer-centric cultures. The future of teams is here, and it doesn't look like the factory your grandfather retired from. "Hierarchical organizational models aren't just being turned upside down," wrote the authors of the study. "They're being deconstructed from the inside out. Businesses are reinventing themselves to operate as networks of teams to keep pace with the challenges of a fluid, unpredictable world."†

The same kind of culture that saved a group of men on the brink of destruction and cemented their names in the history books can save your organization, too. History maximizes the importance of heroes

---

* McDowell et al., "Organizational Design."
† McDowell et al., "Organizational Design."

but minimizes the significance of teams. We want to reverse that. In the work we've done over the years—in small and large businesses, the nonprofit sector, and government organizations such as the Navy—we've seen what it takes to create cultures that win. In this book, we want to share with you what we've learned: from the organizations we've encountered and coached as well as the world-class companies and outfits we've been a part of.

Of course, it's not just any team that can drive a group of dying men to dig their way out of miles of ice, overcoming the unlikely odds stacked against them. What makes a winning unit is adopting the power of self-leadership. We will demonstrate that this is prevalent not only in the world of polar exploration but is also found in successful sports franchises, industry-leading tech companies, and elite military outfits. Nimble teams of skilled individuals can accomplish far more than organizational behemoths driven by a single, dominating figure.

It's not that leadership doesn't matter, of course. It certainly does. It's just that it's highly overrated. And once we understand that, change is not only possible; it becomes inevitable.

Who This Book Is For

It's no surprise that many people are disenchanted with their bosses and careers these days. It's no secret that poor leadership can lead to disengaged team members and even leaders themselves, which can significantly impact a company's bottom line, and not for the better. Billions of dollars are lost each year as a result of a workforce that's become indifferent about its work and fatalistic regarding the outcome.

We need a change in the way we organize organizations.

The problem is not just the leaders. It's how we've come to think of leaders and the teams that follow them. In a sense, we are all to blame for creating this modern monster we call command-and-control leadership, which runs rampant in most organizations. And if we all have had a part to play in creating this mess, we all must accept our roles in fixing it.

If you're tired of the same old books about leadership that offer the same old advice about stepping up, leaning in, or adopting the latest twelve tricks to help you stand out, this book is for you. We have taken a hard look at the leadership industry, exposing its flaws and offering a new perspective on what it really takes to build a team that succeeds and wins in a post-pandemic twenty-first-century world.

Pulling from our own experiences, insights, and research, we address the very real and significant financial cost, human cost, and cost of lost opportunities—for both individuals and companies—caused by a leadership culture that is broken and laughably overrated. If you're ready to shake things up, make a real difference, and transform your life, career, and organization, it's time to change everything—starting with how much control we give the leader.

1
—

KILL THE LEADER

Kyle and Muskrat hustled up the rocky hill, looking for the right position to see what was going down in the village below. The four-by-seven-mile stretch of land in the middle of southern Afghanistan was crawling with Taliban, and the unit's job was to eradicate them.

The team of Marines came to a tiny clearing and stopped. Kyle was the Navy SEAL in charge that day. As he looked through the scope of his rifle, he spotted the Marines below and also saw that the enemy had found the Marines' location first and was making a move on them. Things were happening fast, and the men were about to be blindsided.

Muskrat was Kyle's JTAC (Joint Terminal Attack Controller), the SEAL who directs the air forces should a team need support, and boy, did they need support—and fast. While Muskrat was working his dials and setting coordinates, Kyle talked him through what he was seeing. Then there was a sudden silence. Kyle felt a sharp elbow nudging his arm and looked at his partner to see Muskrat looking back at him with the most solemn face he had ever seen.

"What's up?" he whispered.

Muskrat pointed to their feet.

Kyle looked down and saw two wires coming out of the ground and going back in. It was unmistakable: they were standing on an improvised explosive device (IED). Kyle looked at his compatriot, who stared back at him, both men silent. Muskrat didn't need to tell Kyle what he was thinking. The same thing was going through Kyle's head. Both men had been in many fights, running and gunning and shooting their way out of all kinds of situations. Cheating death was a part of what they did; but now, as they stood as still as two statues on top of a makeshift bomb, facing the likelihood of their own mortality, death made no sense.

"Like this?" Kyle thought. "After all we've been through, we're going down like this?"

Time was running out. Kyle was responsible for the Marines below, and the enemy was quickly closing in. The Explosive Ordnance Disposal (EOD) unit was hours away, and Kyle and Muskrat had been exposed on the hill for too long. By this point, they had probably been spotted, and it would be only a matter of seconds before they were taken out by a rocket-propelled grenade or PKM machine gun.

Kyle looked down as the seconds ticked by. He sent his team member away while he kept his weight on the IED, preventing it from exploding, and tried to figure out what to do next. At that moment, though, he stopped thinking about the mission. He stopped thinking about the team, too. He even stopped thinking about all the decisions, good and bad, he had made leading up to this one, which would likely cost him his life. All he thought about, as any father and husband would, was his family.

Kyle knew his men would be all right. Muskrat would be fine. The Marines would be okay, too. Air support was on its way now, and they'd all be able to go on, a little sad for losing their leader, but they'd make it. Mourning the loss of their friend and fellow soldier, they'd certainly miss him—but they'd live to fight another day. In a way, they'd been expecting it. They had trained for this moment many, many times.

Becoming Dispensable

The second phase of a Navy SEAL predeployment workup is called Unit Level Training (ULT). ULT is a six-month block run by the respective group training detachments in which the SEAL troop trains in its core mission area skills: small-unit tactics, land warfare, close quarters combat, urban warfare, hostile maritime interdiction, combat swimming, long-range target interdiction, rotary and fixed wing air operations, special reconnaissance, and much more.

In 2015, Kyle was in charge of close quarters combat and urban warfare for the West Coast SEAL Teams of the United States. These two blocks of training are the pinnacle of ULT. During this training, the team routinely "killed the leader" to ensure the platoon could complete the mission. The exercise was simple. The training staff would intentionally remove the leader from whatever training they were doing as a way of simulating what might happen should he actually die while on mission.

Success as a Navy SEAL means recognizing that you're not the solution to every problem. The whole team must be prepared to handle whatever obstacle it may face. Of course, every soldier has a role to play, but no single SEAL is indispensable. Because Kyle spent twenty years serving as a SEAL, we will rely heavily in this book on the stories of self-leadership in the Navy SEALs, but these principles can have just as great an impact in your organization as they have had on the front lines of combat.

What the teams learned from this training exercise was clear and unforgettable. If the mission failed after the leader was removed, the team was not adequately trained. The same is true in just about any organization. To create long-term success with any team, leadership must be disposable. It's not that we don't need leaders, but the team should never be too dependent on a single person. In the case of the Navy SEALs, this is a matter of life or death. However, it is just as serious in other environments, albeit with different consequences.

"Killing the leader" is an important training exercise designed to see what would happen if the leader of a platoon does, in fact, meet his end, but it's a useful thought exercise for any team. What happens in your organization when the CEO takes a break, when the person in charge goes on vacation? What does everyone else do when the boss leaves the room? Does the team thrive? Or does work suffer, grinding to a halt until another charismatic person steps up?

It is, in fact, possible to build a team that is not quite so vulnerable. Following the example of the Navy SEALs and other extraordinary organizations, we can create cultures that allow individuals to thrive and teams that come together to accomplish any goal, even when the leader steps down or is removed. We call this type of team "self-led" because of the way it is uniquely organized and assembled. In the rest of this book, we will explore how such a team is made and maintained in any organization. But it begins with what we do with leadership itself.

Every organization has to learn to "kill" its leader before it's too late. If a company cannot flourish after the retirement of its founder, if a team cannot pick up the slack when the boss is sick, then the organization is vulnerable to all kinds of trouble. What we learn from combat is that if you are weak, eventually something stronger will come to take you out.

Weakened teams are often the result of a leader who doesn't know how to step down, as well as a team that hasn't been trained to step up in his or her absence. A good leader is constantly readying his team for the day when someone else can take over. A manager who is fearful of being replaced, who is scared of losing control, is not a leader but a tyrant. And that's the kind of leader who deserves to be "killed."

Kyle didn't die that day in the hills of Afghanistan. The operation was a success. And even though the leader made it out of that situation alive, he didn't have to. The team had trained for his departure many times; it would have been able to go on without him.

This book is full of such stories of men and women who didn't wait for the boss to tell them what to do. These teams were prepared to lose their leader at any moment, precisely because they had trained for it again and again. Self-led teams create innovative organizational structures and world-class cultures that allow both individuals and groups to flourish. These kinds of environments are becoming increasingly popular and attractive. They are no less than the future of business, and we would all do well to understand how they work.

We Don't Quit Our Jobs; We Quit Our Bosses

It was a hot summer day and Chris was sitting in his office, overwhelmed with the work he had to do. He was feeling buried by the onslaught of tasks and projects that never seemed to end, learning and doing at the same time. Worried he wouldn't be able to keep up, he was having a hard time focusing on anything other than the workload that day. As he sat there, feeling sorry for himself, he heard a faint knock on the door. It was his assistant, Karen.

"Hey boss, can I come in?" she said gently, poking her head into the room.

"Sure," Chris said, trying to sound chipper while letting out an inadvertent sigh. "What's up?"

Karen walked in and sat down across from her boss. She looked at him with a serious expression and said, "I'm sorry to do this to you, but I've decided to quit."

Chris was taken aback. Karen had been with him for years. He'd relied on her to keep things running smoothly. "Why?" he asked, not hiding his shock, already feeling a pang of guilt.

She looked at him with what appeared to be a mixture of pity and frustration. "Well, you've been so disengaged lately," she said. "You're always in your own world, and you're not paying attention to what's going on around you. I feel like I'm just a cog in the machine, and it's not fulfilling or rewarding to work here anymore."

She was right. Chris *had* been focused on his own problems so much that he hadn't been paying attention to the needs of his team. He'd stopped asking how others were doing, stopped checking in on team members, stopped demonstrating any real care or concern for anyone but himself. Of course, he had his reasons; we all do every time we become oblivious to the needs of others. But that doesn't make our ignorance of others any less distressing for those who rely on us.

Having been so caught up in his own drama, Chris had missed the early warning signs of a disengaged team member—until it was too late. Karen did end up leaving, and there wasn't anything Chris could have done to stop her. Not at that point. Nonetheless, he learned a valuable lesson that day: His assistant didn't tell him the job was the problem. She said it was her boss. And that tells us everything we need to know.

Most people don't quit their jobs. They quit their bosses.

Ask any person stuck in a dead-end job and the first complaint they raise will usually be about the person they work for. Their supervisor is not nice enough or doesn't pay close enough attention to others. Or maybe she is a control freak. Perhaps the whole executive team just comes off as being stupid, oblivious, or downright rude. Whatever the issue, the real problem with most jobs is far more often not the work itself but the person one works for.

Surveys and anecdotes indicate that the reason people most often cite for leaving a place of work is the manager they report to. Managers, in many ways, shape the work experience of their subordinates, leading them to feel empowered and engaged in their jobs or, more often, frustrated and disillusioned.

According to a 2021 Gallup poll, only 20 percent of the world's one billion full-time workers are engaged in the work they do. This is a study that has been going on for years, and sadly, the numbers don't seem to be getting any better. Roughly 80 percent of the world's workers are in some way frustrated with or uninterested in their jobs, and often, it's the boss who's to blame.

This is not just a soft skills concern. It's costing us more than mere morale. A lack of engagement leads to a lack of productivity, which implies a disastrous impact on the bottom line of every single company that doesn't strive to make its place of work more compelling. In the United States, we lose somewhere between $483 billion and $605 billion in productivity every single year as a result of this lack of engagement. The global number is even harder to conceive: $8.1 trillion in potential revenue is lost every single year because of a lack of engagement.*

Imagine what would happen if we improved this number, if only incrementally. What would the impact of a mere 10 percent increase be? How could such a shift change the bottom line of a company or even an entire industry? What would it change not only for your team but for the world?

Engagement, as defined in most workplace studies, is the emotional commitment an employee has to the organization and its goals. When team members are engaged, they don't work just for a paycheck or the next promotion but on behalf of the organization's goals. They're all in.

When employees care, when they are truly engaged, they use discretionary effort: they stay late, work harder, give more. They do this not because they have to but because they want to. Such commitment is im-

---

* Pendell, "The World's $7.8 Trillion Workplace Problem."

possible to fake or force. You have to nurture it, grow it, and care for it. It can be more difficult than it sounds, but it's not impossible.

The Bad Boss Dilemma

Mia Robinson—not her real name—knows what it's like to have company commitment forced upon her. An Amazon delivery driver in Edwardsville, Illinois, she was told one holiday season that she'd better keep delivering packages despite the tornado warnings swirling in the area. "Just keep driving," her supervisor told her when she texted her concern. "We can't just call people back for a warning unless Amazon tells us to."[*]

Trying to make an impossible choice between her own safety and her boss's orders, Mia texted again, saying that there was no place for her to find shelter where she was and that inside of thirty minutes, she'd be engulfed by the storm. She wanted permission to return to the Amazon warehouse for shelter.

"If you decide to come back, that choice is yours," the supervisor responded. "But I can tell you it won't be viewed as for your own safety. The safest practice is to stay exactly where you are. If you decide to return with your packages, it will be viewed as you refusing your route, which will ultimately end with you not having a job come tomorrow morning."[†]

Moments later, he changed his mind when a tornado hit the warehouse.

The biggest obstacle to employee engagement, more often than not, is the boss. Bad bosses are what keep individuals from feeling a part of the team. We all know this; it's no surprise to anyone. In most organizations, we see far-from-competent individuals somehow applying their skills in such a way so as to not get fired, inevitably making their way up the corporate ladder of success only to settle into a place of mediocrity. At best, they become uninspiring managers of the status quo. At worst, they become intolerably cruel tyrants. Most bosses are somewhere in between these two extremes. What are we doing to fix this problem?

---

[*] Duffy, "Amazon Driver Told She Would Be Fired."
[†] Duffy, "Amazon Driver Told She Would Be Fired."

We invest in bosses. We send them to leadership retreats and encourage them to read business books. We ask them to become better so that their teams can improve.

But this is all wrong. You don't fix an organization by fixing the leader. You begin by addressing the form of leadership itself. Despite incredible amounts of money spent on leadership development every single year, most people still don't like their jobs very much. It's not that they despise the companies they work for. Far more often, the culprit responsible for disengagement by most workers is a manager or leader or some small set of authority figures toward the top of the organization. It only makes sense that we would try to fix these individuals; it's the efficient and economical thing to do. Unfortunately, it doesn't seem to be working.

With billions being spent on books, conferences, webinars, trainings, and talks to turn average managers into marginally better leaders, why are so many of us still so frustrated with our work? With immeasurable tools at our disposal, shouldn't we have, as leadership strategist Ron Thomas wrote, "employee engagement at record levels, turnover at an all-time low, and the innovation pipeline brimming to capacity"?* Yet we don't. We must ask ourselves, then, what do we get for all this money being spent on building "better" leaders? What do we get for all this time spent studying leadership? If the purpose of this exorbitant investment in leadership training is to effect change, the answer is *not much*. Something has to change, and it's not a simple tweak of who to report to.

Reddit has more than two million followers for its subreddit called "antiwork." The social media posts we share about how team members are unappreciated by their bosses regularly get the most likes and comments. Everyone knows this is a problem—everyone, it seems, but those who stand to benefit from not admitting what's wrong. Leadership experts are paid not for the success of their trainings but rather for how many books, conferences, and coaching sessions they are able to sell. They're selling information, not solutions, and to change the way our organizations are run, we are going to need something better. We can't just change the leaders. We have to transform leadership itself.

---

* Thomas, "$24 Billion Worth of Leadership Training and What Do We Get?"

Leadership Is a Class Structure Gone Bad

It's easy to blame the person at the top. Everyone wants to take shots at authority figures, so why pay attention to such complaints? Leadership development has typically focused on making the individual, not the team as a whole, better. All the training, educating, and seminaring we've done has led to an abundance of autocratic individuals who see themselves as saviors. They didn't do this by themselves; we helped. Under the old model, the team exists, at least in the leader's mind, to help the boss get ahead, to increase production, maximize profit, and make the leader look better.

Jim Clifton, chairman and CEO of Gallup and author of *The Coming Jobs War*, wrote, "What the whole world wants is a good job, and we are failing to deliver it . . . This means human development is failing, too. Most [individuals] are coming to work with great enthusiasm, but the old management practices—forms, gaps, and annual reviews—grind the life out of them."* Management styles, which have changed very little since the late 1700s, are due to evolve with the changing face of business. The world of work is changing fast, and management needs to follow.

A true leader goes beyond mere titles and does more than fulfill a role. Leadership is a responsibility shared by everyone that involves working with the right people to identify their strengths and help develop them for the organization's betterment. Doing this job well takes emotional capital, which is one reason why many bosses are so bad at it.

Telling people what to do rather than *showing* them what to do takes a lot less effort. And yet the latter is precisely what we need. Sadly, we may not find the answer at the top. It will likely come from the middle or even the bottom. We are experiencing today a crisis of true leadership. Few are willing to stand up to the cultural problem that wants to put a single individual at the forefront of everything. And no amount of advice from bestselling authors and leadership gurus can fix it.

What we are doing is not working. The days of making the leader better to make the team better, which then improves the company, are over. Change will no longer come from just the top. It'll come from you

---

* Clifton, "Why We Hate Our Jobs."

and me, right here and now, wherever we may find ourselves in the hair ball. But first, we have to assess the damage. By training the leader as a superhero type, we have managed to frustrate the entire workforce, the world over, in our quest to improve the workplace. At best, leadership is overrated; at worst, a complete failure.

What even *is* a leader nowadays? It's not someone respected in the workplace. It's not a particularly industrious person who earned their way up the ranks of an organization, whose experience and expertise are highly valued by peers and subordinates alike. In today's work climate, leadership is practically anything anyone wants to say it is, and leaders are anyone with a label, appointed by someone with a fancier label.

With engagement rates in the workplace continuing to plummet over the past two decades and only being exacerbated by the COVID-19 pandemic, the time for change is now. We are dealing with global failure of leadership that has affected the mental, emotional, creative, intellectual, and even physical health of human beings the world over.

It's time to get rid of our old ways of thinking about leaders and leadership. The bad bosses need to go, and the way to replace them is to become something better than that which we have aspired to. The days of the selfish upstarts who charm and manipulate their way to the top are over. Individual success at the cost of the rest of the team is growing obsolete. It's time for us to recognize that what we're doing is not working and to see what it's truly costing us. Change in our organizational structures and system is closer than we think, but the way it happens will be unlike anything we have ever seen before.

If leadership is overrated, then what comes next? In a sense, we have to kill what we've understood a leader to be so that another, better organizational model can emerge. It is no longer leadership that saves a company or defines a movement—it's the culture—and that's something we all can have a hand in creating. If we don't step up and change things, we may be those bad bosses everyone is complaining about. At best, we will have submitted to another autocrat; at worst, we will have become the leaders who ought to be "killed."

2

CHANGE FROM
THE INSIDE OUT

In June 2016, at the pre-quarterfinals for the UEFA European Football Championship, Iceland beat England 2–1, sending shock waves through the international sports community. What was this nation of three hundred thousand Vikings *doing*, standing up to one of the most prestigious teams in the sport? And how did a nation of more than fifty million people that in many ways breeds professional players lose to a country so small and seemingly insignificant?

It wasn't so upsetting that England lost. These things happen on occasion to even the best of teams. But the loss was to a small Nordic island with a relatively tiny population, adverse weather, an amateur league, and a part-time coach who also worked as a dentist. It was the sort of thing movies are made of. Where, exactly, did Iceland come from? What *were* the contributing factors to its victory? And what *was* the secret sauce in a competitive field in which everything is professionalized, from the players to the coaches, product endorsements, and all the resources used to make a world-class team? It just didn't add up.

After England's defeat, journalists from all over the world flocked to the "land of fire and ice" to find out what was going on. What they found was equally shocking. Iceland didn't have any particularly great players, none that attracted international attention as did the "standards" known around the world. Names such as Messi, Ronaldo, and Beckham are known by even the youngest of fans halfway around the globe. What made Iceland great if all the things we typically think of as ingredients for greatness, quite frankly, weren't there? What's more, Iceland has consistently done far greater than expected in every major team sport played at the international level, including football, handball, basketball, and team gymnastics.

Something curious and interesting is happening in the tiny microstate that most experts and enthusiasts never could have anticipated. Even more curious is that in spite of all this, the tiny Nordic island has not excelled in the same manner in individual sports as it has in group sports.

In the words of Vidar Halldorsson, a sociology professor at the University of Iceland who has been studying this subject for some time, "although the Icelandic teams have done exceptionally well in international competitions, they do not necessarily consist of world-class athletes."[*] This is not only surprising, it's upsetting. In a world where single players such as LeBron James and Tom Brady can lead their teams to victory by sheer force of will and tenacity, it is surprising to see a team reach such heights with no knockout all-stars.

To pull a Jerry Seinfeld, what *is* the deal with Iceland? As mentioned, the Icelandic international sports revival has been the subject of much international intrigue and curiosity, and not everyone agrees on what caused it, but the trend is undeniable. Before vanquishing England in 2016, Iceland tied Portugal 1–1 and, in its first-ever appearance, went toe to toe with Argentina in the 2018 World Cup, resulting in another final score of 1–1. Over the course of four years, it went from being ranked 133 (out of 211) to 23—in the world! Iceland went from being in the bottom fiftieth percentile to being ranked in the top 10 percent of all teams on planet Earth.

---

[*] Halldorsson, *Sport in Iceland*, 8.

This isn't supposed to happen—or is it? Certainly, opinions on why and how this has happened abound, but there are some key factors to pay attention to. In his book *Sport in Iceland: How Small Nations Achieve International Success*, Halldorsson listed a number of contributing factors. "A national sporting success, such as Iceland's," he wrote, "is a cultural product."[*] In other words, you could say it's something in the water—or perhaps the ice.

"I grew up in the northern part of Iceland in a town called Akureyri where there [live] about 15,000 people. I played for a club called Thor—like Thor the god," recounted Arnar Arnason, Iceland's former youth national coach, in an interview for Urban Soccer Park. "During that time facilities were not great, we didn't have these indoor facilities or artificial pitches, so football was basically a summer sport, and the summer in Iceland is quite short. So it was playing handball, basketball during the winter—maybe one football session per week. And during the summer it was purely football . . . my favorite hour of the week would always be the football part."[†]

In 1957, however, the national team got its first grass field, which caused an uptick in play of the game. Then, in the 1990s, the Football Association of Iceland went on a trip to Norway, a country with similar climate issues as Iceland, and returned with a plan to build heated pitches both indoors and outdoors, introducing the possibility of year-round playing. And for all we can tell, it worked. Since 2000, Iceland has built seven full-size indoor football halls, twenty outdoor heated fields, and 150 mini-pitches, the latter of which may be the most important.

"These pitches are absolutely vital," Arnason said, "because nobody, in my opinion, becomes a good football player only showing up three times a week to a training session. You have to be able to play football 24/7. When these mini-pitches came, everyone could go out and play football anytime they want."[‡]

There's the rub. Football went from being something Icelanders did

---

[*] Halldorsson, *Sport in Iceland*, 9.

[†] Arnason, interview.

[‡] Arnason, interview.

on the side, if at all, to becoming a national phenomenon played year-round, with small fields outside every school in the country. It became part of their national identity. "The achievements of the Icelandic national teams cannot be understood by looking only at sports in Iceland," wrote Halldorsson. "They have to be understood through an analysis of the general Icelandic culture as well."* Which is to say it took intention, time, and follow-through. Such a change required radical commitment from all major stakeholders, consistent follow-through spanning multiple generations, and the support of an entire country. And so far, it's worked. Because that's how you transform a culture: not from the top down but from the inside out.

All necessary and lasting change in an organization takes place like this. Certainly, leadership has a role; but it is not the be-all and end-all we have understood it to be. The lesson from the surprising break-through of Icelandic soccer is that all those in organizations who want to see change happen and are willing to take responsibility for the piece of the puzzle they may be in charge of—and are courageous enough to bring others along for the ride—just might be able to create the change they seek.

How to Change an Organization

Changing the course of how an entire nation interacts with a single sport is not altogether easy. In the case of Iceland, it took a lot of time, focus, and energy. The small nation has a fraction of resources available to any of its competitors, especially the more populated and historically more experienced European countries it faces. And yet, in the span of a few decades, its team quickly rose to the top of its category. This is how cultural shifts can take place: starting small and building momentum as they go until the result is undeniable.

"It is actually an advantage this is a very small country," said Lars

---

* Halldorsson, *Sport in Iceland*, 19.

Lagerback, the technical director of the Iceland national football team. "You can find things and make them work in a country like that. . . . If you want something to happen you take care of it yourself." One of the things the country has taken care of is offering great coaching to players at a very early age. "Every coach in Iceland gets paid," said Dagur Dagbjartsson, education coordinator for Iceland's national soccer association, KSÍ, "we don't have any amateurs. Every kid who plays pays an annual fee and can go and train with a professional club. My own kid started when he was three."[*]

This is a big change from traditional leadership methods in which a single person makes a massive pronouncement from on high and watches his underlings carry out the orders. To effect long-lasting change that impacts an entire culture, you've got to start from the bottom up and stay the course. Small teams of individuals can move more nimbly and react quickly to changes as they come so long as they are empowered.

So, when we think about changing our own organizations and teams, we have to begin with the smallest unit possible—the individual—and apply those efforts to our teams and organizations. The transformation, whatever it is, has to be baked into the culture at every level. The effects of such cultural shifts can be extraordinary and long-lasting, as has been the case in Iceland.

"Twenty years ago . . . the main characteristics of the archetypical Icelandic player were physical strength and a 'never say die' attitude," noted Arnar Bill Gunnarsson, head of football development at KSÍ. "Those elements still remain very important, but with the facilities and high-level coaching from an early age, we can add technical skills and passing ability. In the past, we would rarely see one generation bringing through a high number of talented players, one like the generation now playing a key role for the national team. A large number of players in the current national team were around the age of 10 when it all started."[†] Once all the pieces start working together, the change you want to create

---

[*] Ronay, "Football, Fire and Ice: The Inside Story of Iceland's Remarkable Rise."
[†] "Arnar Bill Gunnarsson (KSÍ)."

becomes almost inevitable. Big things can and do happen within a relatively short amount of time when effort is paired with commitment. The results then ripple out in dramatic ways, sometimes faster than expected. Change just takes time, focus, and buy-in at every level. This is true for a nation, corporation, and your local Scout troop. The way we transform an entire culture is by rethinking everything we know about leadership and change.

The way forward is to create cultures of autonomous teams. The business of leadership development is broken, and the only way to fix it is to completely throw it out and replace it with a system for developing organizations that is more in tune with the way the world works today. Currently, we spend massive amounts of money each year training leaders, and the problems we experience in our organizations continue.

The average employee is either punching a clock or throwing wrenches into the system of which they are a part. Everyone in the world wants a job they can love that appropriately challenges and rewards them. We are failing to deliver this to ourselves and to one another. The good news is that we know better, and when we know better, we can do better. Traditional leadership development focuses on making the individual great instead of the team as a whole, and everyone suffers as a result. Fortunately, we have a model we can trust, one that offers a glimmer of hope in an otherwise bleak landscape.

What Is Culture?

Imagine you put a tree in a pot and leave it outside. You don't water it, prune it, or make sure it has adequate sunlight. Perhaps, if the environment is just right and it rains enough, it might thrive. But you have done nothing to ensure that. You've essentially left it to chance.

However, if you put that same plant in a greenhouse, where you've taken the time to make sure conditions are perfect, it will thrive and you'll have very little maintenance to do. You can simply place it in an ideal atmosphere and watch it fulfill its purpose. The plant will feed off the environment created by other plants along with the groundwork you laid a long time ago, which will nourish the plant as needed. You haven't left its success to chance; you've done everything possible to ensure its success.

That's culture.

An organization's culture is not merely a mission statement or a plaque on the wall. It's the environment that's been allowed to take shape—yes, by leadership, but by you as well. Even if you aren't the CEO, you have allowed the culture surrounding you to take root if by no other means than the fact that you stayed. You didn't speak up. You didn't quit. You didn't try to change things. And if you did, you didn't follow your words with decisive action and challenge. Otherwise, things would have changed, or you would have left. But if you, like most people, didn't do either, then you are a part of the problem. And there's no shame in that. We all have a part to play in the dysfunction of the organizations of which we are a part. But it's insanity to look outside ourselves for the solution to a problem we helped create. This is no longer acceptable.

We as human beings can no longer abide cultures we find detestable or boring. We can't continue to support mediocrity when we know things could be better. This doesn't mean you can change every culture you are a part of, but you can do something. You can, at the very least, find someplace better. Maybe that's not something you can do today, but don't read this book, put it down, and say, "That's nice." You and everyone around you deserve better, and change begins now, today, with you. With us. With wherever we are and whatever we can do.

A shift in culture requires more than a pep talk or memo. Wherever you may stand in the existing hierarchy, all change begins with awareness. Take a look around. *Notice* things. See what your culture is and try to understand how you got there. Do you see how the status quo is more often created through tolerance than intentionality? Every time we allow something unacceptable to go unaddressed, it sticks around, inevitably embedding itself in the structure of the organization.

Whether the norm is that people come in late or they all contribute to a project, all culture is created through allowance. And before you can change anything, you first have to recognize it. You have a culture. Like it or not, it contains aspects that have sneaked in slowly, over time, unbeknownst to anyone. But at some point, somebody noticed. It may look like the bad habits of a few or the positive habits of many, but your culture is a symptom of a larger ethos that has been allowed to exist. It is the sum of mentalities, habits, and mantras that exist in a single place, whether *you* introduced those ideologies or not.

When people don't shape culture, it takes on a mind of its own. Because no one is framing it, it will stay that way until somebody cares enough to change it. Now you have to decide: Do you change your culture? Do you want to grow with it? Or will you do what most do and simply allow it to be what it is, pretending you have no control at all, waiting to see what happens?

We Don't Need Better Bosses

No one wants to work in a place where they feel undervalued, so what do most organizations do in response? They focus on creating better bosses. They overtrain, overeducate, and overindulge in training for teachers, managers, and executives. And it's not working. Leadership training isn't making teams any stronger; it's not even making leaders better at their jobs. The reason is simple: We don't need better bosses; we need places where people want to be. We need schools and governments and places of work where people want to serve and lead and learn. We need a mission that motivates us to be more than we would be otherwise.

Something is seriously broken in the relationship between most leaders and their teams, and all the money spent on leadership development has not helped. As we've already stated, disengaged leaders and employees cost the United States hundreds of billions of dollars per year, and if you dive deeply into most companies, you'll find managers who are miserable and teams that don't care. This is not what any of us envision when we imagine an ideal work environment. We all want to work with people who are excited and feel empowered to create change without needing the boss's approval. But leadership alone cannot do this. It takes a village, they say, to raise a child, and it takes a team to create a culture.

Creating better culture is not about offering more perks—it's not the company gym, free coffee, or laundry service that makes a team world-class. We don't need better bosses to change the world, and you don't have to be Google to be a great organization. The ultimate goal of leadership is to create an environment that is so attractive that people will never want to leave. We do this by setting a tone in our workspaces that allows extraordinary people the freedom to do what they do best. Culture does that, not leadership.

The Cost of Failure

Success in any organization comes down to finding people who care and empowering as many of them as possible. Systems tend to fall apart or become soulless bureaucracies when a single person gets a little bit of power and refuses to share it.

A great organization is built on people who believe in the mission, want to contribute to the cause, and are allowed to do so. Just ask Jeff Bliss, a high school student in Duncanville, Texas, whose short speech to his teacher went viral on YouTube in 2013. Here's an excerpt of him "schooling" a nonplussed educator who had just delivered yet another packet to him with lackluster enthusiasm.

"You want kids to come into your class? You want them to get excited for this? You gotta come in here and make them excited. You want a kid to change and start doing better? You gotta touch his freakin' heart. Can't expect a kid to change if all you do is just tell 'em."

As the teacher tells the outspoken young student to leave amid his protests, he continues.

"You gotta take this job serious. This is the future of this nation. And when you come in here like you did last time and make a statement about 'Oh, this is my paycheck,' indeed it is . . . but this is my country's future and my education."*

He then stormed off, but of course, a fellow student was filming it and posted it on the internet. It is not enough, even for a high school student, to have someone tell you what to do. Incensed, Bliss advocated for his fellows, pleading with the teacher to get involved in the culture she had created, to make it more than it otherwise would be. And she

---

* "Jeff Bliss, a High School Student, Gives a Lesson to His Teacher at Duncanville."

refused. Why? Because the status quo worked for her, and that is sadly the case for many of us.

The culture we are in, whatever it may be, often works for us. We don't change things because it's easier to go along with the way things are than to try to rock the boat.

In 2020, years after storming out of class and becoming a media sensation, Jeff Bliss was reported (via a Reddit post) to be working for UPS; according to the post, he was a hardworking but quiet employee and didn't like talking about the video.*

Back in 2013, a few months after the video was covered by multiple local and national media outlets, Bliss tweeted a quote from Aristotle: "Educating the mind without educating the heart is no education at all."† It seems that we—all those who are complicit in a system that causes such things to be normal—have failed the Jeff Blisses of the world. We let them and ourselves down every time we allow a simple packet to be delivered to a desk when an eager mind demands to learn.

If you are a leader, you know this already. You know there are aspects to your culture that you don't like, that you have contributed to and even allowed. And for all the off-site retreats you've done and consultants you've hired, for all the seminars you've attended and courses you've invested in, you just can't seem to strategize your way out of some of the problems you're currently facing. And that's because, in the words of Peter Drucker, "Culture eats strategy for breakfast." Hire good people, set expectations, treat them well, empower them, and you will have a great organization.

But this is harder than it sounds.

Everyone in the business world is talking about culture, but few organizations are doing it well. That is, few are changing the way organizations are run. It takes a tremendous amount of commitment, focus, and reinforcement to change the direction of a culture. Culture creation requires a reimagining of our organizations and teams, and when push comes to shove, it often takes a back seat to sales and marketing, product devel-

---

* "What Happened to Jeff Bliss?"
† Gatollari, "Jeff Bliss Went Viral for Telling off a 'Lazy' Teacher."

opment, and growth. We work our people to death, they leave, and we replace them with new cogs in the system.

But this game is running out. CEOs and managers are killing themselves trying to become world-class leaders when their focus should be on creating places people don't want to leave. With a stronger team, there's no need for better bosses. The team can succeed on its own and thrive without much management. It's time to retire leadership and reimagine what organizational innovation actually looks like. It's time to make culture count.

Our Most Important—and Neglected—Resource

The single most precious resource of any organization, regardless of its size or industry, is the talent inside its walls. The success of any company depends on finding remarkably talented people and keeping them. For years, we thought the key to this issue was training leaders to be better, asking them to improve themselves and their tactics, expecting the impact would trickle down to everyone else. It didn't. As a result, our organizations continue to struggle with a disconnection between management and the people they claim to lead. Quite frankly, many businesses just aren't that fun to work at. Leadership alone cannot fix the problem of retention—we've *tried*. What we need are team members excited about their work and empowered to create change. Such a shift only comes with a complete transformation of the work culture itself.

When people enjoy their jobs, they are happier, don't show up late, don't steal, and work harder—all of which translates into economic success. Bad organizations neglect this important component to their own success and do so at their own peril. And yet, the negligence of talent persists. As with the teacher scolding the outspoken teenager, there's too much comfort at risk to consider upsetting the proverbial apple cart. Nonetheless, when we ignore the culture our allowances are creating, we run the greater risk of continuing to create an unremarkable organization.

Creating better culture is not some pie-in-the-sky ideal; in fact, our work environments directly affect outcomes that can be measured. We see this in employee attitudes such as those reported in Glassdoor ratings, as well as in revenue growth, organizational reputation, and analysts' stock recommendations.* Gallup states that highly engaged employees are more present and productive; are more attuned to the needs of customers; are more observant of processes, standards, and systems; and show 21 percent greater profitability. We can, in fact, see results in action when companies buck the trend and engage their workforces. According to the executive summary of Gallup's "State of the American Manager 2017" report, these companies tend to see an increase in revenue, in some cases to the tune of 147 percent higher than their competitors.† Changing the culture where we work changes how we work.

This is not a problem we are unaware of. In another study, Deloitte reported that 50 percent of CEOs and CFOs named company culture as a top-three predictor of firm value. Eighty-four percent of those executives surveyed believed their culture needed to be improved, and only 19 percent believed they had the right culture. To top it all off, only 28 percent of the respondents believed they understood their culture. Clearly, we have a problem and what we've been doing to solve it just isn't getting the job done.‡

The competition for skilled and talented workers is intensifying as more and more people are leaving their jobs and refusing to settle for a vocation that doesn't align with their values. Millennials in particular care a great deal about working in a place with a culture where they feel valued and respected, and this continues to be an increasingly important qualifier for choosing a place to work. If we don't put effort into building great cultures, we will inevitably face critical challenges in both attracting and retaining talent.

Another source of understanding this issue is kununu, a Europe-based workplace insight website with more than sixty thousand companies listed. Kununu uses employee reviews to rank the best places to work in terms of employee satisfaction. The companies that consistently rank

---

* O'Reilly et al., "Narcissistic CEOs."
† Gallup, "State of the American Manager."
‡ Kaplan et al., "Shape Culture: Drive Strategy," n8.

highest have significantly better company culture than those that rank lowest. When employees give four or more out of five stars in terms of how good a place an employer is, the corresponding company culture average rating is 4.51. Similarly, companies given two or fewer stars have a company culture rating of 1.31.* These results indicate that the value of a company and the quality of its culture are, at least to the employees, virtually synonymous. In other words, a company is its culture. You don't get to have a bad environment and a good company; it doesn't work that way. You are what you do when it comes to organizations.

When most people hear talk of "corporate culture," they think about perks and benefits. Everyone loves talking about better environments, but few know how to create them. Great culture is not about gyms, coffee, or laundry service. It's the bar you set for what is possible, the promise of integrity and excellence that will attract both the right team members and customers.

Culture is the heartbeat of every organization, the result of intentional collaboration and innovation. It's what makes conflict meaningful and productive for everyone involved—the desire to protect what you've created together to make it even better. If you're not the one ultimately responsible for the direction in which an entire organization goes, join the crowd. That's most of us. All of us have someone to report to, someone we are accountable to, someone who needs something from us. In that sense, we've all got a boss, whether it's a manager, a shareholder, or a partner we need to please. We've all got someone to look to, someone who's looking at us, and someone else who, we think, holds the key to our problems.

But where does it begin?

With *you*.

---

* Le Phan, "25 Business Leaders Share Their Own Definition."

3

CREATING CULTURES THAT WIN

Just after college, Chris worked for a design agency, pouring his heart and soul into his job because to do so was part of his work ethic. During the hiring process, the managers promised him they'd pay for grad school, so naturally, he was elated. He gave his all at the new job, not only to show his gratitude but also to prove their investment was worth it. Then, just as he was about to deposit his first tuition check, he was told that money was a little tight. They said that they couldn't afford to pay for school anymore, pulling the rug right out from under him. He was shocked, devastated, and heartbroken—not to mention, that same day, as he arrived at work, he had seen the owner's wife drive up in her brand-new BMW sport utility vehicle.

She didn't have a corporate job, and their family lived entirely, and very comfortably, off the success of the company. Too young to understand much about culture back then, Chris still knew it was a symptom of something bigger. Working diligently while someone else reaps the rewards is the kind of culture many of us have come to expect.

We have seen, if we've been around the block a few times, that we can work as hard as possible, give our all to the team, and even bring in a lot of sales, but in the end our effort is neither respected nor rewarded. We are told that the fact that we get to keep our job is thanks enough. And of course, that's a blessing, but it's not enough, not by a long shot. After all, there's always somewhere else we can apply our talents and passions. It's not enough to offer gainful employment; you've got to work to keep your best people.

In Chris's case, all signs pointed to the business thriving financially, yet he was denied what he'd been promised. That kind of behavior creates a culture that does not encourage people to do their best; quite the opposite, in fact. Back then, he wondered whether all businesses were run that way. *Maybe it's just what everyone does.* Embarrassed for even caring so much, he decided to suck it up, assuming everyone gets mistreated and it's normal to hate your boss. Like an episode of *The Office* or a scene from *The Simpsons*, maybe that was just the way it is and there's no escape.

Then again, maybe not.

After that, Chris worked for a company for almost ten years at which the founder and CEO couldn't *stop* creating culture. Dave Ramsey was the kind of leader all six hundred of his employees at the time would do anything for. He was constantly rewarding team members and blessing them left and right. The team would do company shoutouts for great work, and showing appreciation for one another was second nature. It was inspiring.

That theme started to weed out impostors quickly. The team didn't want to work with gossips, flakes, and people who weren't interested in growing professionally and personally. People who just wanted a "job" were exposed. Employees liked having people around who worked as hard as they did and didn't create drama.

Chris never knew a company could operate with such a thriving and exciting environment. Investment of that much time, energy, and money back into a team is a rarity in the marketplace. For many of those team members, it certainly created a love for their place of work that was foreign to outsiders. If Dave promised you something, you got it, and that trust was more than a simple transaction—it was a mentality and an often nonverbal affirmation between everyone involved. The staff trusted one another; they kept their promises.

Going from a workplace where he was underappreciated and undervalued to experiencing the opposite gave Chris a sense of frustration. "Why doesn't everyone run a company like Dave Ramsey?" he thought. Nobody wanted to leave that place, and isn't that every boss's dream, almost zero turnover and everybody happy? People even jokingly referred to the Dave Ramsey organization as a cult because the employees were so tight-knit and united, which makes sense. Having worked at other places, we can see how important culture is but how difficult it is to create. It's frustrating to care deeply but feel that you can't move the needle on your own. Leaders may say they care about culture, but doing something about it requires discipline and daily attention.

In a great culture, average people become great. A healthy culture can self-police and self-correct. We've seen both crippling and thriving cultures, and what we now know is that what made the difference wasn't the fancy spread at the Christmas party. It was the day-in, day-out small acts of care that were constantly being attended to within the company. It is culture itself that makes a company excellent.

Shifting a Culture

In 2010, Kyle had just returned from a dynamic deployment in Afghanistan and been placed in charge of a platoon with a strong culture in need of a shift. This kind of deployment requires constant action and regular engagement with enemy forces, along with conflicting intelligence reporting and activity mixed with an ever-shifting battlefield. To say such a situation is wrought with stress and anxiety is an understatement. In such a setting, you never know exactly what the situation is, and it changes on nearly a daily basis.

The platoon had been hunting terrorists in Afghanistan for a year, but in the final two weeks of deployment, they had lost a friend. To Kyle's incoming lieutenant, Brendan Looney had been a classmate at the US Naval Academy, his roommate during BUD/S (Basic Underwater Demolition/SEAL) training, and his best friend. Lieutenant Looney was a fierce, up-and-coming officer, destined for great things, when his life ended too soon as a casualty of war. One morning a few months after the loss, Kyle wrote the following in his journal:

> It's the morning of Feb 24th, 2011. I'm pouring my second cup of coffee as I'm getting ready to head out to the range for a day of shooting with my platoon. The air is thick . . . there's a solemnity to it. It's quiet. Fierce. Nobody is talking. Today would have been Brendan Looney's 30th birthday. The boys miss him. We all miss him. We're hungry for payback. We don't want to talk: we want blood. The best we can do is get on the range and take our anger out on paper targets and prepare for war.

The blood ran deep in the platoon, and now they were back in America, eager to get back to the front lines. But this time, it would be a very different mission—not what they were expecting or even hoping for. This mission was named Village Stability Operations, and it was the type of operation where you're living, breathing, eating, and sleeping in communities with the purpose of winning over the hearts and minds of the local population in an effort to establish peace in a region. It wasn't a combat mission; it was a public relations campaign.

With this type of mission, there is often little support. Your closest coalition forces are about thirteen miles away, and you're equipped only with what you've got on your back. You might have a couple of vehicles, but that's about it. The United States hadn't done this type of mission often; the last campaign of this magnitude had been in Vietnam, which was far from a good omen. The officer in charge, Rob, had just assumed command of the platoon and was ready to take the fight to the enemy. These guys were elite warriors, but instead of fighting to remove bad actors from the battlefield, they would be working toward establishing stability through influence.

The goal of the mission was to have an impact on the regional government in hopes of helping it overthrow Taliban control. The SEALs, then, served as autonomous diplomats with lines of operations being security, government, and economic development. The larger strategic vision was to spiderweb the villages together to function at the district level, then regional, then national. It was a great vision, but this sort of thing usually breaks down at the village and district levels. The team had to help ensure that the Afghan people could establish their own sense of democracy. Kyle knew he had to change not only his platoon's warrior culture but also its entire attitude about Afghan culture.

The SEAL community is very different from a traditional military community. Even though there are ranks, file order, and discipline, you have to assemble those. If the guys don't trust a leader, it won't play out like traditional military rank and file. If you don't build real trust, you will be removed from your position because it can be detrimental to the mission. Rank isn't a given.

The SEALs do things differently than personnel in other areas of the navy, and that requires deep confidence and accountability built into the team. Kyle's platoon would need to trust him not only tactically but also philosophically. Since they were going to try to establish rapport with the Afghan population in that region, a major difference in this mission was that they were going to be embedded with the local population instead of living on a Forward Operating Base (FOB) outside of the towns or cities.

In the past, they would live on an FOB and conduct missions in the middle of the night, hunting down terrorists. This time, they would be living near and talking with potential terrorists in the middle of the day—having conversations, sharing meals with them and their families, and living life right alongside the locals. The challenge was to build and cultivate a sense of safety and belonging for the village, knowing they probably wanted to kill Kyle's team and that his team wanted to kill them. It wasn't going to be easy, changing an entire culture. And they knew that before they could change an entire region, they'd have to start with their team.

It Starts with You

While in training, getting ready for deployment, Kyle made himself fully available to his platoon, sometimes even to the detriment of his own personal life. He was an engaged leader and spent most of his time with his men. They worked 90 to 120 hours per week, and he was involved in every aspect of their lives. Such presence bolstered the SEALs' confidence in one another and in their mission. Kyle, although he did not have full authority, started with himself, fully buying in, and others soon followed.

Kyle and Rob worked intentionally with the platoon to develop a deep sense of trust and purpose in the team they were building and in their mission. The first thing they did was introduce a simple slogan to remind the men how they ought to conduct themselves in any scenario. They needed to create a sense of openness and transparency with the locals so that the Afghans would trust them, but they still had to present an air of confidence and power when necessary in the event that the Taliban unexpectedly came to town. They came up with a simple but clear motto: "quietly aggressive."

When practicing their tactics and procedures, the men disciplined themselves to be extremely quiet. In the field, they might walk into a situation in which women or children were present, and they had to be ready. Instead of practicing a more common approach of entering a space and saying, "Get down, get down!," they would approach quietly and ask any women present to take a seat, letting them know they just wanted to talk. That was the mission. That was how they had to be to carry it out effectively. So they set up training scenarios in which the team would be forced to use a quietly aggressive approach, and it started to take shape on its own over time.

None of this, of course, was without its challenges. This was all new to the men, who were still thirsty for blood, and many of the SEALs began asking questions like "Why do we have to be gentle?" It was a confusing slogan in itself, so the next thing Kyle established was a purpose. He explained that they weren't just going to be hunting down terrorists, nor were they going to conduct nothing but direct-action missions. They wanted to establish "white space," areas of calm and peace where people could feel safe and build a life for themselves.

Of course, they wanted to remove terrorists from the area, but the real objective was to push out terrorism from an entire region and return control to the people. The goal was to work alongside the local government to establish democracy, a police force, a security force, and an Afghan army presence that would cooperate with the local police and government. Their slogan began to bolster the team's purpose, and

Kyle started reinforcing it wherever he could. Although aggressiveness is what would remove terrorists from the towns and villages and what would bring them all home at the end of the mission, quiet would ensure that their visit was as peaceful as possible.

In SEAL teams, there are officers who are in command and a senior enlisted tactical leader who is in charge. "In command" means to be legally responsible for the mission—to be in command or in control of the overall mission outcome and the external assets supporting the mission. Being "in charge" means you are responsible for the overall actions of the mission: how everything is executed physically—the tactics, techniques, and procedures. As platoon chief, Kyle was the tactical leader, and Rob was in command.

On that deployment, there were no breaks—it was 24/7, nonstop. They could not kick up their feet, sit back, or ever let their guard down. Someone was always on duty, and for the purpose of keeping their sanity, they had to share roles and responsibilities. The team established leaders for a "red, white, and blue" rotation, which meant Rob was in command and in charge of "red"—the guys going outside the "wire" and conducting an operation. Kyle, then, was in command and in charge of "white"—the guys overseeing the base and maintaining communications with Rob's operation in case they needed support. Then there was "blue"—the guys spending their downtime resting, recovering, and sending emails to family. Rob and Kyle would rotate through operations and base control, each taking turns at playing leader.

They built a culture that not only allowed for a "red, white, and blue" rotation but they also trained four subordinates to take the lead in "red, white, and blue," so six leaders were in constant rotation. This allowed Rob and Kyle to rest and recover and also allowed for innovation. Once the other four leaders had more understanding of their roles—and the subordinates of theirs—innovation began at all levels.

Leadership was happening everywhere. Each SEAL was taking greater ownership of what was in front of him, and they all ended up being more productive as a result. There was no single leader whose removal or death would have devastating effects on the team. They had effectively "killed the leader," and the mission continued. They got more done because the structure of the organization had become more agile and purpose driven. Why they were there was clear, as was what they had to do. And who had to do it? Well, that was everyone.

Because their culture allowed them to replace one leader with another, everyone stepped up, including the men at the top. At that point, titles didn't matter. Leadership, as traditionally understood, was more or less defunct. What mattered was that they had a mission and a culture to support it. And not only did they accomplish what they set out to do, but they were the only platoon, during this period of time, to return home with 100 percent of their men. At that time, Helmand Province was the area most heavily loaded with improvised explosive devices on the planet, swarming with Taliban; soldiers were dying all around them. Not only did they make an impact on the battlefield, but they made it out alive as a result of the level of maturity reached by each guy.

Leadership didn't do that. Culture did.

Where We're Going

Culture reinforces mission. On that SEAL mission, the team members kept lines of communication open, they had a distinct purpose, and their approach was clear. Creating a winning culture, as it happens, isn't leaving beers in the department fridge every Friday. It's not a Ping-Pong table in the break room or company picnics. Creating culture goes deeper than offering a repetitive system of carrots and sticks. It's about creating something worth belonging to, something you just might die for (or at least be willing to sacrifice for).

You probably don't need to take a team of the world's best fighters and turn them into public relations ambassadors, but you can still make a dramatic shift in your organization. You can change an unhealthy organization into something world-class or purposefully build one that wins from the start. As with any serious strategy, shifting a whole culture involves a system in which your team feels empowered, united, trusted, and valued. In the rest of this book, we are going to explore that process together, how we've seen organizations rebuild cultures again and again in a variety of contexts—from Kyle's time with the SEALs to Chris's experience in a number of companies and all the people we've met along the way.

So what's next? Now that we've spent ample time talking about the negative impact of unhealthy culture, let's define what we actually want. In the remaining chapters, we will explore the three essential phases of transforming a culture—whether that's in a Fortune 100 company, in a small village in the Middle East, or in the United States government. The process for changing how a group of people works with one another and functions as an organized whole is simple but not easy. First, we must **define** what kind of culture we want; then, we must **develop** that culture gradually and consistently; and finally, we must **sustain** what we have created for the long haul. Let's start with Phase I.

PHASE I
DEFINE

———

Before you create a world-class culture, you have to define what kind of culture you want. There is no right or wrong, only what you allow. If we want a place where we enjoy working and that attracts top talent, this is not going to happen by accident. We are going to need to develop customs, practices, and traditions as precedent.

To do this, we have to know what we are aiming for. This can feel a little like learning how to ride a bike for the first time. It's slow at first and somewhat arduous, but we are learning to begin well. First, we are going to focus on Phase I of building a culture, which is to define what it is. Before we can establish the norm of a self-led team—one that, in fact, doesn't need the same positional leader all the time—we have to establish what we want this team to look like.

4

VALUES

Who Do We Want to Be?

In 2011, Kyle's platoon was getting ready for deployment to Afghanistan. As part of Unit Level Training, SEALs have multiple training trips and work hard to develop camaraderie in the platoon and in the troop. During this phase, the men went on their land warfare trip. Land warfare is what SEALs do as combat personnel, employing a diverse set of combat skills, weapon systems, and equipment. This can be done in urban or rural areas, but they were conducting this trip in the desert, the Chocolate Mountains of Southern California, where it's 120 degrees Fahrenheit during the day and 100 degrees at night. No matter the time of day, it's hot. The men were practicing rural combat, studying different defenses and types of combined armed concepts with regular troops, conventional troops, and special forces troops.

At that time, the troop was three platoons, and Kyle was the chief of Echo platoon. All three platoons equaled about sixty Navy SEALs in total. They had a lieutenant commander and a senior chief. Kyle's senior chief was his mentor and had been one of his best friends for twenty-three years. His name was Rock 'n' Roll, and the troop commander was named Mike. They were getting ready to go out, and their sister platoon chief, Dan, was doing nighttime operations with Kyle. It was two o'clock in the morning and still hot as hell. Dan was in one area of the mountains with his platoon, and Kyle was in another with his own.

To keep things light, Dan and Kyle developed a competition in which they took a phrase from *Mad TV* and tried to incorporate it into their official communications over the "net" without anyone else catching on. The net was accessible by others who were also on nighttime operations, such as helicopter pilots and their command center, so there were a lot of people listening in. The game was to repeat the phrase from a Key and Peele skit in which they went back and forth about taking things to a "whole . . . 'notha . . . level." For example, instead of just telling Dan over the net that Kyle's platoon was changing locations, he'd say, "Echo2 is gonna move to a whole . . . 'nother . . . level, into quadrant C74J6." And Dan would respond, "Roger that, I see your position, and I'm gonna take my position to a whole . . . 'notha . . . level." Whoever said it the most, or the best, would win for the night. That was the game.

They knew that at any time during rural combat training, something unexpected could happen. They might be creeping up on a target, setting up an ambush or sneak attack, but then the trainers would surprise them with an attack of their own, or they'd find themselves in a booby trap. They might think they were making good progress on a mission only to find themselves getting shot at, taking live fire and rocket-propelled grenades out of nowhere. So throughout the mission and all through the night, they had the net to keep the experience as light and fun as possible while working their asses off and dealing with the stresses of the unknown.

The platoons knew the joke, but no one else did. It was something special they were in on together. Every night, the men would wonder: "Is it gonna be Kyle, or is it gonna be Dan? Who's gonna win?"

One night, Kyle's platoon was ambushed by the trainers, and they were taking live fire down in the makeshift village. Dan's platoon was in a supporting position up high on the ridgeline. He was watching over the village as Kyle's platoon was pushing through. They were shooting from the ridgeline, and wherever you looked, it was like the Fourth of July. Explosions everywhere. Seeing his opportunity, Kyle got on the net and remarked that this ambush was a "whole . . . 'notha . . . level."

Kyle glanced up out of the corner of his night vision goggles and saw Dan on the ridgeline. Dan stood up and silhouetted himself against the night sky, explosions going off around him. He was leaning back with his gun, laughing at the top of his lungs. He couldn't breathe, he was laughing so hard. No one could hear it, of course, because there was gunfire everywhere, but Kyle could see it through his night vision. He won the Coors Light for that night.

In a crazy life-and-death situation like that, how do you get through it all? How do you create a culture that can withstand the stress? The SEALs weren't making light of what was happening during their night-time operations, but they needed a way to keep their sanity. *Mad TV* was how they did it. By the end of the night, the other people on the net had caught on, and the game was up. As they completed the mission, Dan switched over to the line that was private between him and Kyle and, in a whisper, said that he and Dan had taken the game to a "whole . . . 'notha . . . level."

Values Are Who You Are

One day at Burger King headquarters, marketing executive Jeff Campbell and his team decided to introduce a new noisemaker for children in the kids' meal. They didn't test the idea. They didn't consider the implications. As is done in many large corporations, they made a decision independently of how it might affect individual owners and operators of local franchises. And they had no idea what they were unleashing.

Campbell left the marketing department for operations shortly thereafter, seeking an opportunity to work on the front lines of a Burger King restaurant instead of in the ivory tower of its executive offices. During the two weeks he spent standing in as an assistant manager at a local Burger King, he realized quickly how out of touch he'd been to green-light this particular toy. The restaurant was too cacophonous to be hospitable. "Every kid in the store was blowing these noisemakers," he told us in a podcast interview later. "And I'm sitting there going, *Who can I blame for this? Oh. Me. I did this to myself.*"* In retrospect, it's not hard to see how poorly thought through the idea was, but sometimes the most obvious truth is the hardest to see—until you're in the room hearing a hundred plastic hand-clappers go off all at once.

We often don't know how a decision is going to play out until we are on the ground, connected to the real-life consequences of that decision. But when we entrust the future of our organizations to an elite few, we risk losing the nuance that those individuals in the boardroom just can't see. An idea that seems smart at the time can turn out completely differently in the field. Those little noisemakers, Campbell recalled, were "guaranteed to drive you insane." What he witnessed in a moment would have taken his fellow executives months to realize in market testing. What else, he wondered, had he been missing?

The temporarily retired executive learned a lot about the difference between Burger King operations at the corporate level and the individual store experience. Or, in his words, "It's amazing how quickly the 'other guys' are stupid." He spent a lot of time talking to the people who worked in the store to see how decisions at the top affected people throughout the organization. As a leader, Campbell realized that part of his job was to listen to what others were saying and not assume that his way of seeing things was necessarily correct. Paying attention to his surroundings, noticing where things weren't working, and asking both team members and customers why led to a whole new understanding for the executive. To say this stint as an operator was enlightening would be an understatement. After his experience, Campbell understood that even if you are the "top dog," your limited vantage point can cost you a lot.

Years later, when Jeff Campbell became the CEO of Burger King, he remembered these lessons and immediately called his executive team together, placing in front of them a whiteboard and telling everyone in the room, "Tell me what's broken. Tell me what we need to fix." And

---

* Campbell, "Pushing Forward with Jeff Campbell."

they did. But more importantly, he listened, which was something he'd learned from those crazy noisemakers.

Plenty of leadership clichés will tell you, "Ask for feedback. Ask for what's broken." But what's different is how Campbell did it and who he was, as well as what he had learned by then. As the leader, he put himself in a vulnerable position, opening himself up to the honesty of his so-called subordinates, and he did this by creating a safe space for people to share their thoughts and ideas. This is essential to creating a culture people want to be a part of. Everyone has to feel free to tell the truth, and that begins with you doing that now, even if you aren't the CEO.

Does this mean you might get fired or demoted or embarrassed? Yes, it could. But it also might mean you could be the one who shifts the tide from complacency toward something greater. Most leaders won't open themselves up to that level of criticism, but Campbell didn't let his pride, title, or position get in the way of truly engaging with the people he was supposed to take care of. A lot of leaders tend to think, "You're here to serve me," when the real job is to serve everybody else—creating a place where everyone feels welcome to share and grow.

Seek First to Understand

Before you attempt to change something, you need to understand it. In the classic words of leadership guru Stephen R. Covey, "Seek first to understand, then to be understood. Seeking real understanding affirms the other person and what they have to say. That's what they want." You can't change an environment you haven't first attempted to comprehend. You've got to study your people, the place where you all work or serve, and really get to know your surroundings.

What *is* the atmosphere of your organization? Is it laid back and forgiving or rigid and hierarchical? Do you have the autonomy to try new things, or do you have to wait until you're given permission to tackle a new idea? Is failure forgiven or punished? Are your leaders interested in helping you improve your performance, or are they more interested in making you toe the line? All of these are questions of culture, and again, before we can change anything, we have to understand it.

Depending on the team you're a part of, or possibly even lead, you probably have an unintentional culture that, if you asked some of the executives, they couldn't tell you who forged it or how it was created. It just sort of sprang out of the people who were there early on as the organization grew and developed. We're willing to guess that no one planted a flag and declared, "This is our company culture!" That's just how it happens. The culture emerges on the basis of the personalities involved, the preferences of those early stakeholders, and the policies they create early on.

If you have a new company, you have a chance to build your own culture, deliberately and with care. But rarely does that happen. When a company is in a startup season, it's in survival mode, and the leadership often makes the mistake of allowing the hoped-for end to justify the means. So they skip steps and rush through certain aspects of establishing a healthy culture just so that they can go public or get acquired or simply make payroll. But maybe you work for a company that has been around for a few years or even decades, in which case you may be mired in the results of cultural decisions that were not made by you. Or maybe you're somewhere in between. Regardless, we all end up with a culture we don't feel that we have full control over; and yet, it begins here, with us, right now.

We have a chance to dramatically affect the culture in which we work, but before we can do that, we have to understand what our current culture is, then define what we want, and eventually begin creating it. Leadership experts tend to define organizational leadership cultures in one of three ways:

- **Dependent:** Believes people in authority are responsible for leadership

- **Independent:** Believes leadership comes from independent expertise and "heroic action"

- **Interdependent:** Believes leadership is a collective, collaborative activity that works across open organizational boundaries

There's no right or wrong organizational culture. One is not inherently better than the other, although there may be a culture that works better in one setting than another. For example, the military would not function well as an independent culture, and a tech startup might not thrive as a dependent culture. But what about *your* culture in general? Maybe it's dysfunctional, responsible for a high turnover rate among employees. Whether you helped found the organization ten years ago or you're the "new guy," we all need to develop the discipline of taking a step back and looking at our environment as objectively as possible. Whether we realize it or not, we are complicit in creating the situation in which we find ourselves. And we have to be able to look behind the curtain and see the dirt, so to speak, to get an accurate idea of what's really going on in the organization.

If you don't have the ability to do that, to accurately see what's right in front of you, you need to find someone who can. This is why we advocate a full 720-degree assessment with every client we work with. Typically, in most leadership development circles, experts and consultants will advocate for a 360-degree assessment, meaning you get feedback from everyone around you. Think of the old roundtable from the days of King Arthur, in which each person who has a stake in the mission is invited to offer feedback on how the team can work better. Certainly, this is better than a top-down approach, but it's still slightly lacking. We believe that it is crucial for everyone in an organization to not only look to the left and right of themselves but also above and below—not just our peers, but also our bosses, subordinates, customers, and clients. We can and should learn from anyone, and a self-led team is one where we are constantly seeking feedback from everyone we encounter so that the mission can be carried out as effectively as possible.

The question we are always asking is, "What are we dealing with? What does our culture look like right now? How do we operate, and how could we do it better?" This can be a challenge to answer for organizational founders and people who have "been there since the beginning" as they tend to see things how they were or how they envisioned them to be instead of how they actually are. Sometimes, we have to get an outside perspective or a fresh take from someone who doesn't have all the history that we as leaders might be burdened with. For example, it is relatively easy for a new person to come in and see what's wrong with a company that may be stuck in a rut and not even know it. These people contain a wealth of knowledge in their ability to see what others might miss. Nonetheless, to move forward in any mission, we all must develop the ability to seek understanding. Anyone can learn to do this, and you're going to learn how.

Meanwhile, if you feel like you're struggling to see the problem or if something just doesn't seem to be working in your organization and you can't quite figure it out, just know that this is normal. You're right where you need to be. You just don't need to stay there. Being honest with yourself and your coworkers will likely mean admitting some things you're not proud of. You may have to face your role in contributing to whatever mess you've found yourself in. You may be part of the problem—in a sense, we all are—but now you're going to be part of the solution.

Defining a New Culture

When attempting to define a new culture, an organization's people must get clear first on what they have to work with and then on what exactly they want to change. When working with clients at Culture Force, our consulting organization, we walk them through the following process: observe, establish a vision, call a meeting, codify the results, and adjust.

Step 1: Observe

First, if you're starting a new position, especially if you're coming in as a manager, it's important to not just walk in and start making changes or solving problems. Too many people start a new position and feel that they have to make their impact felt during the first week. The best thing to do is to just sit and wait. *Observe.*

Start talking with people. Have lunch or coffee with them. Ask them, "What do you love about this company? What do you hate about it? What do you think the biggest problems are within the company? What are the biggest problems in the industry? What are we missing that could make us great? What do you need to help you succeed in this role?"

Your role at this time is to just listen. Don't change things, don't fix issues, don't make personnel changes. Sure, you want to fix problems like a broken piece of equipment. But you're still gathering information. Once you've got your information and you've started building relationships, which may take a few months, you're ready for the next step.

Step 2: Establish a Vision

Next, *establish a vision* for what you want in terms of performance. Tell people what you expect as far as the quality of work and what it will take to achieve that level of performance. The benchmark should be "Will this make us great?" Be sure to constantly remind people of the standards you set and ask them whether they feel their work brings the company up to those standards. Are they satisfied with their level of quality? It means hiring people who can deliver on that level, including your third-party vendors. Once this is the standard you've set, it should always be the one you meet.

Step 3: Call a Meeting

Get everyone on your team in the same room. Hand them all pens and pads of sticky notes, and have them write down what they perceive as the company's core values. Ask them, "What does our culture mean and stand for? What do you think are the most important things we do here? What are our nonnegotiables in how we conduct ourselves and our business?"

Have them write down as many of these ideas as they can, one idea per sticky note, then start grouping the notes by idea. If several people write "honesty," make a pile for these. If other notes say "fast order fulfillment" or "twenty-four-hour response time," put all of those into a pile. You'll go from a few hundred notes to a few dozen. Group them as much as you can, even if you need to combine a couple of piles.

Let your people vote on the ideas they think are the most important. If you're going to expect them to live certain values, they should get a say in those values. The goal is to distill those down to twelve to fifteen key points about what you want the culture and the organization to be like.

Step 4: Codify the Results

After the meeting, use those points for your hiring process and your evaluations and reviews. How are your staff lining up with these new values? Are they meeting them and fulfilling them?

Step 5: Adjust

After that, adjust your onboarding process for new team members. Adjust your training so it reflects your newly defined culture. You want to begin instilling these values into your new hires from the very beginning rather than trying to break them of bad habits later on. Training should also be ongoing, not just something you do once and then never speak of again. As a leader, you need to regularly remind your staff about your values and hold them (and yourself) to that standard.

Develop Meaningful Core Values

When we say "core values," what words come to mind? Words like "integrity," "diversity," "inspiration," "community," "creativity," and . . . *blah, blah, blah.* Right? This is the problem with most companies' core values.

Too often, they're just empty phrases that mean nothing to the people they're supposed to inspire. Such so-called values are often shaped by good intentions but miss the mark when it comes to the language used and how they're presented. Stringing together a bullet list of words does nothing for a team. In fact, team members may not even know what a core value is or what your core values happen to be.

It doesn't have to be this way. Values are an important piece of any organization and one of the most important operationally—when you understand how to harness their power. Often, someone has to set the foundation with a mission statement, giving the team a rallying cry for why they get out of bed every morning and go to work. This can be done by the leader, but it doesn't have to be. Regardless, once the target is set, how will you get there? What are the rules and guidelines for the road you need to travel to achieve this mission?

This is where your core values come in. Core values are the framework of any organization; they are the rules of engagement for how to achieve your mission, laying out clear expectations and telling the team what behaviors are expected and appropriate in any situation. Can you see now why simply creating a list of words like "helpful" and "dignity" is not going to work? Such words will not be clear enough for the journey ahead. You have to get more specific.

Start with Action

Your core values should always start with a verb, with some action an individual can easily take. You don't want to list a bunch of positive qualities like "unique" or "creative" because these words tend to feel vague. You are building the rules of engagement for how your team members will interact with one another. They need to be clear and easy to apply. If you want your team to focus on taking care of the customer, for example, instead of saying "customer service," say, "We go out of our way to focus on the needs of our clients." This statement has much more meaning and is therefore easier to apply and measure.

Involve the Team

Whereas a vision and mission statement may come directly from the positional leader, the core values of an organization should always be vetted by a team. If you are the one initiating this process, you may start by coming up with a list that you think exemplifies the culture you want. That's well and good, but such a list is useless until you ask the rest of the team for feedback. "Does this accurately reflect who we are as a company?" you might inquire. And if the list doesn't make sense to them, change the verbiage until it does.

Be careful with this, however, because you don't want too many cooks in the kitchen. Some team members will be more outspoken than others, and this doesn't need to be an all-day meeting with people incessantly talking over each other. Do your best to make sure everyone is heard, and then use a subset of the team to craft the final language after all team members have offered their input.

A self-led team doesn't mean utter chaos all the time in which everyone is always deciding where they should go. Quite the opposite, in fact. Everyone has a role to play, and there comes a time when decisions must be made. Be the one who makes the call; just make sure everyone is on board with it.

Use Inside Jargon

It's pretty common for a company to develop its own inside phrases as the culture is being developed. These phrases can be wonderful to integrate into your core values because they embody what makes your business operations so special. It doesn't matter if outsiders don't understand. This isn't about customers; it's not about marketing or even positioning. It's about rallying your team around a few key phrases that make each member feel special and included.

Describe Each Value

Once you get all the information down, write a sentence describing each value to provide some additional clarity. These descriptions should be short but should also establish the expectations for each of your "rules of engagement."

Don't Worry About the Number

Core values are unique. They should define your team, the company, and the culture you are representing, and just like snowflakes, no two sets of values are alike. Some people want to establish a set of three values or a single big one. The number doesn't matter. There may be five nonnegotiable operating tactics for how you conduct business—or twenty-five. Don't try to force a certain number of core values onto the page. What's important is that they become the playbook for how you achieve your mission. The number of values you have isn't what matters. It's how memorable they are, how easily they can be applied, and how bought in the team is to each one.

Ask the Questions

To create your own core values list, start with these questions: What is important in our company operationally? What is unique about working here? What are the things that are nonnegotiable when it comes to how we do our work? Your answers to these questions are the start of your list of values that make this a unique team or organization.

Create the List

Take a few minutes to answer the foregoing questions. Have each person on the team write down every answer that comes to mind, making sure to put each idea on its own separate sticky note or piece of paper. This is best done in person but can happen virtually if necessary. Set a timer, and stop writing ideas when the time is up or when you run out of sticky notes, whichever comes first. These notes will become the beginnings of your core values list, so hold on to them. Display everyone's notes randomly, in no particular order, making sure each idea is visible.

Organize the List

Now it's time to organize the list of potential core values from all the notes collected. Sort the notes into groups that feature similar ideas and concepts. This process is known as affinity mapping and helps us recognize similar relationships between things so that we can begin to identify key trends. For example, if someone wrote "empathy" and someone else wrote "we care," those two ideas are similar and can be grouped together.

Once you've done all of this, you will have a working list of core values that you can continue to develop and get feedback on, because a value is not real unless it is reinforced and lived out regularly. So once you have these values, what do you do with them? You test them. You keep talking about them and practicing them and seeing where and how they hold up (and don't).

Living Out Your Values

An important but sometimes difficult exercise for leaders is to ask each person on the team what they love and hate about the organization. This can be hard because it can be a hit to your ego, but it is essential to getting the data you need on what should stay the same and what needs to change. And the more honest the answers are, the more difficult they might be to hear.

It's going to be hard because what you're going to hear is going to be—or feel like—a direct reflection of who you are. An attack on you as a leader or manager, on the very character of your soul. What you've let your team become. But this is necessary, as painful as it might be, because you can't get where you want to go until you admit where you are. Honesty is the most important quality in this process of understanding what your culture is and defining what you want to create.

If you want your company to grow and succeed, you need to be honest with others and let others be honest with you. This includes "opening up the kimono" and being vulnerable in ways that you don't have to but that will nonetheless generate trust and confidence. Honesty and vulnerability go hand in hand; in fact, being vulnerable is simply being honest about yourself, especially your areas of greatest weakness and struggle. This is so important to earning a team's trust and creating a healthy culture; the more you do it, the better you'll get at it, and the more others will follow in your footsteps.

You can cultivate a sense of safety and belonging by being vulnerable with your team members. That doesn't mean handing out a list of your top ten fears or telling people about that thing you did in high school that makes you cringe whenever you remember it. But it does mean setting aside your ego, admitting you don't know everything, and not feeling that you have to be the smartest person in the room. It means hearing some things that might hurt but remembering that the only way to get better is to hear the truth. You expect your employees to improve after you share harsh truths with them, don't you? Why would it be any different for a leader? Of course, there's a risk in being vulnerable: What if no one believes you? What if you don't have that trust and your staff doesn't feel safe?

It takes two years for a SEAL to become fully plugged in and indoctrinated into that world-class culture. It shouldn't take longer than that for an individual in your organization to feel that they're part of a team. In many cases, sadly, it never happens. To solidify a team takes a willingness to meet regularly with people, plugging everyone in to the team's way of doing things and making sure what they say is important actually is. Your values are not mysterious; you can see them in practice every day. They are what you do and how you do it. And if what you wrote down is not what anyone can see, then something is off.

Who you are as an organization is not something you can put on a PowerPoint slide or a motivational poster and expect it to become the predominant way of thinking around the company. It's going to take continual reinforcement, affirmation, and holding one another accountable to make it happen.

When Chris adopted this approach with an employer, focusing on building a team through active listening and engaged empathy, everything changed. His department went from losing $3 million per year to making $10 million annually—all because he listened to what his department staff wanted, asked questions about what they loved and hated about the company as well as other areas of interest, and helped define their values. What followed were set expectations for the quality of work they produced and the kind of company they wanted to be.

This is not only a good way to define where you are currently; it also makes it easier to know where you want to go later. After you've had your conversations with all your people and had a few months to watch the team in action, you'll know whether those core values are an indication of where you are or where you want to be.

If people are saying they really want to get to a place like this, that tells you something is missing. When people tell you what they're hoping to achieve, it says a lot about where you are at that moment. Take time to get to know the people you work with—whether you're the leader or not. When you do this, you gain influence and perspective, and that's all leadership is. The more you pay attention, the more you'll recognize a disconnect between your perceptions of "what's wrong" and what's actually going on. The observations of a newcomer are in many ways superior to the jaded lens of an old-timer.

When Something Is Off

Once, Chris was working with a company CEO and his entire C-suite, and he brought them in for some training and development. The CEO asked to survey everyone anonymously, and the results that came back were horrible. That is, they roasted the poor CEO in the survey, and it was clear that he was a big part of the problem for his C-level executives. He had created an atmosphere of fear to the point that the only way people felt free to say things was if the survey was anonymous. They were completely honest and savaged the guy. The CEO brought everyone together and said, "Let's have a conversation here. What are you all upset about? What's the problem?" He basically had an attitude of "Man up, and say it to my face so we can talk about it."

Only one guy stood up and said, "Here's the problem: it's really you; you're the problem."

Then something even crazier happened: no one backed him up! Everyone just powered down as if all the other people except them had hammered the CEO on the survey results. They more or less said, "Sorry, we just don't believe that about you. This guy needs to leave."

But the CEO was looking at the survey results, saying, "Well, is it me or not me? Or is it just this guy who doesn't like me?"

So, even though the problem really was with the CEO, no one was brave enough to step up and support the only guy who spoke up. Even when Chris and some of his team spoke with the other team members, they all declined to say anything for fear of losing their jobs. They thought that whatever they said would be reported back to him, so they said nothing. That is a culture of fear and distrust that will engender safe choices that won't lead to groundbreaking work. You won't get fired, but you also won't feel very fulfilled.

In the end, Chris and his teammates shut their operation down and said, "We don't think we can help you. The only way we can help you is if people trust each other and can be honest." The CEO was happy when Chris's company pulled out because he was happy with the status quo: he was still in charge, still running the show. His attitude about his team is one we see in many poor leaders—especially the bullies and jerks. If you're not happy at your job, they reason, you should just be happy that you *have* a job. And if you're not going to be happy, go find another job. So when everyone went back to work after that meeting, do you think they were engaged? Inspired? Do you think they felt like putting all their energy into that job? Or would they do only what they were asked to do, only when they were asked to do it, between the hours of 8:00 a.m. and 5:00 p.m.?

The People Cost

If you want to lead the way for change in your organization, you have to go first—and you must be vulnerable. The way we lead impacts the way people work, so we want to take note of the choices we're making and how they might affect others. Coming out of a pandemic and a shift in the workforce now known as the Great Resignation, there is more and more evidence supporting such a statement.

The "2022 Workplace Belonging Survey" by Ipsos showed that almost half of Americans were thinking about leaving their current job,[*] and that figure was probably conservative. Those who are considering a switch are unlikely to feel a sense of belonging in their workplace. People don't quit things that matter to them. The more something matters to you, the better you are going to perform and the higher your productivity will be.

Productivity obviously goes down the drain for team members who don't like or respect their boss. Are you going to do extra work for someone you hate? Of course not. A recent newspaper headline read, "There's a Cost to Keeping Bad Bosses Around—and It's Rising."[†] It would take a lot to convince workers to stay at a job they loved if they disliked their boss. But productivity isn't the only cost. The Society for Human Resource Management found that employers often have to spend the equivalent of six to nine months of an employee's salary on finding and training a replacement.[‡]

All of this is quite expensive, and none of it should be surprising. Everywhere we look, we are experiencing leadership malpractice, which is creating a real poverty of dignity in the world. Such a phenomenon has significantly impacted the health and family life of those in the workplace, with some statistics implying that changing jobs will only take you to another place of unwanted stress. In 2021, according to a study by the Massachusetts Institute of Technology, more Americans left their

---

[*] Ipsos, "Public Survey Findings and Methodology."
[†] Medici, "Keeping Bad Bosses Around."
[‡] The Well, "The Cost of Replacing an Employee and the Role of Financial Wellness."

jobs within a five-month period than ever before in American history, with a total of twenty-four million resignations from April to September of that year. The reason for such a massive departure? MIT cited "a toxic corporate culture" as "the strongest predictor of industry-adjusted attrition" and stated that it is ten times more significant than what people are paid. Bad corporate culture plus an overall "failure to recognize performance" are the two greatest contributors to people leaving their jobs.* The issue, then, is not compensation but recognition. If you paid people below market rates but gave them a stellar place to work and praise for their contributions, this would be a more favorable environment than one in which they were well paid but virtually invisible and seemingly insignificant.

Everywhere we look, people are burned out on their jobs, and throwing more money at the problem is not fixing anything. The way we lead does, in fact, impact the way people live. It is much more devastating to think of the effect poor leadership has on the lives of the people within an organization than the amount of money the organization spends on hiring and training. How many marriages have ended as a result of poor leadership in the workplace? How has poor leadership affected the way parents treat their kids? How has it contributed to anxiety and depression in the world? We need to realize that every single person within our span of care is someone's child, with hopes and dreams for a future in which they can realize their full potential. They are people, deserving of care and attention.

We all have the opportunity to learn from one another, to listen. The most powerful gift we can offer is our attention, and anyone can do it. To listen shows empathy. It is a demonstration of care and a declaration that the person you are listening to matters. When done with the intent not merely to get information but to meet the needs of another, listening allows us to connect with and understand others. Leaders need to look for the goodness in people and celebrate what they find daily. Traditional management teaches us to look for the errors or exceptions, to look for

---

* Sull, Sull, and Zweig, "Toxic Culture."

opportunities to improve. But we all have a need to be recognized, to be listened to and understood.

None of this is revolutionary, but much of it is rare. All you need to lead well is to care, to see people within your care as human beings and treat them with the respect and dignity they deserve. This is how we move from traditional management to true leadership. Unfortunately, our institutions don't teach such leadership skills, at least not widely. Instead, they offer cold, academic exercises in helping kids get good grades so they can get into good schools and then make good money in hopes of one day getting to live a good life. It doesn't work like that. Unfortunately, what people end up learning is how to push through life, stacking one set of accomplishments on another, killing what makes them human and exchanging it for a plaque with a few words, a yearly raise, or some arbitrary sense of success.

The real cost of the way our organizations are run nowadays is much greater than dollars and cents. We all bear the cost of poor leadership, and therefore we all must be part of the solution. The way forward is by harnessing what makes us human and not hiding it but emphasizing it.

Harness Your Strengths

When consulting with companies, one question we love to ask employees is "How would you spend your day if you could work only to your strengths?" Then we start pairing people off by their strengths. For example, if one person loves using spreadsheets and revels in making budgets and analyzing metrics, while another person's strength is in coming up with creative ideas, we get them to help each other with those tasks. If the creative person is supposed to create a budget for an upcoming marketing campaign, why not let the spreadsheet guru take it over? And if the data analyst is supposed to come up with an email newsletter, turn the creative loose on the project. That doesn't work in a strict you-do-this-and-I-do-that context, but when we flatten our team's structure, allowing roles to shift depending on the need, we end up becoming more agile and productive.

When we learn to harness our strengths and let others do what they're good at (instead of pridefully trying to be average at all of it), each person gets to do the thing they love. Because who doesn't love doing something they're excellent at? More important, people are not wasting time doing something they hate. Chances are, if they were forced to do that task, they could get it done, but it would take a lot more time and the result wouldn't be as good as it would have been if they had traded projects with someone who can do it better. This is the beginning of a self-led team, an operation that doesn't need hard-and-fast titles and positions but can adapt depending on the mission. By having members of a department share their workload this way and play to their own strengths, you can get amazing things done.

Chris has done this with other departments he's led and found that this shared cooperation becomes one of the core values of the team. When people feel frustrated or stuck on a project, someone can say, "What are your strengths? How can you help out here?" This mindset has an amazing effect of shifting the entire culture of a department. Ultimately, of course, this flies in the face of requiring your staff to improve upon their weaknesses—which never makes much sense because you end up with a team of mediocre generalists rather than a squad of high-performing specialists.

Why would you have your copywriter learn budgeting when she could spend that time becoming a better copywriter? Why would you have your data analyst learn to create visually stunning dashboards and reports? Turn that over to your graphic designer so your analyst can continue learning new skills and software to make him even better at his job. By letting people get better at the things they're good at—and enjoy—instead of forcing them to improve upon skills that aren't part of their regular duties, your team can feel better about their work, enjoy it more, and feel happier. Plus, you end up with some of the most talented people you'll ever encounter in the workplace. When everyone is empowered to play to their strengths, they will be more likely to take initiative, lead themselves, and not struggle with tasks and responsibilities they don't enjoy.

Innovation thrives when individuals from all ranks in an organization become official stakeholders in solving problems. Just ask the people at

Pixar. Ed Catmull observed in his book about what made the animation studio such a legendary place to work: ". . . something that sets us apart from other studios—is the way people at all levels support one another. Everyone is fully invested in helping everyone else turn out their best work."* At Pixar, team members would have equal say in certain decisions regardless of who they were. This was meant to encourage individuals, even those who might have completely different perspectives of priorities in a project, to find ways to cooperate and collaborate. Solving a complex problem, after all, sometimes requires a sophisticated solution. This also ensured that people focused on their strengths and found ways to contribute their skills to a variety of outlets that otherwise might not have called for such a diversity of talent. Pixar intentionally creates a culture of collaboration and empowerment, and its output proves the efficacy of such a system. From 1995 to 2016, the studio released seventeen feature-length films, averaging more than half a billion dollars in gross sales for each one.†

The way you conduct yourself affects what you create. Whether you are the leader of the team or someone who simply sees what's wrong with the organization, there are changes you can make, changes that must be made. And if you don't speak up, who will? Remember that true influence always begins with listening, and a self-led team learns to collaborate across myriad disciplines in ways that bring gifts together. It's not easy, but it can be worth the hassle of dismantling an old system to welcome something new and better.

And once you get clear on your values—who you are and want to be—it's time to pay attention to where you want to go.

---

* Catmull and Wallace, *Creativity, Inc.*
† Bahcall, *Loonshots.*

5

VISION

Where Are We Headed?

For years, we've been obsessed with the idea that better leaders create better cultures—but that's not exactly true. More often than not, better cultures draw out the right leaders to take the team into the heat of battle. It is, admittedly, a bit of a chicken-and-egg situation: Which comes first, the leader or the culture? In a sense, the answer is both: good leaders sustain healthy cultures, and healthy cultures create better leaders. But where do we begin? We need a catalyst, someone willing to speak up, to identify some semblance of a vision. And a vision is always a clear answer to a simple question: *Where are we headed?*

Where is this thing going? Who's needed? What does success look like? Ideally, this vision is set by someone who is brave enough to ask the questions. Sometimes it's the founder or CEO. Sometimes it's the janitor. Whoever possesses the courage to ask is often the one we end up listening to. Begin with you. Don't deny the value of your own perspective. Making a culture better is a process involving everyone, and wherever we are in the company, we have our own unique vantage point.

Take Sir Richard Branson, the charismatic founder of the Virgin family of companies, for example. Branson is notoriously hands-off in his leadership style, saying his number one criterion for hiring in his companies is to hire his weaknesses. Branson is famously dyslexic and apparently cannot read a spreadsheet to the point that he doesn't understand simple profit-and-loss statements.

Being CEO and founder of multiple businesses (Branson owns more than four hundred companies worldwide) certainly requires an ability to understand numbers and what to do with them. So what does the infamous rule breaker and bucker of the status quo do? He doesn't attempt to improve these weaknesses; rather, he seeks out people who have already harnessed the strengths he needs.

You could even say that Branson's deficiencies have given him a certain advantage as a leader. The fact that certain business functions are incredibly difficult for him has kept him out of the weeds, forcing him to hire those who can perform them much better than he can and allowing him to stay focused on the vision of his companies.

As for where his companies are headed, Branson said in an interview that he has three simple but powerful principles that guide every company he creates.* In addition to the vision of all Virgin brands that they will disrupt the status quo with products and services that the market demands, Branson attributes the following essentials to their organizational success: listen, learn, laugh. That's it.

"Learning and leadership go together," he said in an interview.† "Too much credit goes to me for what we have achieved at Virgin but the successes happen from working and learning with some of the world's most inspiring and inspired people." That's a culture of empowerment, a truly self-led team.

A healthy culture is one that not only allows but encourages people to speak up and to listen to one another, sharing ideas that help the

---

* Schawbel, "Branson's Leadership Principles."
† Schawbel, "Branson's Leadership Principles."

organization's mission move forward faster and in better ways. To begin such a process, it often takes a bold, forward-thinking leader to break the ice and get people to speak up, moving the team in the direction of openness and honesty. Such a leader needs to be secure enough to let other leaders emerge from the process—to take the initiative for their own work, as long as it's aligned with the vision and values of the organization. To get to that point, it's important that people define and understand their core values and their true nonnegotiables.

What Is Nonnegotiable?

Every organization should have its nonnegotiables, its list of values or ideals its people bring to the table that are not up for debate. These are the most deeply rooted values, and they are embedded into the very cornerstone of every great business, team, and organization.

Let's say having integrity and doing the right thing is one of your nonnegotiables, and one of your customers makes a mistake on their shipment. They don't buy the necessary shipping insurance for the final leg of a journey on a full container load of product. The shipment gets damaged on that final leg, and a lot of the product is unusable—nearly $100,000 is lost.

Normally, the shipping insurance would cover those losses, but the customer forgot to get it before they scheduled the shipment. So they ask you to fudge the paperwork on your end to show the insurance was already purchased and will cover it. Of course, you say no, because it would be dishonest, not to mention illegal, but your customer stands firm. You need to do this for us, they say, because we can't take the hit. If you don't, we'll stop buying from you. What do you do? Do you help them out and keep them as a customer?

This is where you discover what your true values are.

Everyone loves talking about these concepts—values, culture, empowerment—but the truth is that in practice this stuff can be messy. It's scary to let go of control, to invite chaos into a system that may be dying but is nonetheless controlled and somewhat predictable. Your values are not a placard on the wall; they are not a memo after an off-site retreat. Your values are visible, clearly seen by anyone who interacts with your organization on a daily basis. You are what you believe in; you do what you value. Your team is the lowest common denominator of whatever you tolerate. That's just how it works.

Ray Dalio, who founded and runs Bridgewater Associates, the world's largest hedge fund, has a process he calls "looping" that is, at least in part, the reason for his team's long-term success. Looping is the art of taking problems and turning them into progress. How Ray and his colleagues do this so effectively, and have done so for more than forty years, is by enforcing their value of an "idea meritocracy" in which anyone is free to contribute a potential solution to a problem at any time.

"Great cultures," Dalio wrote in his bestselling book *Principles*, "bring problems and disagreements to the surface and solve them well."* The staff at Bridgewater does this by paying attention to problems, following the causes back to the original issue, and then coming up with a new solution and pushing through to a new result.

This process of looping allows teams to get to the root of their problems, break bad habits, and change the trajectory of where they're headed. A more "flat" management style makes this easier to do without unnecessary bureaucracy or red-tape hiccups. Failure to do so can result in obsolescence.

Looping, for Dalio, is essential to the evolution of an organization. For him and his team, values are not necessarily static; they are simply the result of a group of people who work well together pursuing a common goal in a way in which they are constantly adapting to new information.

Values are almost always implicit before they become explicit, meaning you have to observe what matters most to you and your team members. This takes time and practice and a little awareness. When Dalio started Bridgewater, he did so in a two-bedroom apartment with a friend with whom he played rugby, and who had no previous knowledge or experience in the markets. It felt like play to him, and he didn't want to bog himself and his company down with stuffy pretensions like

---

* Dalio, *Principles: Life and Work*.

a list of core values. "I never set out to manage," he recalled, "let alone to have principles about work and management."* But as the company grew, he saw the need to codify that which was already happening, making it clear for all that the way they did things as an organization was not accidental. There was an intention to everything, even if it was an evolving one.

At the outset, he saw his team members as an extension of his family, sending them all birthday cards and gifts that he personally picked out—until the organization got so large that this was no longer manageable.

He invited his colleagues to stay at his house in Vermont on the weekends, celebrated their most significant moments in life, and chose to work only with people whose company he genuinely enjoyed and whose opinions he sincerely respected. The more caring team members were to one another, he observed, the harder they were on one another.

Investing in the lives of others, it seems, gives you the opportunity to hold your colleagues to greater accountability, not less. When you clearly care for your teammates and are invested in a common cause, work becomes more meaningful and therefore more important to each person involved. You don't want to let someone down, and you don't want to be let down. You help one another reach a level of excellence that would otherwise be unapproachable.

In 1996, Dalio wrote in a memo to his team: "Bridgewater is not about plodding along on some kind of moderate standard. . . . Our overriding objective is excellence, or more precisely, constant improvement, a superb and constantly improving company in all respects."† He went on to say that conflict is a necessary part of this pursuit of excellence, as is thoughtful and considerate criticism of one's teammates and oneself. In the memo, he prized "the intolerance of substandard performance" and long-term relationships. Money is not the point of such an endeavor; rather, it is a by-product, an important and necessary outflow of the pursuit of greatness.

---

* Dalio, *Principles: Life and Work*, 303.
† Dalio, *Principles: Life and Work*, 306.

"Each person at Bridgewater," he concluded, "should act like an owner, responsible for operating in this way and for holding others accountable to operate in this way."* Because he has given so much to his team, he can expect so much of them; more than that, though, he can ask them to expect it of one another. The key word in that memo is "intolerance."

As bestselling author James Clear said in *Atomic Habits*, "You do not rise to the level of your goals. You fall to the level of your systems."[†] We might say that all great work environments do not necessarily rise to the standards of their values but rather fall to whatever they are willing to tolerate. And that is, in fact, what a person values: whatever they are willing to engage in conflict over. Anything else is just talk. According to Amy Edmondson, author of *Teaming: How Organizations Learn, Innovate, and Compete in the Knowledge Economy,*

> [P]roductively engaging the conflict that teaming creates is not done by avoiding emotions and personal differences, but rather by developing a willingness to explore different beliefs and values. Leaders hoping to employ teaming, and to promote the learning that accompanies it, need to develop the leadership skills necessary to engage conflict effectively. Doing so has very real consequences for the way teaming occurs, or fails to occur, in work teams of all kinds. Fostering an atmosphere in which trust and respect thrive, and flexibility and innovation flourish, pays off even in the most deadline-driven work settings.[‡]

Or, as Dalio himself said, "In order to be great, one can't compromise the uncompromisable."[§] Think back to your core values, and use them to inform your decisions. What are you not willing to compromise about? What does your team currently tolerate? Why is no one speaking up about it?

---

* Dalio, *Principles: Life and Work*, 306.
† Clear, *Atomic Habits*.
‡ Edmondson, *Teaming*.
§ Dalio, *Principles: Life and Work*," 305.

Core Values Create Culture

When we work with other organizations, coming into companies for a short while usually as consultants, we work to understand what the core values are. We don't do this by reading the website or the company's articles of incorporation; we just watch and listen. If you pay close enough attention, you'll start to see what people care about. It's not that hard to notice. Watch what people say and do; see what they tell you regarding what is important to them. They do it every day.

Something we often see is people focusing on areas that are not essential to the mission of the organization but are easy ways to keep busy. They believe these tasks to be important, but they are often a waste of time and resources. Still, they are difficult to simply stop. These "firewall defenses," as we call them, are things people do unconsciously; they're automatic behaviors and are hard to recognize unless you're looking from the outside in.

Breaking through these defenses can threaten the homeostasis of a team. "This is the way we've always done it" is a common response when you are in this phase. But once you can move beyond such formalities, you'll get to the heart of what matters most. Breaking down bad habits and replacing them with new ones is essential to determining a team's values and rebuilding them in alignment with the mission. Once you do that, the automatic responses that were inefficient or were competing with the mission can be converted into automatic responses that now get us to where we want to go faster.

Think of the way the employees at Chick-fil-A say "My pleasure" whenever you thank them at the drive-through. This is rarely conscious; it's so deeply ingrained in the ethos of what they do, they can't help it. But the value is not "my pleasure"—it's hospitality.

In simple but clear ways, almost every interaction you have with employees at Chick-fil-A involves their going out of their way to make you feel at home and taken care of. And when this value is reinforced over and over again, stated and demonstrated, and called out when not met, soon the behaviors become automatic, trained. That's how values work; they are reflections of deeply held beliefs and convictions, leaking out in sometimes unexpected and surprising ways.

Nearly every company would say it wants to serve its clients and customers better than everyone else, but when it comes down to values, few organizations do this so reflexively that they literally can't help but go out of their way to overserve you.

If you work for a company like that, when someone asks you a question, whether a customer or colleague, you stop what you're doing and answer it. You don't just answer, however; you go above and beyond what's expected. If someone asks you where the restrooms are, you don't just point and say, "Down that hall, third door on the left." You say, "Let me walk you over there," and you do.

Similarly, if your core value is "We're a family" and there's an emergency—someone is going through a divorce, a family member has died, a child is sick—this is the sort of thing that everyone around you is concerned about. Your teammates don't complain about having to carry the extra load; they do so gladly and gratefully, knowing their time will come, too.

To determine a company's core values, we often ask people, "What are some of the things you love around here? What are your core values, even if they are just for your own department?"

The question gets answered in a variety of ways: at an organizational level as well as departmental and down to an individual's core values. We write down each value on a sticky note, group the notes, and share what we found with the leadership team. "Here," we say, "are your values—not what you wrote down somewhere in a meeting once. This is what we've observed; this is what your people are doing. These are your values." Our values are our benchmark; it's where we're starting from. But knowing your values is not enough. You also have to know where you're going—you have to have a destination in mind.

It's not as simple as "I want to do X more and Y less." You need a clear goal with measurable outcomes and a reasonable schedule. You have to be willing not only to dream up how you'd like things to be but also to face your problems head-on. Because whatever ideal you are striving for is going to have its set of obstacles. There is a reason why your goal hasn't been met yet—it's hard to get there. So you'll want to consider adopting the practices of looping and listening. Don't walk away from a problem or pretend it's solved if you haven't gotten to the heart of it.

Be willing to hear from those who can help you see what's broken and fix it.

If you strive to do this, to attempt to improve anything systemic in your organization, not everyone will like the changes. Human beings as a species are not always fans of novelty and change. Our entire existence is contingent on a rigorous stability in both our environment and our biological makeup. If, for example, your body temperature were to rise or fall suddenly by just a few degrees, the results for you could be deadly. Change is not comfortable; yet stasis is a myth. Every organization is always evolving or eventually dying. So conflict is a necessary part of growth, and people disliking change is to be expected. There will, of course, be moments when you as the instigator of change won't have time to get everyone on board with the vision. Others may be happy with the way things have been going, but if that team hasn't been succeeding, if they've been beaten by the same struggle for some time now, the most responsible thing you can do is shake things up.

When you turn the wagon, you just might throw a few people off, but you're also going faster. You're headed somewhere. Some may not like the new direction, which will create an opportunity to clarify the vision. People often aren't challenging change as much as they don't understand it and therefore resist it.

To create change, however, you cannot merely mandate it. You have to talk to people, get into conversation with your team members, find out what they personally value and care about. Ideally, you want to do this in a private, one-on-one setting whenever possible. You need to sit down, especially when you're new to a team, and talk with people.

Of course, that's not always possible.

When Jeff Campbell was the global head of Burger King, he couldn't have one-on-one conversations with all his staff, so he had to have group meetings with his managers. But he did get his managers in a room and run through the same exercise, asking people to be honest and share their ideas. Group meetings accompanied by the sticky note exercise is one way to do this. Just try to keep the groups as intimate as possible. When you get too many people together, they can start to create the dysfunction you are trying to dismantle. Groupthink begins to take over, and it's harder to get a pulse on individual frustrations.

So, as much as possible, we try to sit down with people in small groups or individually. We ask them what they like and don't like about their place of work. What fuels them? What frustrates them? What are their hobbies? Do they have a family? Do they have any pets? Why would one person have so many cats? And so on.

After a time, they start to talk about the job they're doing, and we ask, "What would you change? What frustrates you the most?" It's important in these conversations to create a safe space for team members to speak up. They need to know they're not going to get in trouble or incriminate someone by simply being honest.

Why do this? Because the numbers speak for themselves. At least one study indicates that when employees feel heard, they are more than four times more likely to feel empowered to do their best work. They are more motivated, more driven to produce. Melanie Curtin, a writer for *Inc.* magazine who documented this study by Salesforce, put it clearly: "When your people feel heard, they feel motivated. They feel like they can do a good job. They know they've got what it takes."[*]

The Team Creates the Culture

A leader doesn't define the culture, at least not all alone. A good leader observes the culture, the way things are, before beginning to imagine how things could be. He or she becomes a student of the status quo, digging deep into the causes of certain dysfunctions and discontents among team members.

Granted, it is not always the "boss" doing this; it can be anyone who is willing to step up and start listening. The true catalyst of change in any organization is the person who takes note of all that's happening every day—the many vocational variables, personal agendas, and other values emerging in an everyday environment—and decides to start shaping it intentionally and collaboratively.

Each member of a team will inevitably have their own set of values

---

[*] Curtin, "Employees Who Feel Heard."

and nonnegotiables, those which are important to them. Every person has an agenda, something they want to contribute to an experience or even get out of it. We all have our own respective goals, and it's the job of a true change maker to figure out what the goals are for the team.

Even if someone on the team understands the mission and can recite the values of the organization, it does not mean they are on board yet. It doesn't mean they've bought in so much that they're willing to set aside their own agendas for what's best for the team. It takes great care and attention to do this well.

A good leader will never come into a new organization and plant a flag, saying, "This is our culture now. Everyone get on board!" It doesn't work that way, anyway. Instead, a good leader will start small, with a single department, or even smaller—with himself or herself. The best way to incite change is by setting an example.

When you start with yourself, you rarely have to worry about recruiting top talent. People start knocking on your door and begging to be a part of whatever you're building—inside and outside of the organization. This is how self-led teams get cemented; a catalyst is often required to begin the process, but once people see that they can have a hand in shaping the culture, they'll want to participate in the experience. You can, of course, guide people when they need it, but be ready to hand over the reins once they understand what they can be a part of.

When Kyle went back to Afghanistan to work with the population and government to try to establish a local democracy, the platoon gelled so well that they were known around the area by other Navy SEAL platoons. In fact, one member of another platoon wanted to be a part of Kyle's Echo platoon. He loved being around them because of how tight they were, how natural and attractive their camaraderie was.

This SEAL became known as their Plus One, and other guys in the team would say, "There's Echo platoon and Plus One." Eventually, it became a thing other guys wanted to do, too; it became competitive.

"Oh no, no, no," they would say to one another, "I'm the Plus One this week."

"No, no," another would reply, "*I'm* the Plus One."

This happened throughout the entire SEAL team—other guys wanted to be a part of Echo platoon. The reason? Kyle; his lieutenant, Rob; and the fire team leaders had nurtured an environment of approachability and trust. They were actively engaged with the team, open and honest with them as much as they possibly could be. They joked together, ate meals together, and spent time with one another after work. They genuinely cared about their platoon, and as a result the platoon members cared about one another. It was something special they all wanted to be a part of, and this was evident even to outsiders.

There can, indeed, be challenges to being part of a tight-knit group of professionals all committed to a single goal. Sometimes you can get too comfortable with one another. Sometimes you can forget that your team is not all there is in the world. Rob and Kyle would often preach about "time and place."

As the book of Ecclesiastes says, there's a time and place for everything. There is a time for joking and having fun, and there's a time to be serious. If the general or admiral is about to walk in and the team is going to brief him, this is the time and place for everyone to sit up straight, have a smile on their face, and be quiet, calm, cool, and collected. In the end, that attitude of sharing, caring, and being approachable—plus understanding there was a right time and place for everything—spread to other platoons, and everyone wanted to be Echo platoon's Plus One.

When we build an environment in which others are free to approach even the boss and offer feedback or ideas on how to improve things, we create something everyone values. And as we give one another more responsibility, allowing our weaknesses to be complemented by others' strengths, we build a team that we want to protect and defend. It becomes something others recognize as special and want to participate in.

Approachability, trust, and openness: these are the keys to getting a group of people bought in so deeply that they are willing to lay down their own goals and agendas in pursuit of something greater. That's how you lead people somewhere new: by focusing on the values of the team and not propping yourself up as the leader.

6

BECOMING SELF-LED

When hordes of pagan tribes were ravaging western Europe, destroying the remnants of what was the Roman Empire, a small group of Celts somehow saved much of what would have been otherwise lost. What we think of as Western culture—including those prized ideals of truth, beauty, and justice—would have been all but wiped off the face of this earth were it not for the efforts of a band of brave Irish monks.

Yes, monks. Not warriors or politicians but largely peaceable men and women, loosely organized in interdependent communities, were the ones responsible for the preservation of Greco-Roman thought, art, and literature.

Through a decentralized network of abbeys and monasteries, mirroring the factious tribes that came before Ireland was Christianized, these Celtic monks preserved many ancient documents that would have otherwise disappeared. According to Thomas Cahill, the historian who wrote about this previously untold story, it wasn't just the seclusion of the Emerald Isle that made it an ideal haven for cultural artifacts such as Plato's *Republic*; it was also the makeup of the people who sought to preserve such relics. In other words, it was cultural.

How exactly did a ragtag group of mystics from a largely unknown and "uncivilized" part of the world save what an empire could not? Was it the work of a Roman slave named Patricius, who returned to his native land to preach the good news and become the island's patron saint? Was it the Celtic people's seemingly natural proclivity for conflict and hotheadedness that allowed them to resist barbarian hordes?

Was it, dare we say, *magic*?

No, not exactly. What saved Ireland from the Dark Ages and allowed it to preserve Western civilization for posterity was the way the island itself was organized and had been for many centuries.

Information Wants to Be Free (and So Do Teams)

Since the advent of the internet, the world of organizational behavior has changed. The old way we used to organize information—a single authority sharing truth from on high and then disseminating it through groups, communities, even countries—is practically defunct. Like Moses coming down from the mountain, those of us who would prefer to go back to the old ways of leader-driven organizations are now looking at the world in confusion and maybe even disgust. It wasn't supposed to be this way, was it?

As we've seen, the workforce experienced this on a global scale during the COVID-19 pandemic. Historically, hierarchical leadership worked when trying to avoid uncertainty. However, when offices were closed and everyone worked from home, "teaming" became a life raft for talent and organizational strategies.* It wasn't just about the boss anymore. We saw the importance of a self-led team.

To quote Stewart Brand, a pivotal figure in the counterculture movement of the 1960s and 1970s in America, "information wants to be free." Brand ran a magazine for many years called the *Whole Earth Catalog* and lived by this axiom. Some thirty-odd years later, he was

---

* Deloitte, "2020 Global Human Capital Trends."

right. With the rise of the internet, information that was once stored for safekeeping in libraries, sometimes guarded by gatekeepers (or maybe just a librarian), is now available for all. You don't even have to leave your house to get to it! Not surprisingly, entertainment soon followed this trend.

Tools such as Napster upended the music industry forever, and it's no wonder—why would people pay for something they could readily get for free? It didn't stop there, of course. Books, articles, and even movies became practically free in a matter of decades. Some authors caught on to the trend and used it to their advantage, as in the case of Brazilian novelist Paulo Coelho, who used the internet to pirate his own out-of-print book. His guerrilla marketing tactic eventually led to the runaway success of *The Alchemist*, now one of the bestselling books of all time. Even Andy Weir, author of the massive bestseller *The Martian*, started the whole thing as a daily blog—the science and space geeks would edit all the space, science, and astronomy things he got wrong, as well as suggest things for him to add.*

If information wants to be free, authority wants to be shared. The democratization of content inevitably leads to increasingly democratized societies. The reasoning goes something like this: as societies become more free, so does information; and as information becomes more free, so does society. In other words, as you empower people's liberties, they look for ways to take on more responsibility. It's no wonder that free-market cultures created opportunities for more people to have access to information; and that very access to information is now changing the way many of our organizations are structured.

Take Wikipedia, for example: at the time it was started, many people mocked the website for its lack of centralization. No one was in charge of Wikipedia per se; there was no boss, just a collective of writers and editors who cared about providing information for themselves and the world. Of course, Wikipedia didn't just appear out of thin air; it was, in fact, created by someone. But there is a difference between a creator and a leader, and we'll be exploring that throughout this book.

---

* Dees, "Series of Blog Posts."

Starfish Versus Spiders

In the words of Ori Brafman and Rod Beckstrom, authors of *The Starfish and the Spider*, it takes a catalyst to create what they call a "leaderless organization." But the magic of these types of organizations is that their founders often give up authority rather quickly and eagerly. They don't want authority; they want to share the responsibility. That's a good catalyst: someone who sees the potential for something and says, "Hey, let's do this." The person who begins it and the one who manages it are rarely the same. This is not to say that a self-led team is a socialist utopia. Every worker is not equal, and teams will not exist in a perpetual state of kumbaya. They will, however, have voice and value that are not undermined or shouted over by an oppressive leader. In many ways, the internet caused a surge in what Brafman and Beckstrom call "starfish organizations," groups of people who are organized but not around a central figure. If you cut off the head of a spider, they reason, it dies; but if you cut off the arm of a starfish, it grows a new arm. These organizations are much harder to stamp out, beat, or sometimes even find. Examples include Al-Qaeda, eBay, and Alcoholics Anonymous (AA). Such groups are not chaotic, nor are they recognizable to the typical Western mind, which thinks in terms of hierarchies and top-down structures. This is an entirely different way of doing things, and to be sure, a leaderless organization is not always appropriate—but more and more, we are seeing their efficacy in certain settings.

One of the reasons Al-Qaeda was so difficult to weed out in the days following the terrorist attacks of September 11, 2001, was the way many Americans were approaching the problem. Initially, the hunting down of terrorist cells was based on American ideals of leadership and organizational structures. They were looking for a leader, but that's not how the group was organized. Al Qaeda was set up more like a group of Apaches spread throughout the American Southwest, banded together in small tribes connected in loose associations. One group did not depend on the other, but they mutually benefited from one another. If you got rid of a single group—even the leader—it meant little to the rest of the organization. They would simply replace what was lost and keep going. This is a leaderless organization. This is a starfish.

From Pyramids to Circles

Of course, this is not exactly news; however, such organizational structures are becoming more popular and far more useful today. Many of history's greatest innovations—in the arts, sciences, and even politics—were brought about by small groups of people operating without a single, centralized leader. The women's suffrage movement, catalyzed by Susan B. Anthony and Elizabeth Cady Stanton, was one such group, as was the abolitionist movement, with which those women were also closely associated. The French Impressionists were another decentralized group, starting as a small faction of outcasts who wanted to treat art differently from their contemporaries. In fact, we can go all the way back to the Dark Ages and find cadres of people embracing this seemingly novel organizational structure in those old Irish abbeys.

Human beings have always organized themselves in small groups to ensure their survival and success. But what's happening now in the world's organizations is not just a resurgence of tribalism; it's something more than that. What we see now in successful, innovative organizations is not necessarily leaderless organizations but rather pockets of people loosely assembled around a certain goal or mission who come together to propose a singular purpose and then either disband at the completion of the project or start a new one.

These were what we call self-led teams, and they very well may be the future of self-led work. The Irish were able to "save civilization" (that is, reproduce many ancient documents and protect them) because of the way their people had been organizing themselves for hundreds, if not thousands, of years. When Ireland was Christianized and Saint Patrick allegedly chased all the snakes off the island, factions of warlords and tribes were replaced by an interdependent network of monasteries and abbeys. In monastic societies, there is no charismatic leader on whom the whole organization depends.

Certainly, in any group of people, there is often someone who has to start it; but this is not a leader in our traditional sense of the word. This is, to employ the term Brafman and Beckstrom use, a catalyst—someone who can begin an organization, which others can lead in his or her place. What makes organizations, terrorist groups, and even entire nations resilient is their ability to endure change and weather conflict well.

When all authority and responsibility are not tied up in a single individual, groups of people have options. Take the Ford Taurus, for example. The team that designed the jelly bean–shaped car was not a top-down group—it was made up of engineers, designers, and marketers all collaborating to build a car that would defy the status quo and dig Ford out of its previous year's $1.5 billion loss. The team's collaborative effort became *MotorTrend*'s Car of the Year in 1986.*

Granted, some things may be harder, since there is a reason we've organized ourselves in tribes and kingdoms and societies since the dawn of time. But there are risks in relegating all leadership abilities to one purpose. When that happens, all you have to do to take down that organization is take out the leader.

And people have been doing just that for centuries. One especially talented warrior brings together other warriors and begins taking over more and more land. He eventually becomes king, maybe even declares himself emperor; and now he is vulnerable. All his power—and it is a lot—is wrapped up in a single family lineage. After all, he can't really trust anyone else. So he builds himself a castle or a palace and walls himself up in there with the few people who will carry out his legacy. Naturally, someone soon comes along who wants that power, finds a way to take down the king, and gets it. Thus, the cycle repeats.

It's not always been this way, though. There have, in fact, always been groups of people who have organized themselves differently, not on pyramids of power but in circles of trust. Take our Ireland example from earlier. Monks are typically not concerned with power, at least not good monks. They are most interested in dedicating their life to the pursuit of spiritual disciplines. In the case of early Irish monasticism, cells of men and women were organized in loose but efficient collectives of shared responsibility. Each community existed independently of the others, but a common cause united them. And so they wrote, copied, and shared countless documents, copies of which we still have

---

* *Fortune*, "Six Teams That Changed the World."

today. This is a starfish kind of organization: it's a network full of nodes that connect to one another, but if one disappears, the whole network doesn't shut down.

An Organization Is Like a Human Brain

In Hindu mythology, there is a concept called Indra's net, which says that all of creation is a web, and every node in that web is a gem, reflecting back to the other gems what they are. Those gems—the points of connection in the web—are conscious beings (i.e., people). They are at once separate and connected, experiencing and influencing one another.

If this sounds familiar, it should, because that's how the internet works. Today, we take for granted that there is no central hub of what we used to call the World Wide Web, but when it first began, the idea that the internet was not living on a single person's computer was incomprehensible. It took years even for very smart people to understand that such a thing could exist.

But the truth is that you don't have to look any further than the human brain to understand this phenomenon of simultaneously independent and corresponding nodes in a network that all affect one another but are not necessarily needed. The internet began, essentially, as a group of connected computers mutually sharing information, usually for free. If you were to destroy one of those computers, especially back in those early days before the "cloud," you might lose some information, but you would not lose the whole web. Just as in Indra's net, each piece contributes to the whole; but remove one of those nodes and you still have a net.

This describes a self-led organization. It is a group of people committed to a particular purpose who are all working together to accomplish their mission. We argue in this book that more and more organizations are moving in this direction, creating a culture of self-leadership where people are not only empowered to create change but expected to do so. As we said earlier: history maximizes the importance of heroes but minimizes the significance of teams.

But how does a culture of self-leadership actually work?

Building Self-Led Teams

To begin, we would do well to understand that this is nothing new. Academics and sociologists alike have been studying organizational behavior for decades, if not longer, and their findings all point to a not altogether surprising reality: human beings perform better in groups than in solitude. Professor Keith Sawyer's work points to this repeatedly in his most notable book *Group Genius,* which posits that much of the creative process and what we understand artistic genius to be is rarely the work of a single person.

At the same time, innovative and creative work is not the product of a committee. If the ego of an individual can destroy what would otherwise be good work, the bureaucracy of a crowd can do the same. But in between the extremes of absolute solitude and full-on mob mentality is what one sociologist calls "collaborative circles."

These circles are relatively small groups of people who often start out as misfits. They are in many cases the "secret" behind major cultural breakthroughs, whether in the way we understand the human mind, the future of art as we know it, or whether or not all men and women should be free. Disaffected individuals find one another usually as a result of the charisma of a single person who, often in partnership with a "gatekeeper," organizes them around a stable but agile set of principles and standards.

One example of such a group is the Inklings, that literary mastermind of such notable historical figures as J. R. R. Tolkien and C. S. Lewis, who started the group somewhat accidentally when Tolkien sheepishly shared some of his writing with another Oxford professor. It wasn't long before they were meeting once each week to smoke, drink, and share their poetry, stories, and literary ideas with other peers. The group continued for decades and largely influenced much of what became the greatest works of literary achievement in the twentieth century. Alcoholics Anonymous is another such group. Bill W. founded it and started the meeting format that continues today. But there is no leader of AA, no president or king whose removal would cause the whole thing to crumble.

And so it starts with a circle. Then that circle gets a little more organized. They start meeting, start sharing ideas, start gelling with one another. The group points its intention toward an outcome, something it hopes to accomplish: the abolition of slavery, the right of women to vote, or even the liberation of an Afghan village.

At this point, the circle is more of a team, guided by its principles in pursuit of a common goal. The catalyst who started it begins to share responsibility, either out of necessity or because of an understanding that what the team is doing is bigger than the efforts of a single individual. Other leaders come in to help stabilize the outfit. The organization grows, and so does its influence. Eventually, it accomplishes its purpose or it fails. Then it either disbands or finds a new mission.

This is the magic of a self-led team: it doesn't need to exist. It exists to serve a higher purpose, and when that purpose is fulfilled, there is no need for a team anymore.

Embracing the Future of Work Now

Taking cues from such organizations, as well as our experience of working and talking with Navy SEALs, we believe this is how many of the world's most elite organizations work. They are nimble, purpose driven, and practically egoless. People switch from bitching, gossiping, and positioning for power to fighting over goals, direction, and success metrics. They go from focusing on an individual leader or themselves to focusing on the team's goals and the whole organization. For instance, now I don't care that Daniel and LaTonya are also trying to one-up and position themselves, bringing in elements of team drama to battles over whether we should buy television ads or billboard ads. The former has nothing to do with success; the latter is all about it. That's not to say there aren't issues anytime you deal with people; of course there are. But this is a completely different model for organizations and one worth paying attention to as we consider what it means to create a place of purpose and meaning in which we can work and share and grow.

How do you create a self-led team? We are going to walk you through how Kyle did it with the SEALs and how we see this happening in successful companies and organizations all over the world. If you want to create a better organization, you have to focus on the culture; but what does that mean? Culture is what you do and perhaps why you do it. We are advocating for a certain kind of culture, one that empowers every single individual and expects more from all of them. This is self-leadership; these are the kinds of teams we need to create for our organizations to thrive.

A self-led team requires a leader, at least initially; as mentioned, we think of this person as the catalyst, the one who rallies the troops and gets everyone fired up about a mission. This is often best done with a compatriot of some sort, someone to carry the burden of starting things from scratch. It's no small thing to revitalize a culture, after all; it takes a leader but not leadership, at least in the way we've defined it. What you want in a catalyst is someone who can step up, use their voice to get everyone on board with a mission, and then step aside so the team can begin to lead itself. At this point, you begin moving from chaos to a disciplined kind of loose order. It's not disorganized by any stretch of the imagination, just held together by a different structure from one guy at the top incessantly barking orders left and right.

The days of kings are over. The world is hungry for a different way of being led and organized. Human beings more than ever want greater autonomy, more trust, and, yes, greater responsibility. They want to be a part of something significant and feel that they have a part to play—and they do. We all do. So why not give our organizations and peers—and ourselves—what we all want? Which is not another boss or tyrant telling us what to do but the invitation to change things for the better in whatever context we choose to do so. We don't need another shiny leader; we need a different way of leading.

The internet forever transformed the way we access information by organizing it in the same way our brains do. Thirty years later, our schools, governments, and businesses are following suit. They have to, or soon they'll be left behind, another empire reduced to rubble. To succeed, our organizations must make a dramatic cultural shift: from leader-driven bureaucracies to self-led teams.

To make such a shift, we've observed in our work, most organizations have to undergo a reinvention of sorts. As stated earlier, whether you're just starting out or seeking to revitalize the group you currently are a part of, you will need to follow three phases—define, develop, and sustain. What it takes to build a great organization that does good things in the world is to decentralize control and unlock the power of the self-led team, just as those monks did so many years ago.

7

CREATING A CULTURE
OF EMPOWERMENT

Aretha Franklin wasn't always the queen of soul. It was a calling she had to grow into, an artistic style that, in a way, had to find her. And she didn't necessarily get there all on her own. She, like all of us, was a product of her environment. And like a true master, she knew how to take control of even the most chaotic of situations.

It was 1967. Before she mesmerized generations with "Respect" and other such classics, Aretha Franklin was a twenty-four-year-old singer trying to make it in a world largely run by men. "She was a very shy, introverted lady at the time," recalled David Hood, a bassist and trombonist who played trombone during one of her recording sessions.*† The daughter of a preacher, Franklin had just wrapped up a contract with Columbia Records and been signed by Atlantic Records with the aid of

---

* Taylor, "The Day Aretha Franklin Found Her Sound."
† Hall, *Man from Muscle Shoals.*

her manager and then husband, Ted White. Jerry Wexler, a well-known record producer working with Atlantic, saw something in Aretha that just needed to be unlocked. He called his friend Rick Hall, who a year before had produced a hit with Percy Sledge—the instant soul classic "When a Man Loves a Woman." Bolstered by this success, Hall was eager to try again.

Wexler, Franklin, and White flew down to Hall's studio in Muscle Shoals, Alabama, where they spent two days recording a couple of songs they hoped would become big hits. What happened at FAME Studios that day was nothing short of a disaster—but also a miracle. Franklin's husband started drinking heavily and by midafternoon was completely drunk, demanding that Hall—who was managing the studio that day—fire a couple of musicians he insisted were hitting on his wife. While that was happening in the background, something else was occurring among the band members.

Seated at the piano, Aretha was trying to figure out how to do this first song she was tackling. The band was a group of white men who would later be called the Swampers by Lynyrd Skynyrd and immortalized in the song "Sweet Home Alabama." Together, they were working on "I Never Loved a Man (the Way I Love You)" and having trouble with its waltz-like rhythm. They couldn't figure it out. The manager, producer, and sound engineer were busy arguing over perceived slights and trying to put out relational fires while the young singer struggled to realize her potential. The session seemed doomed. It was then that session musician Spooner Oldham started playing around with a five-note riff on the electric piano. "Everyone fell in line with that," said Hood, "started playing, and that saved the song." Meanwhile, Aretha's husband grew more drunk and antagonistic; halfway through the recording of the second song, Wexler called off the session for the rest of the day. Everyone went home.

That night, Rick Hall decided to visit the hotel where Aretha, her husband, and Jerry Wexler were staying. Still perturbed by the behavior of Ted White, he wanted to confront the man who had made a mockery of his studio—in spite of Wexler's insistence that he not do exactly that. Arriving at the hotel later in the evening, a little intoxicated himself now, Hall began by trying to talk some sense into his client, but soon the two started to fight. White threw Hall out of the hotel room, cursing him, as did Wexler who had apparently overheard the commotion. The sound engineer cursed them both, screaming in the hallway as he was expelled from the hotel. The incident forever burned a bridge in the recording industry. Hall later recalled in his own autobiography, "I hated him and he hated me, they hated me and I hated them. It wasn't good for the industry, it was not good for me, I made a terrible mistake going over there and getting into it with Ted, and for all that I was sorry, but you know, things happen."*

The next day, a note was posted on the studio door saying the session had been canceled. Franklin and White left town, and shortly after that Wexler flew everyone, including the musicians from Hall's studio, to New York and finished the record. "I Never Loved a Man" climbed the Billboard charts, reaching number nine, and became the title track of Aretha's breakthrough album. Wexler set up a studio across town with the Swampers as the studio band. Those four country boys—Barry Beckett, Roger Hawkins, David Hood, and Jimmy Johnson—ended up producing multiple hit records for the likes of the Rolling Stones, Elton John, Willie Nelson, Paul Simon, and so many others seeking that "Muscle Shoals sound," which soon became a fixture of the music industry.

And it all began with Aretha, a talented woman in the thick of a few men's egos, working with a ragtag group of musicians fiddling around on instruments that were not their primary tools for musical excellence. And somehow, something beautiful emerged. It was chaos, of course, but sometimes that's how it goes—too much order and you end up with tyranny; too little and it's chaos. That day in the studio, and many days after that, the Swampers became a self-led team, offering an antidote to the extremes of total order and total chaos.

Creative work is a dance, especially when you're collaborating with others; no one knows exactly what ought to be done because people are all listening to one another in a mutually beneficial and informative way. They're watching one another, getting into flow with one another,

---

* Hall, *Man from Muscle Shoals.*

trying things that may or may not work to see what emerges. They are Indra's net, each glancing at others and being glanced at, seeing what they're sharing reflected back to them—just as musicians respond to what they hear other musicians playing. They were jamming; and in that jam, they found something sweet and good.

How Self-Led Teams Work

Working in self-led team is a chaotic process, but it's not anarchy. There's a goal, of course; and everything the team does should support that mission. In the case of Aretha and the Swampers, they wanted a hit. In this story, you see the conflict of two organizational worldviews: one was the top-down structure of the men in the back of the room, debating over who should get fired. Up front, the musicians were there to work and try to solve a problem. In the midst of confusion and chaos, they figured it out because even though it hadn't been explicitly stated, they were all empowered to figure it out. And they did. When left to their own devices, a good team full of individuals who are willing to lay down their own pride in the service of a greater vision will inevitably make magic.

Leading a team is often an exercise in extremes. On one hand, you could be the "boss," the tyrant ordering people to do what you want, micromanaging them to make sure they do it the way you want and punishing them if they fail to complete every task to your satisfaction. This manifests in the form of a heavy-handed middle manager, an untrusting CEO, or even a drunk and jealous husband of a soul singer.

On the other hand, you could be a laissez-faire leader. The term literally means "leave it be" and refers to an attitude—really, an economic philosophy—that essentially means "hands-off." You let people do their own thing and you're a leader in name only. That's not leadership, at least not the kind we recommend. The ultimate goal for a leader should be to get their team as empowered as possible *while* feeling supported without requiring a hands-on approach. You want them to do it in the best way they can with as little interference from you as possible; and ultimately, you want to make the leader as replaceable as possible.

Leading like this requires striking a skillful balance between the two extremes just mentioned. Most managers struggle with this: they're either too soft or too controlling. Either they can't motivate others at all or they're downright bullies. And the result is self-evident: people quit. CEOs and managers are killing themselves trying to become world-class leaders when that's not where we should be focusing our attention. In the corporate world, we overtrain, overeducate, and overspend on leadership training—and it just isn't working. The solution to workplace dissatisfaction doesn't lie in high-functioning leaders; it lies in high-performing teams.

A Self-Led Team Must First Follow a Leader

It may seem counterintuitive that a self-led team requires a leader. But a castle on a hill isn't built overnight, and it requires coaching and oversight to set a team up to be self-led. There are four stages to any team-building effort: forming, storming, norming, and performing. In the storm, however, is where most outfits fall apart. Self-leadership is the practice of getting a team to, in many ways, lead itself—to move beyond the storming into the orderly stages that follow. This was something Aretha and her cohorts fell into while the rest of the "team" gave in to the forces of entropy. To resist such temptations, you have to find a way to connect around a purpose or mission that is bigger than any single person.

Self-led teams don't need to look to leaders to tell them the next thing to do: they are empowered, equipped, and trusted. In self-led teams, less oversight and hand-holding is needed; people know what their jobs are and they do them, with a clear understanding of what success looks like. Team members work on projects that not only help the organization but also allow individuals to excel in their areas of strength; they all hold one another accountable. It's a common occurrence for someone to speak up, having found an issue worth addressing, and work to immediately resolve it. When we get lost in our ambitions, we risk the health of the organization and our place in it. Being self-led means not just working on the things you think should be done—those could be working against the overall goal of the company or at least not aligning perfectly with what the organization needs. Being self-led means knowing the goals everyone has agreed to and taking initiative to align yourself with and work toward them.

A self-led team doesn't need an individual leader because it can have leadership at all levels. It does thrive on the energy of catalysts who can help it come alive and step fully into its purpose for being. Everyone on such a team can manage their own sphere of responsibility and work collaboratively to bring together their thoughts, ideas, knowledge, resources, and assets in a productive manner. In this sort of team structure, everyone works together to achieve the end goal and no one has to be told to do it or even told *how* to do it.

But self-led teams don't just happen; they must be cultivated, like any good culture. For a manager, cultivating a system of new norms means helping your teammates create the vibe you all want to do your best work. It means helping others identify the best goal to guide the team and empowering each person, in their own way, to accomplish it. It means giving them the tools and trusting them to be smart, capable, and competent without a direct overseer.

Legally, and even practically, you may require a leader, but the leader of a self-led team is different from a head of a fiefdom. It's not the same as the stereotypical manager in an office setting. The leader empowers a team to do their best work free from interference; a manager (especially a bad one) hovers over that same team, making sure they're doing everything they're expected to do. A leader praises success; a manager looks for failure. The self-led team is too busy carrying out the mission to worry about any of that.

What It Takes to Motivate

Most leadership training seminars, conferences, and workshops get a leader motivated and inspired, but there's no actual plan. So this "leader" goes back and drops all these changes on the team. It's not a discussion—after all, *they* were the ones at the training. The problem is, the team hasn't been appropriately prepared, motivated, or inspired themselves. They just know the boss was gone for a few days and now they have all these ideas to implement until the next time the boss disappears for a few days.

This is obviously counterproductive, creating a more significant divide between the manager and the team. Navy SEALs and professional athletes never stop training or being coached. Not only does SEAL training last two years, but SEALs are in constant training and drills between deployments when they're stationed back in the United States. Similarly, professional athletes are constantly training and working out to stay in peak physical condition. They have a coach who trains them, runs them through practices and drills, and helps keep their skills sharp.

The same is true in the civilian world. The best leaders aren't standing in the back of the ranks, shouting orders and trying to steer the ship themselves. The best leaders equip their fellow teammates to practice self-leadership and work with others. SEALs have leaders in place, but there is flexibility in that there will be different leaders for different missions, so they're not too reliant on a single person. The mission is the priority, and that's what dictates the people and resources they use.

Self-led teams work to accomplish the goals they themselves have helped create, not just the ones that were put there by their bosses. These team members, of course, care about what their bosses care about and take the initiative to work for the betterment of the company as a whole. Because selflessness has been modeled for them, they often model selflessness themselves and are no longer fixated on their individual accolades. As self-led teams start to gel, the appointed leaders of those teams should focus more of their attention on workplace culture, not only how it affects the well-being of those involved but also how it will affect the bottom line. If you're a manager, this takes sharing your goals and vision with your people and getting them to go along.

If you're not in management, then it's a matter of finding out what your bosses want and making sure they get it. In fact, the first step in changing things about your workplace is to stop thinking about how and what you're doing and start thinking about how it affects others. That may mean even asking your boss and your teammates, "How can I help you succeed?"

This is one of the biggest limitations of people advancing in an organization. They don't see how they can make their boss and colleagues do better and perform better. The ones who do? They're the ones who are brought up through the organization and take others with them. Your boss gets a promotion and thinks, "I need to bring Kyle along with me because he's always concerned about how to help the whole organization." A rising tide does, indeed, raise all ships; and no one does this better than a self-led team.

Treat Others the Way You Want to Be Treated

Everything changes when you start thinking more about what your team needs from you and less about what others can do for you. When you consider how you can impact those around you, you're stepping into a place of self-leadership, regardless of role or rank. You start being noticed more, as well: getting more recognition and building better relationships with others. People will see you as a leader—a fortunate by-product of the self-led approach that will soon spread throughout the team, changing the culture as others cannot help but follow your example. They'll look to you as a person who is reliable and trustworthy, someone who can solve complex problems and isn't waiting for the boss to tell them what to do.

You can do all this just by switching the way you think about and approach your daily work. Instead of waiting to be led, get proactive and find out more about your boss's or team's vision and goals—and how to support them. According to a 2015 Gallup report, almost half of employees in the United States do not know what's expected of them at work.* We think it's actually worse than that, as many are afraid to admit they have no idea what goal they are actually pursuing. In our experience, most team members seem to suffer from a lack of clarity and vision for the future. As a society, we have placed far too much emphasis on the role of the leader, and as a result we've robbed individuals of their own self-directed purpose and agency. This must stop if our organizations are going to thrive. Change occurs when individuals step up and

---

* Nink, "Many Employees Don't Know What's Expected of Them at Work."

take responsibility for what they can. This is how we all can create better cultures in our workplaces today: not by waiting for the leader to step to the podium and deliver a speech for the future, but by choosing to lead ourselves.

Other members of your team may also step up and take initiative. They may become leaders, doing what needs to be done without being asked. Sometimes a four-man SEAL team will head out on a mission without an officer, each team member knowing what to do and when to do it. This is not a completely chaotic unit where each man is in it for himself. Rather, the idea is that titles and positions are much more fluid. There is always someone to make the call, even if it's just a sniper and a spotter. The point is that depending on the mission, the person who makes that call may change. Self-led teams can work the same way, each member knowing what needs to be done for a particular project and then doing it, sometimes giving up authority if that's what is needed—or taking it. Of course, you need to know in which direction to go first before you can make a call, and that often requires a willingness to ask the right questions.

When Chris worked in the events department at Ramsey Solutions, he was frustrated that no one seemed to know what he was doing, even though *he* thought it was important. He went to his boss and asked, "What do you need me to be doing around here?" Surprisingly, the boss had never even thought to ask that of himself and his own work. So he told Chris what he wanted him to concentrate on, the things he needed from Chris. Chris followed up with, "That's what you need me to do. So how do I help you win and meet your goals for *your* boss?" He was even more taken aback, telling Chris what his own goals were and how he wanted to meet them.

At the time, Chris oversaw the planning of different events around the country, but they weren't performing well. Many weren't even making much of a profit, and the team could never be sure where they were effectively spending their time and money. One of his boss's goals was to increase traffic to the live events, so Chris began to focus on that goal. He developed a data analytics matrix that pulled in radio market data from the company's affiliates, website traffic, calls into the radio show, and other elements. From there, they ranked the cities in terms of importance and traffic, and used that to decide where to book the events. This was when things began to take off. They used the advertising money they saved by dropping the less profitable cities and put it toward events in the more profitable cities. The tours, which had occasionally lost money in the long run, were now a moneymaker for Ramsey Solutions. By prioritizing the top cities in terms of radio metrics and web metrics, they sold out nearly all their live events, something they had not often done before. It didn't require that Chris be a great data analyst; he was just using common sense to help his boss meet his goals of increasing traffic. He didn't wait to be told what to do, and he also didn't just blindly take initiative. Instead, Chris took the time to ask the right questions, considering the goals and problems facing his team and superiors, then went to work on a solution. That's what it means to be self-led: You don't just do what you want, and you don't just sit idly by. You take the time to learn what your organization's goals really are and do what you can to help accomplish them.

Once he accomplished this, the company realized Chris had more to offer. They immediately offered his team a graphic designer and video producer to help with the work he was doing. Later, he hired an assistant, and it continued to grow from there. His superiors began to trust him with bigger and greater responsibilities, and they let him establish cross-departmental relationships with email marketers, copywriters, and creatives in other departments. This was when Chris's personal trajectory started to develop and grow. His boss started seeing him as a leader and began giving him more responsibility, seeing Chris as one of the people on his team who would help him win.

When Chris stopped worrying just about his own goals and started focusing on his boss's goals, his thinking about what was possible expanded. With this expansion, he realized he needed more help, because the target of what he wanted to accomplish had now increased. He needed more people. The team grew from just a few people to eventually twenty-five, and soon everyone wondered how they could be a part of this group. At the time of this writing, Ramsey Solutions has a team of over seventy-five video production people and another sixty to seventy-five graphic designers, and it all started with Chris asking a simple question of his boss.

Together, they created a culture of outsiders who were unusual in that they wanted to do the things no one else was working on. They didn't wait for the company to change; they began to change the culture within their little sphere of influence. At first, it was just Chris and his small marketing department focusing on their boss's goals. Then once they had the chance, they brought on more people who could focus on those goals, and that began to change everything. As the department grew, so did the company, which led to Chris moving up in the company, affording him more influence and the ability to change the culture even further.

This kind of change is something anyone can create, not just the people at the top. Self-leadership is for everyone, and it starts with not just being the person who shows up on time, leaves on time, and does exactly what is expected of you. It means being the person who looks at the current situation, figures out how to support your boss's vision and goals, and determines how to win in that area. In this way, you can slowly begin to morph and change the organization, all by simply changing yourself first.

The Self-Led Leader

No team is without a leader, even a self-led team; but this type of leader isn't the typical corporate diplomat we've been deplatforming. Instead, she is someone who acts as a catalyst for her team, regardless of position, igniting a spark in others. When Kyle was with the Navy SEALs, there was always an ad-hoc leader: the person whose specialty was dealing with whatever issue came up at the time. This was the person who had the most experience in that area and was able to handle the parameters of the mission. The leader would arise from within the team depending on the situation. As in the case of Chris's experience at Ramsey Solutions, the leader wasn't the "boss"; it was the person who chose to step up and solve the problem. That is always the definition of a leader.

Every team has to have a leader. Someone has to be responsible if things go wrong. With the SEALs, however, that someone may change as the mission and priorities of the mission change. Nonetheless, there is always a leader who is given responsibility over the team; and their job, if they do it right, is not to hoard that responsibility but to steward it well and sometimes share it. Someone must be accountable. In the absence of a defined leader, however, someone almost always emerges. Whether or not they have been given positional authority over others is irrelevant; true leaders find a way to get others to buy into a vision.

Studies of jury selection have found that the first person to speak or the person who says "We need a foreperson" is often the one who ends up being selected as foreperson. We've even seen it happen in small committees: the person who says "We need a committee chair" ends up being chosen for that role. The self-led leader and self-led team are different from regular leaders and teams. Even self-led teams have leaders, but they're a different kind of leader from the ones you're used to. They're the ones who are going to make things happen for your organization—by empowering everyone around them to make things happen as well. If you're wondering who should be leading your team on this next mission, consider looking to the person who says "We need a leader." It might not be who you think.

The Bottom Line

As a concept, creating a better culture of self-led teams sounds nice, maybe even idealistic, but it is one of the most financially prudent things you could do in an organization. And the good news is that wherever you are in the organizational hierarchy, you can always do something. Creating a culture of empowered team members has been proven to add to the bottom line in significant ways.

Whether you're a manager wanting to give more responsibility to your team or an eager newbie looking for more authority, self-leadership is an important and necessary discipline. According to a recent article on LinkedIn, self-guided teams are 30 percent to 50 percent more productive than conventional teams. AT&T was able to increase the quality of its operator service by 12 percent as a result of innovating its organizational structure. FedEx saw a 13 percent decrease in errors. Johnson & Johnson reduced its inventory by $6 million. The statistics go on, but the lesson is the same: the way we structure and lead our teams matters—and not just in how it feels to be part of such a team but also in the actual output of these organizations.*

In Chris's case with Ramsey Solutions, there wasn't necessarily a team or a department involved, but there was a mission. Chris had a goal (his boss's goal, which he took the time to learn) and figured out what he needed to accomplish it. To his credit, Chris's boss empowered him by giving him the tools and training needed to accomplish his mission.

As Chris grew in responsibility, he was able to start picking his own projects and his own missions, and he started assembling his own team, sometimes even bringing in people from outside the department. He was able to empower them by giving them their mission and then getting out of their way. He didn't micromanage or demand hourly progress reports. He set goals and deadlines, and his assembled experts made it all happen.

But most important, he was able to set them loose on their own projects, which aligned with the company's goals. They were trusted to identify issues, challenges, and opportunities and to come up with solutions that met the organizational goals. By doing this, Chris was becoming an effective leader because he was empowering self-leadership in his team. He also made sure they understood that they had those opportunities and they were expected to find their own opportunity to self-lead.

If you were to ask every manager, every coach, every leader of a team if they would approve of such behavior, they'd probably all say "Of course! Yes! I want everyone to take on more responsibility." But if you are in the position of manager or team leader and fail to explicitly communicate such a norm and demonstrate it with your actions, such sentiments are going to be misunderstood. Our team members don't follow what we say as much as they pay attention to the norms we allow. If people have to ask for permission to take on responsibility, then you're doing it wrong.

Roughly seven out of ten employees do not feel engaged at their jobs. Part of the reason for this is lack of recognition, which is often cited as

---

* Cody, "Self-Directed Work Teams."

one of the top reasons people leave their employer for a new job.* This is more important than we might realize—and if we want to change the cultures in which we work, compete, and learn, we've got to start taking on more responsibility and sharing it with others.

What If You're Not in an Ideal Situation?

Again, this all sounds nice, but we recognize that some people just don't have the chance to disrupt an entire department, organization, or culture. Maybe you work in an organization in which initiative is tamped down as if in a game of Corporate Whack-A-Mole.

Maybe you have a leader who oversees what you do and is afraid that you might outshine them. Maybe the whole place just feels oppressive, and without anyone saying so, initiative just doesn't seem to be a very positive thing: you do what you're told, don't ask too many questions, and stay in line. Otherwise, you're going to end up in a whole heap of trouble. Most of us are just trying to not get fired. We want to stay on the team, keep our business going, and have a paycheck next month. And there's nothing wrong with that. But at some point, you've got to decide what you're willing to put up with and what would feel like an ideal team environment for you, whatever your circumstance might be.

So, you have options. For one, you could try to find a new team: a new place to work, a new group of people to partner with. If you're not able to thrive or are in a culture that values you and your intelligence, go somewhere else. Find a new company that will value you. There's no need for you to spend forty, fifty, or sixty hours per week at a place where you are not appreciated for your ideas, initiative, and skills.

Of course, that may not be an option for everyone. In this case, you can begin by leading yourself. Let's assume you've got a bozo for a boss; you don't get the direction you need, the mission isn't clear, and there is no vision beyond what needs to be done today.

You can spend all day every day complaining about it, growing more

---

* Pendell, "Tomorrow Half Your Company Is Quitting."

and more resentful of whoever's leading you—or you can decide to be different now. You can summon a little courage, tackle a problem nobody seems to want to solve, and offer to help.

You might try, as Chris did, to subtly win over your boss's affection by getting clear on what their needs are. Leaders are people, too; and they often have very few others asking what they need. Helping someone get what they want is the best way to get what you ultimately want. It might take a little longer, requiring sacrifice and selflessness on your part, but that's okay. You'll be a better person in the long run for it.

When you identify a problem, don't just tell your manager there's a problem and ask or expect them to fix it. Bring a few solutions yourself. Show the options that will save the most money or lose the least money. If you can at least say, "We can do A, B, or C, and I think B is our best option because we'll save the most money," then you've shown some initiative, you've engaged your own skills, and you've shown that you're trying to achieve your boss's goals. You have to understand that your boss is probably feeling as frustrated and distrustful as you are. So you need to work in a way that the boss will get what they're hoping for and realize that you're not going to take advantage of them.

Ultimately, creating a better culture comes down to hiring good people and letting them do their thing. But it also means making sure they understand the boss's vision and goals, as well as the overall mission of the organization. It means the boss needs to step out of the office once in a while and say, "Can I buy you a cup of coffee?" Think about what kind of culture a company could create if managers did only that, thanking their team for doing a great job once in a while. Such a simple effort just might change everything. Employees don't just need a raise; they need acknowledgment. They don't want a gym membership; they want appreciation. We all do. We want to feel like what we're contributing is valued and valuable. It's human nature to crave such affirmation, and there's nothing wrong with that.

When someone doesn't shape the culture of an organization on purpose, culture will shape itself until somebody cares enough to change it. You have to decide: How do you define a healthy culture within your organization? Do you want to redefine and change your current culture? Do you want to embrace it and grow with it? Or will you wait to see what happens and let it organically develop? Healthy workplace culture has become a thing many leaders talk about but few practice well. And there's a simple reason for that: they're still running top-down organizations.

Leadership doesn't start at the top. Sure, you may have someone "in charge," but the travesty behind Aretha Franklin's first hit can teach us that just because you're the boss, it doesn't mean you're the one people should be listening to.

Despite what the attendance criteria of those "leadership training seminars" tell us, you don't have to be anointed as a manager to be a leader within your organization. In fact, sometimes the best leaders are not the ones with the titles; and yet, we still need those people to lead. As Seth Godin wrote in *Tribes*, "The secret of leadership is simple: Do what you believe in. Paint a picture of the future. Go there. People will follow."[*]

You can begin demonstrating leadership skills at any level within an organization, starting with the simple skill of self-leadership. As Walt Freese, then CEO (chief euphoria officer) at Ben and Jerry's, told us: "Start with the branch you're on." No one is going to change your culture without you, because you are a part of that very environment. In order for it to change, you have to change, too—and you have to change first. Whatever you do, just don't go knocking on someone's hotel room in the middle of the night, drunk and angry. That never ends well.

---

[*] Godin, *Tribes*, 108.

PHASE II

DEVELOP

———

If you read many of the top-trending business books on the market right now, you'll find a few definitions of the word "culture." It can be a nebulous term with a variety of meanings, but most sound something like this: "Culture is the behavior of individuals within an organization and the meaning people attach to that behavior." It sounds right, accurate even, but it also feels pretty stale, reeking of business-speak. Not to mention, it's unhelpful to anyone trying to *do* something about the culture in which they find themselves.

Nobody, after all, aboard the *Belgica* was saying, "Hey guys, we need to change the culture around here." They were, in fact, fighting to stay alive. This is often the case when culture shifts are needed most. It's not simply a shift in preference (e.g., "We want free laundry!") but a matter of actual survival. This is the kind of culture we want to explore in this book, the kind that can topple dictatorships, turn around failing companies, and even save a ship full of slowly starving sailors.

How *do* you create a world-class culture, one that changes things for the better? And what *does* it look like to build a team of people who can do the impossible? Or does it even matter anymore in this world of remote work and human disconnection? Does it even make sense to be a part of a team anymore? We argue that it does, but everything we thought we knew about teams is essentially wrong.

We don't need more autocratic leaders with minions running around at their beck and call. We don't need more "rock stars" winning over the crowds with their charisma. No, to truly change things, we need teams with a mission that is greater than any single individual. We need a cause that calls greatness out of each person involved in the project. We need something more than what we've had before.

Yes, the word most often used here is "culture," but the typical definition just doesn't seem right. It doesn't tell us anything about how you create and shape a culture, not to mention why it matters in the first place. In the corporate world, "company culture" has become yet another buzzword, devoid of meaning.

Culture, as we define it, is the environment that leadership allows to take hold in any organization. It is the collective personalities, values, and interactions of team members and is far more often allowed than it is created. What *are* your shared values and norms? If you're like most people, you don't know; or, at least, the question is a hard one to answer. But the truth is that whether or not you can define it, you already have a culture that is driving everything you and your peers do. Do you know what is guiding you? Because it's there, even if you don't see it. That's how culture works.

The most important question you could ask of a team, organization, or company is *"What is our culture, and how do we shape it?"*

Developing a culture is what happens after we define it. Thus far, we've been looking only at the value of self-led teams and what it takes to transform the culture of an organization from the inside out. To change a place, you first have to figure out what it's made of, what the core components are. Then, once you understand that, you can begin to truly change things.

In Navy SEAL training, Hell Week happens in the middle of First Phase of BUD/S (Basic Underwater Demolition/SEAL) training. First Phase takes eight weeks, and if you complete that, you have earned the right to continue training to become a SEAL, but finishing Hell Week, or even First Phase, doesn't mean you're done. You still have to finish the rest of your six-month basic training period, and then you've got almost two more years of advanced training and unilateral training before you're ready to go on your first mission.

For many, this phase of training is intense. The lessons are hard, the habits become difficult to maintain, and people begin to drop off. The dropout rate during the first portion of BUD/S training is around 75 percent to 80 percent. Of those candidates who enter Hell Week, another 75 percent to 80 percent drop out. The complete dropout rate between the time a SEAL candidate signs up to join the US Navy and when they complete Hell Week is above 95 percent. Becoming a SEAL is hard. Changing yourself is difficult. But it is essential if you want to go off somewhere in the world and try to change an entire culture.

This is where we struggle the most, where we are most likely to lose our battle against the status quo: right in the messy middle. At this point, we've defined the culture we want to create by tapping into our own personal and professional values and asking other team members what they want and what is important to them.

Now is the time to start growing what we defined in Phase I of this book. You can't just plant a seed, walk away from it, and expect it to grow, any more than a manager can attend a weekend seminar and expect to come back to his team capable of changing an entire company. You can't take up jogging for a few weeks and then expect to become a Navy SEAL. This is hard. It requires discipline.

This is Phase II. It's time to develop your culture. Like a potter shaping a piece of clay, you're going to create the basic form and then mold it and shape it until it becomes not what *you* want but what you and your team decide together it will be.

A SEAL goes through all kinds of physical and mental conditioning just to get through Hell Week, but it's not the toughest part of basic training. The toughest part is the week that follows Hell Week—which is called Pool Week. That's where we are.

Pool Week is when you're put through multiple underwater tests and the instructors tie knots in the oxygen supply lines of your scuba gear while your goggles are blacked out, simulating that you are on a dive in the middle of the night. Or they'll rip off your dive mask, turn off your air supply, and violently spin your body around, simulating chaos. They will mess with you constantly to test your composure, keep you adaptive, on your toes, ready for anything.

The first part is over; the second is about to begin. And if you can make it, you'll be miles ahead of where most people ever reach. You'll be prepared to handle the final phase of this process, sustaining what you've built. Let's dive in together.

8

GROWING A
SELF-LED TEAM

In the winter of 1939, as the whole world erupted into chaos and conflict, an army of about half a million Russians invaded Finland. Under the harsh regime of Joseph Stalin, the Soviets had just conquered eastern Poland, taking the land with fewer than four thousand casualties. Outnumbering their Finnish enemies by at least two to one, they expected a quick and decisive victory. They experienced anything but that.

Storming the tiny Nordic country with tanks and infantry, the Red Army was caught completely off guard. In spite of coming from inhospitable conditions themselves, the Soviets were ill prepared for the challenges found in those frozen forests. In the winter, temperatures in Finland regularly dropped below −40 degrees Celsius (−40 degrees Fahrenheit)—at the time, the Red Army did not train in conditions lower than 15 degrees Celsius (59 degrees Fahrenheit). The soldiers wore traditional camouflage and stood out as easy targets in the snowy terrain. In spite of its size, the army was quite clumsy and disorganized, an unfortunate consequence of the Great Purge of 1937, which had eliminated most military experts to solidify Stalin's power and prevent other ambitious upstarts from taking his place. Though strong in numbers, the Soviets were far from ready for what was to come.

Their native counterparts, on the other hand, were a force to be reckoned with. Wearing all white, the Finns could easily blend into their surroundings and maneuver over the land. Armed with rifles, they would speed by on skis, striking like cold, white death and disappearing before the Russians knew what had hit them.

The Finnish Army was a scrappy bunch of no more than two hundred thousand farmers-turned-soldiers, wearing whatever they could find because there were not enough uniforms for all the men. Though meek in presentation, each Finn was adaptable to his harsh conditions and prepared to protect his land at all costs. One such soldier was Simo Häyhä, who, like many of his countrymen, had been enlisted in compulsory military service at an early age—and who, like other Finns, surprised the Russians.

An expert marksman, Häyhä was unusual in his combat strategies. Instead of using the standard-issue rifle provided by the army, he opted for his own rifle, which had an iron sight instead of the traditional scope.

Buried deep in layers of snow, the thirty-four-year-old assassin would wait in silence for the enemy to approach, his mouth full of ice so they could not locate him through the exhaust of his breath. Highly feared by the Russians, he soon became a figure of mythical proportions, acquiring the nickname "the Magic Shooter" because of the deadliness of his aim. But there was a method to his madness. Häyhä's choice of an iron sight allowed him to avoid the glare of the winter sun reflecting off the glass of his scope—one more way he could stay hidden from the Russians and strike with surprise.

Much of that brief war was like that. One of the largest armies of the twentieth century suffered tremendous losses at the hands of a ragtag band of farmers who refused to let their country go without a fight. After a month of embarrassments, Stalin increased his numbers and sent even more troops into Finland. The Red Army, totaling well over six hundred thousand at this point, aggressively bombarded the Finns every single day for a week and a half, seeking victory at all costs, even if it meant near devastation of its own forces. Three and a half months after the initial invasion, the Soviets prevailed but not without experiencing tremendous losses at the hands of their underrated enemy. The Finns had begun to suffer significant losses themselves and sought a peace treaty in March 1940, unable to endure the casualties of war—sadly, only days before France and Great Britain were to deploy an intervention.

Although the numbers vary, experts estimate the Finns suffered approximately 25,000 deaths and 43,000 casualties. The Russians lost around 135,000 soldiers and had another 150,000 wounded. During the brief but bloody Russo-Finnish War, also known as the Winter War, Simo Häyhä is reported to have killed over 500 Russians. He was wounded at the tail end of the 105-day war and hospitalized. To this day, he is credited as the deadliest sniper who ever lived.

In 1941, Finland took back the land it lost.

Self-Led Teams Are Grown, Not Built

The Finnish Army, in almost every respect, was a self-led team. It was not a particularly well-trained group of soldiers. They didn't have the latest equipment or even, necessarily, the best leaders. Can you name the president of Finland at the time of World War II? And yet, who doesn't know the name Joseph Stalin?

What allowed the Finns to stand up against one of the cruelest leaders of the twentieth century and ravage his army wasn't leadership, at least not in the way we are typically used to thinking of that term. It wasn't the drive of a single man that propelled those Nordic soldiers to eviscerate nearly one-quarter of a million Soviets—it was their will to survive, a familiarity with their environment, and an ability to adapt to their conditions. Which is to say, they had a mission and a purpose, a reason to live and fight—and the advantage of meeting the enemy on their own turf.

And they nearly won.

In fact, you could argue that in the long run, they did, though not without experiencing their own losses and discouragements. Still, it is a marvel to understand the sheer magnitude of the numbers. By the end of the conflict, the Red Army outnumbered the Finnish Army by nearly four to one, and despite pulling out all the stops, they struggled to break into a small and seemingly insignificant country.

One army was organized around a single leader who had his sights set on victory. The other was sleeker and knew how to use their surroundings—in many respects espousing the values of what we now call a self-led team. The Finns, for most of the fight, were on their own, working with their environment to outsmart the invading army. The Russians, on the other hand, expected to conquer by blitzing through the land—a strategy that nearly destroyed them.

As we can see, what makes an army mighty is not sheer numbers. Bigger is not better. Braver is not even better when it comes to building a team that will win. More often than not, the team that wins is the one that knows how to work with whatever conditions it is given, organizing itself around its circumstances instead of fighting against them.

What we can learn from this lesser-known war that is often overshadowed by the outbreak of World War II is that tenacity, as well as leadership, can be overrated. What makes an organization great is its ability to adapt to its environment, for all of its members to use what is available to them, making the most of their surroundings to accomplish a central and important goal. Or, to quote Kevin Costner in the film *Robin Hood: Prince of Thieves*, "One free man defending his home is more powerful than ten hired soldiers."

Self-led teams are grown more than they are built, necessarily. Like a garden that requires tending, a self-led team is not something you create out of thin air. It is developed with careful attention. No matter how great a leader you are, one person does not create a culture. Leadership, in the words of General Stanley McChrystal, "is a choice," and when you empower an entire group of people to make that choice, you have the beginning of a self-led team. In his book *Team of Teams*, the general said this approach to culture development is similar to gardening. "The temptation to lead as a chess master," he wrote, "controlling each move of the organization, must give way to an approach as a gardener, enabling rather than directing."* This is exactly what Stalin was trying to do:

---

* McChrystal et al., *Team of Teams*, 232.

drive an army across a national border, thinking like a chess master. In contrast, the Finns were acting like gardeners, using their surroundings to outsmart a seemingly impervious enemy.

Successfully developing a self-led team is a recipe of sorts, one in which you want to strike the appropriate balance between the ingredients, making sure all the flavors come together in just the right way. It's an organic process that requires the right amount of time, care, and attention. The right amount of pressure at the wrong time will ruin the very thing you're trying to make. This is true in the development of any organization you want to take on qualities of self-leadership. Cultures are developed by paying attention to both your environment and the people in it.

McChrystal, now a retired army general, headed the Joint Special Operations Command in the early to late 2000s and led all forces in Afghanistan from 2009 to 2010. Called by former defense secretary Robert Gates "perhaps the finest warrior and leader of men in combat I ever met,"* the general warned against following the "plan" at the cost of what matters most. In his book, McChrystal argued that adaptability is the most important aspect of a team with a mission. "Efficiency remains important," he wrote, "but the ability to adapt to complexity and continual change has become an imperative."†

From a complex situation in Afghanistan, where one of the greatest armies in the world tried to fight a seemingly invisible enemy—Al-Qaeda—General McChrystal learned a few humbling and important lessons. First, he understood that to take down a network, you needed a network, or in his words a "team of teams," instead of a monolithic organization. Second, he argued that to be effective—defined as doing the *right* things instead of simply doing things right—you need small teams organized around a central mission. Third, these teams need to be able to adapt quickly to whatever new factors may present themselves in an unstable environment. This is the nature of instability: anything can and may happen. And this is the world in which we now live, as well as the state of many modern organizations. You can't make

---

* Satell, "Famous General Says Redefine Leadership."
† McChrystal et al., *Team of Teams*, 81.

a team do things just because the boss said so. It doesn't work that way anymore—not if you want to be effective.

Moreover, according to McChrystal, appointed leaders should submit themselves to intense scrutiny by their subordinates to create a sense of buy-in. For your team members to care as much about the mission as you do, they need to see your willingness to be challenged and criticized. How can the team get better unless each and every member is submitted to the same process of observation and review?*

Developing a self-led team often means watching one come together and choosing to intentionally nurture the process. You work with what is already unfolding and tend to it as you would a garden, paying attention to each living thing. Developing a culture is not a game of chess; your team members are not pieces you move around. They're individuals with a set of values and opinions that will inevitably affect how they act. And if this is something military leaders are paying attention to—in an institution that is categorically understood to be about taking orders—then how much more important is it on your team, in your organization?

Smith School of Business at Queen's University in Kingston, Ontario, demonstrates that each individual on a team has one of two main "goal orientations" that will determine whether or not the team will be able to thrive autonomously. If the team members share the same goal orientation, the team will work well autonomously. With diverse goal orientations, the team will not work well autonomously and will need more management.† We build healthy teams by not thinking of it as building; we grow what we want to thrive. And, of course, the opposite is true: the best way to destroy a team is to apply too much pressure all at once, to not give it space and time to grow into what it might become. This carries a risk, of course, because too much open space can cause unnecessary chaos, just as too much structure can be stifling. Striking this balance is a careful art and is contingent on multiple factors.

---

* Coauthor of McChrystal et al., *Team of Teams*, Dave Silverman was Kyle's troop commander in 2005 and 2006. Much of that book has excerpts from their deployment together.

† Morantz, "Trouble with Self-Managing Teams."

Death of a Self-Led Team

Development of a self-led team can seem contradictory. For one thing, a self-led team can't—or shouldn't—be managed. At least, not in the traditional sense of the word. Micromanagement is the death of morale for any team, and the progress of self-led teams is rarely linear. So to cultivate self-leadership, we have to entrust our people with a sense of ownership and responsibility; we have to, in fact, give others the freedom to criticize those of us in the acting role of leader.

A self-led team is one with a general sense of purpose and freedom. Team members know what the mission is, know the resources available to them, and are capable of carrying out their purpose with minimal check-ins and accountability. You don't have to hold people's feet to the fire; they know what is expected of them because each individual on the team expects it of themselves. They know how they are being evaluated and what winning looks like. They are intrinsically motivated to succeed because they believe in the mission, not because it's something the boss says is important. We see this illustrated in military conflicts in which one side doesn't understand what, exactly, it is fighting for and soon becomes disillusioned with whatever cause its leaders purport to be following. In the case of the Winter War, Stalin had enlisted soldiers from the ranks of other conquered Soviet lands, sending inexperienced and ill-equipped soldiers to fight his war. His reason for fighting was power; theirs was fear. And many men died for one man's ego. Finnish citizens, on the other hand, needed no grand speeches or fear-based campaigns to be called to arms. They had a much nobler cause: freedom.

Development of a self-led team begins with a cause bigger than any leader's personal ambitions. The team must have a purpose so simple and clear that individual team members can organize themselves around it and be entrusted to do whatever is necessary to fulfill the mission. In many ways, the end justifies the means—that is, so long as you do not violate core values of the organization itself. Doing so will undermine any long-term trust and credibility you've built with the team, and it will inevitably self-destruct (see the example of any tyrant whose oppression of his own people eventually led to revolt).

To successfully grow a team that manages itself, you need the following: (1) the leader must entrust the team with a clear purpose and mission; (2) the team must understand and believe in this mission; and (3) each individual on the team must be given the leeway to make whatever arrangements they deem appropriate to accomplish a given task.

This is how Navy SEAL teams operate. First, they identify their objective, their overall mission. Next, they figure out what the team needs and determine the assets they have available: personnel, equipment, finances, energy, transportation, and so on. Then they identify the specific personnel they need on the basis of mission requirements and the individual team members' skills, capabilities, and qualifications. From there, the team is given the latitude to accomplish its mission in any way it sees fit. Based on its members' training, experience, and individual capabilities and the assets available to them, the team is given its mission and allowed to amplify and support its own culture.

In a self-led team, it is assumed that the leader doesn't have all the answers but that the collective group has the wisdom and experience needed. Different members can step up to contribute their skills and take charge temporarily, but when their part is done, they step back and let the next person step up. It is, admittedly, a little messy. But according to American journalist and author James Surowiecki, this is how we get the best information from a group of people. In his book *The Wisdom of Crowds*, Surowiecki argues that under the right conditions, the collective is almost always smarter than any given individual. He makes a distinction between groups and crowds, pointing out that without the right self-corrective conditions—namely, creativity and flexibility—a mob of human beings can quickly descend into unproductive and unintelligent groupthink.

To get the most out of a group, then, you have to empower all individuals to share their best ideas—and you must allow that group to quickly cut out the bad ideas. "Groups are only smart," Surowiecki wrote, "when there is a balance between the information that everyone in the group shares and the information that each of the members of the group holds privately. It's the combination of all those pieces of independent information, some of them right, some of them wrong, that keeps the group wise."*

In other words, when individuals aren't allowed to practice independent thinking and ideation, the group's ideas will be only as good as the strongest, or perhaps loudest, voice within it. This was the short-sightedness of Stalin's attack on Finland. Having removed anyone who would challenge his authority, he also reduced the group to a homogeneous mob of mindless soldiers who were good only at taking orders. This does not typically lead to success and, one could argue, ultimately led to the downfall of the Soviet Union. Diversity, and the ability to exercise thinking that diverges from whatever the masses might be saying, is what allows any organization to thrive.

In a less extreme example, Chris and his team at Ramsey Solutions had meetings with one of his bosses to give presentations on whatever project they had been working on. Invariably, the boss would ask a lot of questions, especially if he perceived a weakness in one of the members. This man seemed to have an uncanny sense of when someone didn't know something and would exploit that weakness, asking about it first. It wasn't enough for one person to know the right answers because if he asked the question directly of a single person and that individual failed to respond to his satisfaction, it looked as if the whole team was ignorant, and the presentation was a wash. The team was only as good as its weakest member.

So Chris made the call to get his team into a conference room a day or so before the official presentations, and he would pepper the team with any questions he expected from the boss. As a result of this extra preparation, everyone on the team was ready to answer nearly any question or objection the boss could come up with. Because of this training to adapt to an uncontrollable environment, they usually hit it out of the park once they got to the real meeting. They were ready for almost anything. Best of all, the team got so good at preparing for these meetings, even if Chris wasn't able to attend, he didn't worry because he knew they were prepared. A self-led team is not merely a band of

---

* Surowiecki, *Wisdom of Crowds*, 253.

minions following orders; it aspires to be more than a group of efficient rule followers. A team that wins is one that knows its mission and can respond to the unexpected, whether or not the leader is present.

Finding the Right People

So how, practically, do you develop a self-led team? How do you hire the right people and train and empower them to do more than stay in line? Clearly, you can't just select any group of individuals, stick them on a team, and expect them to perform at the level of, say, an elite band of soldiers sent into the Middle East with a challenging goal and little else. It comes down not only to getting the right people on the bus, to quote business author Jim Collins, but also getting them into the right seats. Beyond that, however, you have to ensure that you are driving in the right direction and, ideally, that all those on the bus have their commercial driver's license. Which is to say, it takes training.

Finding people who are not only teachable but also flexible in all the right areas, understanding both the mission and the resources available to them to accomplish it, is essential to growing teams that win. You don't want a group of perfect clones who do whatever the leader says. Again, to quote Surowiecki, diversity is key: "Groups that are too much alike find it harder to keep learning, because each member is bringing less and less new information to the table. Homogeneous groups are great at doing what they do well, but they become progressively less able to investigate alternatives."[*] The goal is not to have one leader and nineteen mindless followers, nor is it to have twenty individual leaders who go off and do things their own way or who all think they should be in charge. You want a mix of different types of individuals who all understand and are bought into the mission, aware of their place in it at any given time.

So how do you find the right people?

First, identify the mission. Then figure out what the team needs and determine the assets available to you right now. You may not have every-

---

[*] Surowiecki, *Wisdom of Crowds*.

thing you need or want, but you have what you have, and you need to be able to work with it. The Finns didn't have uniforms during the Winter War, after all, but they knew a lot more than their enemy did. They understood that wearing white in winter was a better form of camouflage than green and brown. They had an awareness of their surroundings and a wealth of experience in the harsh cold. They knew how to work with their environment instead of fighting it. They were entrusted with a mission and empowered to do whatever was necessary—no matter how unorthodox—to accomplish it. After all, the survival of their nation was at stake. Use what you have; work with whatever resources are available to make the mission work.

Then determine each individual's capabilities. You can't make people into something they're not, but you can understand their strengths and weaknesses. Once you grasp the various competencies the team members bring to the table, you can accomplish your mission by working with each of these factors—allowing each individual to shine. As the leader, you don't need to quash bad ideas; if you allow all team members to focus on their strengths and contribute what they have, without prejudice, the cream really will rise to the top. A good team progresses when it is allowed to freely explore alternatives, even deviating from the original plan. So long as it accomplishes the mission, little else matters.

For example, let's say you need to hire an executive assistant, and you've spoken with three qualified people. They've got the right experience and the right skills. They could do the job just fine. But what you need is someone who's going to contribute to your company culture and team. So how do you choose between these three equally qualified candidates? We are big proponents of holding multiple interviews, not just by the managers but also with members of the team, executives above the hiring position, and even those under—their direct reports. Short interviews don't reveal a person's character. It's hard to do a 720-degree assessment of an individual in a thirty-minute interview. If someone brings a lot to the table and they have a high level of capability, you're not going to learn all of that in half an hour, no matter how good your questions are. Some questions could take fifteen to twenty minutes to answer.

Take time to get to know the people you're asking to join your team. Allow multiple members on the team to interview the prospect, giving them the margin to ask questions you may not have even considered. "The more power you give a single individual in the face of complexity and uncertainty," Surowiecki wrote, "the more likely it is that bad decisions will get made."* So let your team interview a new team member; don't make your team building another failure of leadership. Let the team grow itself. Cultivate an organization of individuals who want winners and won't tolerate losers. Make the process long and somewhat arduous, like a boot camp of sorts. Give your candidates time to shine, and don't let the process be driven by any single person. Ultimately, the result of a pressure-tested team member will be worth its weight in gold. You're looking for a person with whom you're going to spend forty-plus hours per week, every week, for the next several years. You can't find out enough about that person in a single meeting, and you can't grow a self-led team on the basis of one person's impression of an individual. Yes, we know this is out of the ordinary. And time-consuming. However, we aren't asking you to create average teams but self-led teams that will thrive and dominate. This takes more time and effort.

There are different hiring and management philosophies depending on who you are and what kind of team you're developing. Undoubtedly, you have heard the phrase "Hire slow, fire fast." But we've tried to work under the principle of *hire slow, fire slow.* You can't grow a garden overnight, and even pulling weeds takes time. A leader shouldn't be the only one making hiring decisions; therefore, the process will take time. And because you aren't growing this team by yourself, you shouldn't *un-grow* it all alone, either. Both hiring and firing should involve processes driven by more than a single decision maker. This is what it takes to create a culture that sustains greatness over time. To rush the expansion or contraction of a team invites chaos into a process that should not necessarily be completely ordered but should certainly be organic. If we want more than individual-driven organizations, we need team-led hiring and firing processes.

If you hire fast *or* fire fast, you end up creating an unsafe environment

---

* Surowiecki, *Wisdom of Crowds.*

for your fellow team members. (Not to mention, the actual cost of a new hire is $4,000!)* Your team will not trust you, and they will think you don't trust them. So they'll keep their résumés polished and their LinkedIn profiles up to date. But when they know you're hiring slowly and involving others in the process, they'll trust the team that comes together.

The goal of a leader, after all, is not to get a thousand helpers at his beck and call. It is to share his leadership with others so that the team, ultimately, can lead and manage itself. Don't hire for the leader; hire for the team. Almost every leader would agree with this, but few actually do it. Leading at this level, or rather organizing a team at this level, makes you better than the competition. Take the film *Miracle*, which tells the real-life account of the 1980 USA Olympic hockey team, which beat the seemingly invincible Soviets. How did they do it? In the words of coach Herb Brooks (played by Kurt Russell): "I'm not looking for the best players . . . I'm looking for the right ones."†

A great team is made not by assembling the best individuals but by getting the team to work together to understand and accomplish a clear mission. Do this and you can beat even the unbeatable. Don't do it and you'll fail to get the gold.

Enabling your team to do the work you could do is demonstrating trust in others, even if it means allowing them to fail when you might succeed. This doesn't mean there won't be a time for drastic action. If you've somehow pulled a bad egg into your group but allowed the team to help you in the process, they'll let you know. And it will quickly become evident that this person doesn't belong. To once again pull from Surowiecki's *Wisdom of Crowds*, "what makes a system successful is its ability to recognize losers and eliminate them quickly. Or, rather, what makes a system successful is its ability to generate lots of losers and then to recognize them as such and kill them off. Sometimes the messiest approach is the wisest."‡ A team made up of individuals who all understand the mission and are empowered to do whatever it takes to achieve what's

---

* Fahey, "Real Cost of Bad Hiring Decisions."
† "Tryouts for USA Team."
‡ Surowiecki, *Wisdom of Crowds*.

best for the team will quickly correct itself—without needing the boss's approval.

If you find you've somehow made the wrong choice, that you've hired someone who can't keep up with the work, someone who isn't trainable, or someone whose personality just doesn't mesh with the rest of the team, then you've got a decision to make. But understand that this isn't just your decision to make. The decision to hire that person was made in whatever way it was made, and now a seed has been planted. Either it will grow and fester, running roughshod over the entire system, or the decision must be rectified. Regardless, you may not want to rush. To take a decision you made slowly and then try to unmake it quickly may break other things. That's not to say there aren't fireable offenses. If an employee is caught stealing, committing safety violations, continually being late, or repeating other offenses after being given write-ups and warnings, you absolutely should fire them, fast.

But if you are considering firing someone because they're not figuring out the work quickly, or they seem quiet and reserved and don't fit in with the team, or they're missing some important knowledge, there are ways to work with the situation for the benefit of the entire team. More often than not, the decision to fire fast is unfair and is often driven by a single individual. It's often unkind and unexpected to yank out the rug from someone without advance warning and an opportunity to correct their behavior. It's unfair to the team because it sends a message of instability, and one of the most stable aspects of your team should be the team itself. Yes, you respond to unstable conditions, and you should do so with responsiveness and agility; but the team itself should be a well-oiled machine, each person willing to trust the other. When we honor the process of bringing someone new onto the team, or leading them off it, we honor the team. When we honor the team, we honor the mission. When we honor the mission, we honor what we are a part of.

Even if you have to quickly evacuate someone, the way you share this with the team should be a process, not just a memo sent via email or something that gets talked about once. Your team members need to understand how and why these decisions are made, what part they have to play in them, and what warning signs they may recognize if the writing is on the wall for themselves.

When it comes to performance, fire slowly. After all, if nothing else, you have a vested interest in helping this person work out, since their performance is a reflection on you and the team you are growing. That means they need training; they need guidance, coaching, and mentoring—from you or someone else on your team. If they need a little more hand-holding than most, find a way to provide it. If you want to see improvements, make sure they understand what is expected of them and that they are clearly empowered to do the work. Proper handoffs need to be made, and they need to feel supported not just by the leader but by the entire team. If or when someone needs to vacate the team, it should be seen as a failure not only of an individual but of the whole team. Why did we allow this person to join us if they couldn't hack it? What did we not see? How did we not properly train or empower them to fulfill our mission? *Shame on us for letting them fail.*

And of course, at some point, you may have to get rid of someone for the good of the team. That doesn't mean firing fast; it means first communicating that they're facing removal from the team. Chris once had an employee whom we'll call Bart. He was the most talented, creative person on the team, but he was always off doing his own thing. He didn't want to be a part of the team. It got so bad that Chris took Bart out to lunch and said, "Bart, I love you, and you're doing great. But you have to work with the team, or you've got to go. This isn't the vision I have for the team. You're going off and doing some amazing stuff, but you're frustrating the team because you don't want to work with them. When there are issues, you try to solve them on your own, which creates bigger problems for us all." Chris told Bart this was the last straw and gave him an ultimatum: *fix the problem in thirty days or you have to go.* Bart was stunned and hurt. He thought he was doing a great job, so he was surprised to hear that people were frustrated with him.

Chris was willing to let the best person on the team go—for the sake *of* the team. But it wasn't just his decision, and it didn't happen immediately. The team itself was letting him know that Bart was a problem. You have to be willing to let go of anyone who is not willing to work well within the structures your team has established. All team members need to know their role so they can do their work, but you can't have someone who doesn't want to be a part of that team. Otherwise, no matter how talented, they will end up being the biggest cancer you have, eroding the organization from the inside.

Fortunately, this wasn't the end for Bart. Chris and the rest of the team offered additional coaching and guidance, and Bart, who took the ultimatum seriously, turned things around. Some time later, he even stepped into a leadership role, overseeing the entire team. All that is to say, hiring and firing are team affairs. Leading is a process that involves the whole team and should include every member; therefore, growing a team should involve the same. A trustworthy team is one in which all members are able to lean on one another, sometimes even in circumstances of life and death. Everyone needs to know what is expected of them and be willing to lean on the others for support and call one another out when they see someone failing to uphold the mission-critical values of the organization—even if that means confronting the person who hired them.

Elite teams are grown slowly and carefully; they are maintained in the same way. And that is why it is so important to start today. Few organizations want to dedicate the required time to creating something great. This is how high turnover rates slowly kill organizations. With people constantly moving in and out, how can you expect to build an elite force or win a gold medal? It just won't work.

Creating Cultural Magnetism

When Kyle and his SEAL team were in Afghanistan, one of their first objectives was to establish a police force in Helmand Province, in the village of Malozai, from scratch. As soon as they landed, they began attracting local interest and found a local leader, who we'll call Khalil, and put him in charge of the police force. This made Khalil the first member of that police force, and the SEAL team quickly gave him ownership of the entire process. After some recruiting, another man joined the team, but he was disgruntled, out of shape, and untrained. He was joined by a second individual who had similar issues. This didn't bode well for the long-term success of a police force that would, it was hoped, ward off the presence of the Taliban. Something had to be done.

One of the first things the SEALs did with Khalil and his team was teach these new recruits the importance of physical fitness and proper nutrition. The most important step of the training process was to earn the trust of everyone on the team, so they started building that trust and helping train the new police force by building camaraderie within the unit. They created competitions and started getting everyone to compete with one another. There were actual prizes involved, and there were winners and losers—no participation trophies. The guys all learned to work hard, and if they lost, they learned to go home and come back the next day to try again. Through this competition, camaraderie increased and others took notice.

Two recruits grew into five, five became ten, and ten turned into twenty-five. Soon, there was an active police force of sixty-five people. The central theme running through the entire operation was trust, camaraderie, and a sense of belonging. It was a magnet culture they had created together, a team built on hard work, competition, and fellowship. Kyle and his SEAL team knew they could return home and leave the force in good hands. When they eventually left, there were tears all around. A local elder and landowner gave Kyle and the team a camel as a gift of gratitude for establishing peace in his region, allowing his businesses to thrive and his family to grow. They named the camel Harry, and he stayed around the camp for a couple of days before they had to give him away. It turns out that camels don't make for very good pets—at least Harry, who smelled terrible and defecated everywhere, didn't. But the gesture is what matters: never underestimate the value of building a culture so attractive that people will want to sacrifice almost anything to become a part of it.

If you are so fortunate as to find yourself on such a team, do whatever it takes to protect it. Preserve the specialness of it and tend to it as you would a garden. By building a sense of camaraderie among the police recruits, by helping them excel at something they cared about, Kyle and his team were able to grow the force into something much bigger than they had originally envisioned. People like being a part of something bigger than themselves. They get to contribute to something that will have a longer-lasting effect than their own individual efforts, and this makes individuals feel that they are significant, that they have a purposeful part to play in a greater whole. To find people who love what you do, create something people will love and want to preserve. Talent recognizes talent. As you create a magnet culture, the entire team will get excited about what they're building and what they get to be a part of. They'll tell their friends and invite others to join them.

After Chris figured out the benefits of helping his boss achieve his goals for the events department at Ramsey Solutions, he started to wonder who else he could bring along for the journey. Soon, with a couple of colleagues, he formed an ad hoc team, which they called the Brand Wagon, to share ideas and collaborate to make the department even more successful. It began with a graphic designer and a video production person regularly meeting with Chris for breakfast at a local Cracker Barrel restaurant. Soon, as others began to see their results and the fun they were having, more wanted to join. This was an unofficial team that was meeting outside the office to talk about work. They weren't getting paid anything extra to do this; it was just something that had a clear purpose, and that clarity attracted others. Talent recognizes talent, after all, and everyone wants to be a part of something special.

What had started out as a few people sharing ideas over coffee turned into a squad of twenty-five, with even more people wondering how they, too, could be a part of the crew. The breakfasts got so large that they had to hold them in the company's warehouse with catered food brought in. The team grew because every individual who was a part of it cared about the success of the mission. That's the sort of thing that's contagious.

In such a scenario, it's not long before a self-led team attracts the attention of an entire department or organization, sometimes an entire nation. It all starts with individuals loosely organized around a core purpose that clearly matters to them, with each person empowered to fulfill the mission, doing whatever they can with whatever they have. After all, those who succeed are not those who wait around to be told what to do. Rather, it's the teams of empowered people who care deeply about a cause that otherwise might go unnoticed or at least unaddressed. And whether that's a band of farmers protecting their country from hordes of invaders or a clan of creative professionals grabbing breakfast, it's true that the ones who change things are those who are bold enough to try.

9
—

EVERYONE NEEDS
EMPATHY

Winning at all costs for an organization is not really winning at all. Many leaders lose sight of their teams when consumed with a massive vision for success, and as a result everyone loses. For example, take Amazon. What was once thought to be a powerhouse of productivity and innovation is now understood to be a "bruising workplace," according to the *New York Times*, which recently reported on the company's work culture. "It's the greatest place I hate to work," said one executive.* The now-largest retailer in the United States is receiving ample and due criticism for its workplace culture.

By interviewing hundreds of previous employees of the online super-store, the authors of the *Times* article painted a picture of the company as a wolf with teeth bared, ready to bite into the jugular of anyone unwilling to work eighty-five-hour weeks. Amazon has garnered and

---

* Kantor and Streitfeld, "Inside Amazon."

earned its reputation for being a cutthroat place of work by regularly culling its employees in an effort to mine for diamonds, separating the best and brightest from the "duller" ones. "Dull" is actually a term the leadership has used to refer to those who don't work overtime and whose work suffers for personal reasons, such as delivering a stillborn child.

Pardon the pun, but Amazon is a *prime* example of how to burn out good people. One former Amazonian, Elizabeth Willet, who was also a US Army captain, reported being criticized by her peers for not doing her work when she left at 4:30 p.m. to pick up her newborn from day care. Her coworkers didn't know that she'd arrived at work at 7:30 that morning, and the manager refused to defend her. Amazon creates an environment where workers are pitted against one another, having to outperform their colleagues constantly and be willing to report on them. No one knows whether their job is safe. The focus of every dedicated employee, therefore, is to work as hard as they possibly can so as not to be sent to the chopping block. Although this is likely an intentional strategy of leadership to weed out all but the best employees, it more than likely will burn people out, even its most loyal employees.*

Achieving greatness at the cost of the people who helped you get there is just not worth the cost. This isn't how humans work. You can't beat a person into submission and expect them to love you. That's not how love works. They'll fear you, but *love* you? Probably not. And fear always breeds a kind of insecurity that makes long-term success precarious at best. As a corollary, take the story of Zappos, the fun and quirky online shoe store founded by the late Tony Hsieh and eventually sold to Amazon. Having sold a previous company, Hsieh walked away from tens of millions of dollars to start something new, something interesting. He didn't do it for the money. He did it so that he could have a fun place to work.

Long before the billion-dollar acquisition and plenty of years before the

---

* Kantor and Streitfeld, "Inside Amazon."

Harvard Business Review was bragging about the company's culture wherein it paid new employees a bonus of $1,000 to quit, Zappos was just a boot-strapped startup struggling to get off the ground.* Like any good founder, Tony Hsieh believed so much in his vision that he put nearly every dollar of his own money into the company, covering the cost of overhead when the company was far from profitable. When the startup was in its infancy and had to choose between paying its vendors and employees, the company chose to pay the team. Whenever in doubt, you always want to take care of your people first. The alternative is unsustainable. Zappos employees were paid above market rates and given, in many cases, free rein to make the company into what they thought it should be. Similar to Ray Dalio, Tony Hsieh believed the best idea should win and encouraged team members to contribute their opinions about what would make the organization better. And they did. With that kind of feedback, the company was able to create something unique and extraordinary.

What made Zappos into the company it is today was a series of small but significant decisions, starting with its leader giving every-thing of himself to the team and the organization, doing everything he could to commit to this vision of his. He wasn't sure it would work, but he knew he wanted to try. And when he had the chance to either invest in the company or invest in his people, he chose the latter—because every company is nothing more than the people it's composed of. As Hsieh once said in an interview, "If you pour into your team, the team will pour into your customers."† That was what made the company great.

At Zappos, Hsieh and his leadership team created a culture of safety and empathy, which showed in every call, email, and tweet the company's world-famous customer service team became known for.

They created a phenomenal organization with a work environment that attracted global attention, all because they started with a focus on people.

---

* Taylor, "Why Zappos Pays New Employees to Quit."
† Hsieh said this to Chris during an interview.

More than Emotion

It takes more than a goal to make a great company great. You've got to be able to accept and embrace the humanity of your fellow team members, to celebrate them. You have to give them time and space to be who they are, not just who you need them to be. These are not robots you're dealing with; they are complex human organisms who don't just run a single directive into the ground. They aren't easy animals to control.

When you unleash the true power of a human being, you get more than someone who follows orders. You get innovation. You get creativity. You get a self-led team. Understanding the power of soft skills is the only way to create an organization of people who learn to lead themselves. But to do that, we just might have to change everything we know about management and what we have been taught about strong leadership.

Traditionally, in most types of organizations, we are trained to think of the leader as a special person and his or her subordinates as just that: lesser than the person with the most positional authority. But this burns out organizations (when so much pressure is on a single person, few individuals can stand such pressure over the long term) and bleeds out its innovation. Having a mission is not enough. You have to have empathy. You have to be able to connect with other humans if you ever want to try to lead them and bring them along for something other than a sense of duty and obligation.

Every team is only as strong as its weakest link, and the way we build teams of leaders is by allowing every person to feel that their experience and opinions are valid and just as important as anyone else's. This doesn't mean every meeting has to be an emotion-fest, but it does mean that all those you work with, if you want them to trust you and one another, need to feel that they are understood as individuals and that they understand others on the team.

Empathy is not just about feeling; it's about understanding and communicating other people's emotions back to them. When someone knows you understand where they're coming from, and you can demonstrate this to them, they will relax. They will become more of themselves, open up, and start trusting you. They'll also bring more of what makes them special to the table. When we allow those parts of our personality that may be emotionally charged to bubble to the surface, all kinds of creative ideas may come. And this is where we find some of the best solutions to our problems.

When you think about corporate America or the US military, you probably don't think about empathy. In this book, we've talked about the Navy SEALs, some of the toughest soldiers in the world; we've talked about multinational corporations, some of which contain the most unforgiving environments in the workplace. We've learned about surprisingly successful sports clubs and midwinter skirmishes in which the victor surprised us. When we think about some of the most successful and productive organizations in the world, we may think about qualities such as perseverance and discipline, but it is doubtful that the first strength you'd pick would be empathy. Yet empathy is exactly what you need to win.

In the past, leadership was bossy, literally. When the boss said to do something, you did it. No questions, no contributions—just a blind willingness to adhere to the status quo. Even if you didn't agree, you didn't typically object to the boss, and if you did, you were cleaning out your desk the next day. To this day, many companies are run exactly like that: there's a CEO or founding prodigy who drives the team with an authoritarian zeal and all the blindness that accompanies it.

In this model, the bigwig on top knows everything and acts as if he does. Everyone sincerely believes him and sometimes trusts him; but it's a precarious place, to be sure. In these environments, employees quickly catch on that they should never question their supervisor because in this model, authority and intelligence have become equated. To be ahead of one person in the organizational hierarchy means you know better than anyone lower in the hierarchy about everything at work. Otherwise, why would you be on top?

There are, of course, some glaring errors in this model.

Smart leaders will never tell you that they are the smartest people in the room; they know they are not. A good facilitator of a group is not trying to maintain his status at the top of the pyramid; he's trying to share his position and responsibility so that the work he is doing may be multiplied. Smart leaders surround themselves with people who have the potential to become leaders themselves. And they start by connecting with those people, not as bosses barking orders to their subordinates but as one human to another.

Things have changed. Empathy is not some special gift reserved for school career counselors and psychiatrists. It is a necessary tool for the progress of every self-led team. Empathy will not only allow us to go further faster. It'll save our operations from utter ruin—and not only that; it just might be the means to lasting success and meaning in any place of work.

Developing Tactical Empathy

The Center for Creative Leadership conducted a study in which it analyzed data from 6,731 managers in thirty-eight countries.[*] What it found, unsurprisingly, was that empathy in the workplace is positively related to job performance. The more empathy a manager has, the better an employee's performance. And the better the employee's performance, the more revenue generated. This also has a "trickle-up" effect in which managers who practice empathetic leadership with their direct reports are viewed as having better job performance by their own bosses. Everyone wins with empathy. "Although an important factor, the benefits of empathy extend far beyond employee satisfaction to all corners of a business—including its bottom line," the authors wrote. "Promoting a work culture centered on empathy is one way to ensure actively engaged employees and increase overall productivity."[†]

Empathy is not just a feel-good aspect of workplace culture; it also has a significant financial impact. According to Rae Shanahan, chief strategy officer at Businessolver, lack of employee engagement costs businesses more than $600 billion in lost productivity per year.[‡] In contrast, an organization with an engaged workforce experiences higher employee

---

[*] Gentry, Weber, and Sadri, "Empathy in the Workplace."
[†] Trickle, "Link Between Empathy and Productivity?"
[‡] Shanahan, "One Word Is the Solution."

satisfaction, lower turnover, greater productivity, increased profitability, and higher levels of customer satisfaction and loyalty.

In fact, according to Businessolver's "2017 Workplace Empathy Monitor," 60 percent of employees would be willing to take slightly less pay if their employer showed empathy, and 78 percent of team members would leave their company for equal pay if the other company was empathetic. Additionally, 77 percent of employees would be willing to work longer hours for an empathetic employer, and 92 percent of employees would be more likely to stay with a company if it empathized with their needs.[*] These statistics demonstrate the financial value of fostering empathy in the workplace.

A lack of empathy can lead to employee turnover, which can be costly for businesses. The Businessolver report found that 72 percent of employees would consider leaving their current company if it displayed less empathy, with 78 percent of millennials and 66 percent of boomers willing to do so.[†] A high level of employee turnover such as this can result in costs associated with recruiting and training new employees, as well as lost productivity during the transition period. By prioritizing empathy and creating a culture that values and fosters it, businesses can not only improve employee engagement and retention but also save money in the long run.

Empathy is an essential element of a successful and financially stable business. By understanding and sharing the feelings of their employees, businesses can improve workplace engagement, productivity, and retention, leading to increased profitability and customer satisfaction. The financial cost of a lack of empathy can be significant, making it crucial for businesses to prioritize empathy in the workplace.

It's no longer a question of whether or not being a "nice guy" leaves you behind. Clearly, it gets you—and your team—far ahead of selfishly looking out for number one. Failure to connect with the human element

---

[*] Businessolver, "2017 Workplace Empathy Monitor."

[†] Businessolver, "2017 Workplace Empathy Monitor." This story was also covered in *Forbes*. See Hyken, "$600 Billion Employee Engagement Problem."

of leadership often leaves individuals on a team feeling unmotivated and uninspired.

One need only read the Malicious Compliance subreddit to see story after story of employees who feel underappreciated, working fifty to sixty hours per week only to be berated by their managers for showing up two minutes late. When this happens, people feel unsafe and revert to making boring choices that prevent them from getting fired. A team member afraid of getting in trouble is not going to take many risks, which will only cost you in the long run.

When Chris worked at a church, there was a leader who never seemed satisfied—he was more often than not disappointed. The church once held an event that was its most attended event ever and another that was equally successful. After both events, the leader said he was disappointed and suggested to Chris that he might have to let him go. The whole of the organization was over the moon with excitement and energy about their successes, but the leader couldn't see the good, only that it wasn't what he wanted.

This is an all-too-common scenario that goes beyond mere unchecked ambition. There is a difference between wanting to improve and showing no appreciation or empathy for how hard a team has worked, regardless of the result. When the team members involved in the two events heard how the leader felt, they felt frustrated. What was the point, then, in trying again, in putting themselves out there and going for something even better? Clearly, it would never be good enough. Suffice to say that neither of those events happened again, and to this day, that organization struggles to retain top talent.

Of course, it's great to be kind to your coworkers and attempt to meet them emotionally wherever they may be. But this goes beyond morality and hits right at the core of what makes organizations successful. A cultural value of empathy allows leaders the opportunity to understand who they're working with, what motivates each individual on the team, and how to get the most out of every person.

This is not just a key part of developing healthy emotional intelligence; empathy creates a more innovative culture. We might think of this as "tactical empathy," a strategic and intentional choice to make each member on a team feel valued and heard. Such an approach to communication can save a relationship, focus someone's vision, or simply remove any guesswork about what the objective is. A manager who lacks empathy can destroy an entire team and ruin a company. The days of "no more Mr. Nice Guy" are over.

Tactical empathy means recognizing each team member's perspective, working to gain each person's trust and to know them well. This helps your colleagues feel understood and often affirmed, which ultimately can result in an atmosphere of unconditional positive regard. Having tactical empathy means you can lead others with more effective communication and achieve positive outcomes in both your output and the way you connect with others on the team. This builds both engagement and retention on the team, with individuals feeling more bought in at every step of the way.

To overlook this important approach to team communication is to miss a huge opportunity to keep the right people on your team. The modern means of managing people as if they were machines is just no longer a safe bet. Those individuals will leave and find an organization where they can be treated like humans instead of robots.

Empathy is not pity. It's more than simply giving someone a hug when they've had a rough day. It means being aware, and acknowledging, that your team members are complex human beings with rich personal lives and social needs the effects of which will sometimes spill over into their state of mental health and well-being at work. It means watching for signs of overwork; it means understanding when someone has an issue arise and needs to leave work early or show up late. It means being compassionate and genuine when people tell you they're hurting and why. If you can show people that you care, they'll reciprocate by working harder and often more gratefully. We all appreciate feeling appreciated.

On the other hand, when people believe someone is not looking out for them, if they feel misunderstood or just not heard, they tend to not care as much about what they're doing. They "phone it in," not giving their best effort. They're disengaged. In contrast, when teams are built on mutual trust and respect, the camaraderie only grows over time. As the norms and values of the team are reinforced, members become more engaged, trusting their team and committing themselves to the mission even more.

Practicing tactical empathy means going out of your way to show team members that you care about them and who they are. This can be as simple as going to lunch or taking a walk around the building with them or any number of one-on-one engagements. If you are the leader of a team, such an offer can have a stunning effect. *Wow,* we think, *the boss really cares about me. I had no idea.* We all want to feel special, to know someone is looking out for us and thinking about us. That's empathy, and it's not as hard as it sounds; it just takes a little effort.

Bottom line: if you show you care about the team, the team will care about you—even when you're not around. Loyalty is a two-way street. It goes "up," but only if it goes back down, too.

Without empathy, we have no true loyalty. And without loyalty, we will fail at developing a self-led team.

Is Empathy Weak?

Some people see empathy as a soft, mushy quality—a negative attribute. That's dumb. Empathy is not a problem or distraction; it is the lifeblood of all true and good leadership. We already discussed how a lack of empathy can lead to lower engagement in an organization, translating into billions of dollars' worth of lost productivity. Empathy is not weak or soft. It is essential.

Having empathy for others means you try to understand their situation. Walk a mile in their shoes. Have some idea of what they're going through and recognize that things may be tough for them right now. They may not necessarily need tough love. They might need someone to watch out for them today and let them know that it's okay to have a hard time. Even in the Navy SEALs, empathy in leadership is important.

In Kyle's first role as lead chief petty officer, he was the tactical leader for a platoon at SEAL Team Three. During their training period in the United States, when they were getting ready for deployment to Afghanistan, Kyle was very hard on his guys when they asked for leave. He was kind to his men overall but hard on them when they wanted to visit their families. "If I do it for you," his thinking went, "I will have to do it for everyone else." At the time, he and his wife, Candice, didn't have any kids, but a couple of the men did. Once in a while, they might have a family activity—a kid's birthday party or recital—and would ask politely, "Hey, Buck, could I get some time off to see my kids play soccer?" Kyle's response was always negative. "It's Tuesday night, it's 6:00 p.m., and we've still got three hours of work left to do. No, you can't go see your kids when the rest of us have to stay here and work."

Two guys in his platoon regularly asked for time off to be with their families, and Kyle never saw what the big deal was. He was very hard on them and continually said no. The rest of the platoon was not very empathetic because they didn't have kids, either. They just didn't get it.

Kyle believed he was holding the two guys to the same standard to which he was holding everyone else, even though they didn't have the same circumstances. He thought he was being fair and thought he was establishing a stronger culture by being consistent and tough. He believed that if the other guys saw him creating a special circumstance for the two, it would be viewed as favoritism, that those two would be working less than everyone else because of a situation they had created for themselves, and it would rip the team apart.

Fast forward a year and a half and Kyle became a dad. Things changed dramatically in a short period of time. His viewpoint on a lot of matters changed, including how he led his men and dealt with personal matters in the platoon, especially extra time off to see family.

Suddenly, he had empathy for the two men who had wanted to see their kids as much as they could. Today, he can see that he didn't handle that well and was too hard on those fathers. He didn't have any empathy; he was too busy being the boss and not taking enough time to be the leader. Kyle has since apologized to those men, and they're still best friends: he loves them and they love him. But he knows he could have handled that issue so much better.

Those two teammates were frustrated with Kyle, but they were also frustrated with the rest of the team. The team would give them grief for wanting time off, which was caustic and degraded the culture Kyle was trying to create. He was so focused on his teammates accomplishing everything together, finishing their work together, that he wasn't meeting their individual needs. He was sacrificing empathy on the altar of efficiency. The result was that it cut down on their contributions and reduced their engagement—the same problem many leaders who lack empathy create for themselves and their teams.

That can be a problem for a SEAL team, in which much of your support network is your family. What do you think it does to someone who is expected to have the back of a team that doesn't have his back? What do you do when a poor decision over a small issue makes the team resent your leadership? Luckily, the team was able to work through the issue and rebuild that trust. But that's only because these were men who had spent years together building up rapport in a way very few teams on Earth ever do.

Leaders need to understand that they may have a gap in their tactical empathy if they are not in a place to fully understand what their team members are going through. If you grew up without grandparents, you may not understand why someone is heartbroken when their grandmother dies. If you never had pets growing up, you won't understand why it's an emotional gut-punch when someone's dog is sick. If you have never walked in someone else's shoes, don't base your decisions on your own feelings. Be aware that you lack the experience they have. Recognize when you don't understand their problem, and do your best to give them what they need.

But what if they abuse that trust? What if they lie? If they abuse your trust, deal with it when the time comes. Have a serious talk with them about integrity and reliability; if necessary, tell them it's time to seek their fortune elsewhere and wish them good luck. But for now, it's not worth destroying the morale and trust of the entire team because someone *might* take advantage of you. When in doubt, err on the side of empathy—remember, you could be making a billion-dollar decision.

Empathy Can Be Taught

Consider these seemingly contradictory statistics from the *Harvard Business Review*'s "Impact of Employee Engagement on Performance."* In

---

* Harvard Business Review Analytic Services, "Impact of Employee Engagement."

2013, Harvard Business Review Analytic Services surveyed 550 executives, including in-depth interviews, and the findings were surprising. Seventy-one percent of executives ranked employee engagement as very important to organizational success, whereas only 24 percent of executives said that employees in their organization were highly engaged.

Nearly three-quarters of all the executives surveyed claimed employee engagement was important to their company's success, but only one-quarter *of those same executives* admitted that their employees were highly engaged in the work they were doing. Nearly half of all the executives surveyed were not engaging their employees, even though they knew full well how important it was to their organizational success. How do we know the executives were not engaging their employees? Because they had created an environment that allowed team members to not dig in and engage with the work in front of them.

Self-led teams are teams of empathetic people who look out for one another up and down and across the organizational chart. So wherever you are in the pecking order, if you want to be a part of such a team, you're going to have to lead the way. Take the first step in trying to understand someone else. Empathy is innate, but it can also be learned and practiced. One way you can learn empathy and teach it to others is through proper engagement.

The more you engage with people, the more you're going to have empathy for them. The more you listen to them, communicate with them, the more naturally you will empathize with their struggles. Kyle admits he didn't have empathy for his teammates who wanted to leave early and see their kids play sports. But once he had finally walked in their shoes, having become a dad himself, he understood why family time was so important to them. More experience begets more empathy.

Practicing Empathy

If you don't think you have enough empathy, you can certainly grow in your capacity. We don't recommend faking it as much as practicing it. Demonstrate care and understanding to others and they will do the same for you and their teammates. Empathy makes everything better, and to begin making this a cultural norm on your team, you can begin practicing it in several ways.

Ask questions. One of the best ways to get to know people is to ask a lot of questions and listen to their answers. This shows people that you're investing in them: you're taking time to get to know them, to learn who they are and what makes them tick. It might just be a matter of two or three questions per day for some people. It might be a conversation once every week or two for others. And it might even be weekly one-on-one meetings with certain individuals.

The point is that when others see you being open and vulnerable, they will realize that they can do the same. They can see that this sort of behavior gets rewarded and repeated, and it can grow just like that. This sort of care and compassion can be contagious.

Practice active listening. Active listening requires more than just not looking at your phone when someone is talking to you. It means paying attention solely to that person and focusing on what they're saying. Don't think about how you're going to respond or wonder when the conversation will finally end. Pay attention and hear what the person has to say.

Be vulnerable and transparent. This means being willing to admit that you don't know something or that you're afraid of something. It might even mean asking for help. One of the hardest things for many of us is to admit we need help.

*Request weekly reports.** One way to learn more about people is to get weekly reports on what they've done—not just what they did at work this week but on a personal level. Ask them, "What was your high point this week?" It might be "I worked on a thousand-line spreadsheet." Or it could be "I got engaged." Maybe it's "We closed a million-dollar deal." Whatever it is, be sure to ask about their low points, too. The highs tell you what went right, but the lows tell you what's real: "My low point is that Adrian is quitting" or "My kid has been sick" or "I'm getting a divorce."

You can do the highs and lows as part of an email report in which

---

* Chris learned this from Dave Ramsey and began instituting it in his own business.

each person sends you that status update. Or maybe you can have a team huddle near the end of the day in a gathering in the conference room or on a call to share your reports.

Spend time with new team members. When Chris brings on new team members, he tells them, "Hang out with me for a few days to get a good sense of everything that's going on around here." It gives them a unique perspective on the team and, more important, on Chris's leadership style. They get to see him in action, watch him make mistakes and recover from them, and ask questions about why he did things the way he did. This also allows Chris to be vulnerable and open, which enables his teammates to trust him more and vice versa.

Give positive feedback. Is it really so hard to say something nice to people? Is it really so painful? No, it's not. But that doesn't mean it's not rare. David Novak, retired chairman and CEO of Yum! Brands (owner of Taco Bell, Pizza Hut, and KFC), started a company called OGO (O Great One!) and commissioned a survey that found that 82 percent of American workers don't feel their supervisors recognize them enough for their contributions. The survey also showed that 40 percent of workers would put more energy into their work if they were recognized more often.[*]

Recognition is where so much ambition comes from. When we acknowledge people, when we look them in the eyes, we honor their humanity—and they feel motivated as a result. Humans work harder when they're rewarded for their work, even if it's just a few kind and encouraging words. We are all human, and empathy is the act of realizing this. You need to talk with your team members face-to-face, thank them for their contributions, tell them you appreciate their work, publicly recognize and praise them when they complete a project. Don't assume they know. Don't take it for granted that they feel appreciated. Pay close attention to how they work and what their strengths are so you can speak to their individual efforts and needs. Praise them in deeply personal ways so they feel seen and known. You can do this no matter where you stand in the organizational pecking order.

---

[*] Novak, "Recognizing Employees."

When Chris started his leadership journey, he was a team member without any leadership responsibilities or direct reports. He started working with people on projects to improve his team's results, but in the process he started practicing empathy. On the Brand Wagon, that little cadre of creatives who got together once a week for coffee and to share ideas, he was taking his time getting to know everyone. Chris would ask these people questions, do his best to understand who they were, and provide support when they needed it. This earned him a lot of influence and trust with this group. He was practicing tactical empathy without even realizing it, which might be the best way to do it.

Empathy is not just an emotion, and it's just not for leaders. Empathy often starts well before you ever reach a leadership position—it's built into the very core of who you are. And it can be learned. How well you practice empathy depends on how engaged you are with your coworkers, how much you know what they're up to and what's going on in their lives. If you engage with them, they'll engage with you and their work. When you treat others with respect, they will respect you. They'll look out for you and one another because this is the example being modeled for them.

Self-led team members care about one another; it's what makes them strong, loyal, and willing to work harder, work longer, and search deeper for solutions. Leadership is overrated. It's not hard or based on some silly paradigm, and you don't need to bruise a team into action; you can listen to your teammates.

10

—

NOBODY'S LISTENING (ARE YOU?)

When Malcolm Muggeridge put Mother Teresa on television, he had no idea of the movement he was about to incite. In 1967, the well-known and controversial journalist conducted a half-hour interview with the future saint for the BBC. The interview was not particularly compelling, at least in terms of normal broadcasting standards, and at the time nobody had any idea who this woman was.

The Albanian nun, visibly nervous and clearly lacking in formal media training, spoke quietly and somewhat meekly about her work. Muggeridge, a critic of organized religion, claimed to have been transformed by his experience of meeting Mother Teresa, but their conversation was difficult to understand and follow, further obscured by her accent and her inability to take up any more space than absolutely necessary. Neither seemed to know what they were getting into, and it was doubtful whether the interview would even be aired. The show aired late on a Sunday night in what was dubbed the "God slot."

The response was nothing short of overwhelming. Although neither

Muggeridge nor Mother Teresa had made any appeal for funds, people responded in droves, sending letters, cash, checks, money orders, and more. After the broadcast, a total of £25,000 flooded into the BBC, the equivalent of £410,000 in 2022—well over half a million US dollars. The letters echoed Muggeridge's own claims of transformation.

Mother Teresa had an effect on almost anyone who experienced her, and just as the once-skeptical journalist's eyes were opened to wonder and mercy in her presence, many others remarked in ways that were reminiscent of his first impressions: "This woman spoke to me as no one ever has, and I want to help."

How did she do this, this penniless nun living in India, relying on the kindness of strangers? It was all in the way she communicated.

The Power of Walking the Talk

To lead an organization well, you must first demonstrate the standards you expect others to adhere to. The words you share carry tremendous weight. Mother Teresa and the order she founded—the Missionaries of Charity—sparked a global interest in helping the "poorest of the poor." She turned the hardened minds and hearts of more than one generation away from modern cynicism and toward a greater awareness of the less fortunate. And she did it without saying very much at all.

A year after that BBC broadcast, Muggeridge, now completely transformed by his experience, flew to India with a film crew to make a documentary about Mother Teresa's work with the poor. Normally, this sort of project would take a month and a half to complete, but Mother Teresa allowed only five days. During those days of filming, the crew visited the Home for the Dying Destitutes, an abandoned Hindu temple previously dedicated to the goddess Kali.

With the help of the Indian government, the Missionaries of Charity restored the building and turned it into a free hospice facility. At this home, anyone who had nowhere else to go was welcome. Those who were dying and suffering from incurable or untreatable diseases were encouraged to receive a comfortable exit from this life. Whether Hindu, Muslim, or Christian, the patients received whatever care could be provided and were offered their final sacraments and rituals according to the customs of their respective religions. "They lived like animals," Mother Teresa would say, "but die like angels."

During the film crew's visit to the home, they experienced what some considered a miracle. Kenneth MacMillan, the cameraman for the project, thought the trip to the home pointless because there was little light to work with in the building: there were only two small windows high up on the walls to light the large room. The crew attempted to film the goings-on inside the hospice and were surprised by what they captured. In spite of the little light available, and against all natural explanations, the scenes from this location are filled with an unearthly glow that softly illuminates the entire space, something reminiscent of a Renaissance painting. It may have been a divine moment, or it may have been the new kind of film MacMillan chose to use for that environment. Regardless, this event convinced Muggeridge he had witnessed the first miracle captured on film and televised for the entire world.

The result of those five days in Calcutta was a film called *Something Beautiful for God*, which was turned into a book. Both received widespread attention, attracting millions of eyes, hearts, and minds to the work of Mother Teresa and her sisters. Many novitiates joined the order over the coming years because they first heard of the work from either the film or the book or both. But that was just the beginning. Following the broadcasts of the interview and documentary, the attention of presidents, popes, and innumerable volunteers from all around the world was directed to India. People came to see the earnestness of her cause and wanted to help and participate in whatever way they could.

Muggeridge later wrote that "the wholly dedicated . . . do not have biographies. Biographically speaking, nothing happens to them. To live for, and in, others, as [Mother Teresa] and the Sisters of the Missionaries of Charity do, is to eliminate happenings, which are a factor of the ego and the will."* People like that don't often get biographies because they're too busy working at their cause. And this is true of all great leaders, catalysts, and change makers. They are doing the work that others

---

* Muggeridge, *Something Beautiful for God*, 16.

are content to only read and talk about. But what we learn from Mother Teresa's example is that if you want to start a movement, you have to start moving. Or, as she once put it, "Peace begins with a smile."

Who, then, was this woman, and why does her example of what we might now call "servant leadership" still matter today?

When she was forty years old, Mother Teresa (born Anjezë Gonxhe Bojaxhiu) received what she considered a "call within a call" and left her appointment to a monastery to start a new order with the intent of serving those whom the world had rejected or ignored. Such a bold move took years of appeals to her superiors but eventually resulted in her starting a new order, recognized by the pope. Where the call brought her was none other than a location Rudyard Kipling once called "the city of dreadful night." Calcutta was a desolate city full of abject poverty that many had never seen until they witnessed it firsthand. This was the world that the Missionaries of Charity wanted to reach; it was the world that had been crying out to Mother Teresa, a call she couldn't avoid.

She once called her order "the most disorganized organization." There was, however, a design to the disorder. There was a code of conduct, an understanding among all who served there—a way of communicating what mattered most without saying a lot of words. Mother Teresa never asked anything of her sisters that she wouldn't first require of herself. In fact, she often didn't ask at all; she simply modeled the behavior she wanted to see practiced.

Throughout the day, Mother Teresa would work with a tireless joy that was palpable and seemingly supernatural. Nothing overwhelmed or daunted her. At night, she would stay up late, doing all the ministry's paperwork and correspondence, and then go to bed for a few hours and rise before dawn the next day to begin again. She never seemed to lag, always eager to wholeheartedly dig into service each and every day. This was her work, the task God had laid on her, and she was going to do it as best she could.

And it was hard work. The nuns labored daily, adhering to a strict schedule: waking before dawn, eating a light meal, and then leaving in the early morning to go out into the city slums, where hope was sorely needed. They returned for a light lunch and brief time of prayer and rest and then headed back into the streets until evening. As arduous as the sisters' work was, many of them did it with the same joy exemplified for them. "In Mother," one sister recalled, "we saw really the living Constitutions: the joy of being poor, of working hard." When that same sister had arrived new to the order, she found the communal toilet dirty and instinctively recoiled in disgust, hiding herself away from the responsibility of cleaning it. Mother Teresa happened to be passing by at that very moment, noticed the mess, and immediately grabbed a brush, cleaning the toilet herself without complaint. There were no words spoken, no chastising of the less-experienced sister, only loving and dedicated service and a desire for others to join her.

Another time, when one of her former pupils won a medal for her studies, Mother Teresa told her to give it to the second-place student. This was how the Missionaries of Charity operated. They did not labor in ego. They did not jockey for position or praise. They had a cause that was bigger than any of them, and most were fully committed to it. Why? Because someone showed them how. As Kathryn Spink wrote in Mother Teresa's authorized biography, "The visionary fervor that burned in her was not the kind that invited compromise, but she asked nothing of those around her that she was not prepared to do herself. She coached them, worked late into the night long after they had gone to bed, and was constantly protective of them, keeping to herself, for example, the knowledge that the small tin box in which she stored the money for their daily needs was once again empty."*

They had little, gave much, and dedicated their lives to unfathomable service and sacrifice for those whom the world had forgotten. When asked how many nuns left the order due to the difficulty of the work and harshness of conditions, Mother Teresa said, "Very few . . . very few."

The Misconception of Communication

When we think of leaders nowadays, we think of people who talk for a living. We see a president, king, or prime minister deliver a speech

---

* Spink, *Mother Teresa*, 48–49.

on television and think, "This must be what leaders do." We see bosses stand up in meetings and declare a new mission or direction for the company. We hear the CEO go on and on about "what's next." And we may wonder if any of that talking is doing any good at all.

Granted, part of leading an organization is communication. And this is important. After all, where would we be without Martin Luther King Jr.'s "I Have a Dream" speech or the paradigm-shifting keynotes of Steve Jobs? The world would be a very different place were it not for the words of Sojourner Truth and Susan B. Anthony. Talking is important—to an extent. It just happens to be the *least* important thing a leader does. Of course, we're not saying no one cares what you say. We're just saying leadership doesn't make people listen. You may speak and others may politely nod along, but that is not the same as listening.

To get someone to really believe your words, to trust your vision and follow your direction—well, that's something else indeed. You need more than mere words to get people to really care. You need action. As General Stanley McChrystal wrote, "A leader's words matter, but actions ultimately do more to reinforce or undermine" the mission of a team. Good leaders exhibit complete and utter transparency in their communication. Like Mother Teresa, they go first; they don't ask others to follow them until they have allowed their teams to see them walking the talk. "This is the new ideal," McChrystal continued.* More than bossing people around or directing others on what to do, he advocates a policy of radical openness to guide people to a common goal.

Good communication begins with listening. We must create a culture of individuals who hear one another, notice what the others are saying, and take it seriously. This doesn't mean everyone gets a vote or that every decision must be made via committee. It just means that if we want to be part of an effective team, we have to learn to listen to one another. Team members want to know they are not just consigning themselves to the ranks of an organization but are actually becoming part of a team. They want to step into a vibrant, growing organism, and they want some of what they've witnessed to rub off on them. To

---

* McChrystal et al., *Team of Teams*, 232.

develop a self-led team, you have to attract more than you recruit. You have to listen more than you command. You have to share more than you want to know. If you require a lot from your team, whatever your role may be, you have to give more. This is how self-led teams thrive.

At one point in his career, Kyle worked as the tactical lead for the West Coast Navy SEAL training for assaults, combatives, and Special Operations Urban Combat. The team ran special training exercises on an island, where they built a fake city to run people through different scenarios and missions.

As part of the training, they would have post-mission debriefs. The lead petty officer would give his debrief, then a chief named Mike would give his. Each man would list his top and bottom three performances of the day. After they were done, Kyle (the senior chief) would give all his notes and areas of improvement. After Mike was done, though, no one really wanted to listen to Kyle. Fatigued by the details of the meeting at that point, they just seemed to stop listening. Mike was not a very good public speaker, rambling when he spoke and unable to keep it "short and sweet." But he was a great tactician who had been on several extremely high-profile missions, and all the men loved and respected him. Despite his lack of speaking skills, they listened to what he had to say. When he delivered his debrief, the men scribbled notes and soaked up every word.

Then it would be Kyle's turn. What Kyle had to say at this point was just not that interesting. It's not that what he had to say didn't matter; it's just that they didn't listen to him as well as they listened to Mike. After a few weeks, Kyle realized it didn't matter whether he conducted the debriefs or not. The fact that he was the leader didn't mean the participants were hanging on his every word. His position wasn't relevant. No one cared at that point that he was the leader; they wouldn't have interrupted him, but they certainly weren't listening.

A person's position in itself doesn't make them worth listening to. When Kyle realized this, it was freeing. He didn't get mad, didn't cuss them out, didn't even move himself up in the order of the meeting. Instead, he gave his notes to Mike and asked him to deliver them.

"Are you sure?" Mike asked. "These are really good notes. You should be saying these things." But it didn't matter who got the credit. People were already listening to Mike, so it made sense to let him be the bearer of whatever notes Kyle had. So that's what they did—and it worked. Over a period of nine months, you could see how much of an impact this move had on all the West Coast Navy SEAL platoons and teams. They absorbed more information because they wanted to hear from Mike. They knew him, respected what he'd done, and were open to what he had to share.

The Choice to Communicate

When we think of communication on a self-led team, we need to re-imagine what "talking" and "being heard" actually sound like in the real world. As Canadian philosopher Marshall McLuhan once remarked, "the medium is the message." What is said is as important as how it is said. In other words, people aren't just listening to the words you say; they're also watching your life and the example you set with it. If you say one thing and do another, the message won't be received very well. Communication, then, is about much more than words. It includes verbal and nonverbal cues alike, and if we want to build great teams, we have to learn to master this art form.

Communication is the key to improving any organization. Asking someone for a favor. Providing feedback. Getting to know someone better. Exploring and deciding on your core values, establishing a common sense of purpose, even getting a raise—everything depends on what you say and how you say it. Healthy and effective communication requires effort and discipline. It's not for the faint of heart and may require humility. But it's also the only way to get a team to understand the vision and how to accomplish it. Being open, honest, and transparent, without being cruel or making things personal, is how you create the kind of environment in which a self-led team can thrive—that's healthy communication. Good leaders create an environment where the sometimes brutal facts can be aired without hesitation. In such settings, team members feel safe to add their own ideas, and the result is progress. The more everyone feels free to share, the more the whole team grows.

Of course, you don't have to do this. Any so-called leader can order people around. It doesn't take someone special to be a boss who micromanages a team, snapping at people when they're not doing things exactly the way they should. That's still communication, but it's not effective—not even in the military. People have different communication styles, but some are more effective than others. Building a team, telling people you value them, and getting others to trust you requires actively listening and expressing yourself clearly.

Much of the so-called leadership we encounter nowadays, especially in corporate settings, does not communicate effectively. Leaders are not taking the time to be open, clear, and honest with their people; as a result, more and more teams are increasingly skeptical of authority figures. It is not enough to be merely effective at communication; you have to excel at it, which requires tapping into your humanity. One of the main problems of the much-touted leadership training in corporate culture today is that it rarely addresses the nuances of all kinds of communication. Companies can send their managers off to learn about modern management techniques, but when they come back, they can still be jerks. The command-and-control style that worked fifty years ago doesn't align with today's workforce.

Of course, most leaders aren't total jerks. They want to do a good job and want their team to do well. But they get lost in the pursuit of becoming better leaders, thinking everything is about them. They go to leadership workshops to develop *their* skills and learn how *they* can become better leaders, when really it's about the other people and developing a better understanding of them and how they work. That all starts with understanding how communication works.

Think about how much it costs to onboard just one employee and get them fully trained and immersed so they can be productive. Some experts put that cost at $3,000 per employee.* So take the number of employees who leave because of your management style and then multiply that number by $3,000. That's what unhealthy, ineffective communication costs you. As we know by now, disengaged employees are costing US companies $600 billion in lost productivity, whereas companies with engaged employees achieve 10 percent higher customer ratings, 17 percent

---

* de Haaff, "$3,000 to Onboard New Employees."

higher productivity, 20 percent higher sales, and 21 percent higher profitability.*

These are the facts. Ineffective, unhealthy communication affects your bottom line—without fail. Disengaged employees bring down productivity and sales, and eat up profitability. Communication is key to building trust, and trust is key to financial performance. Getting this right will save you time, money, and a lot of future headaches.

How Does Communication Work?

Communication seems pretty simple. I talk, you listen. We write, you read. Someone with a smartphone broadcasts and the world watches. There's a sender, a message, and a receiver. We all learned some version of this formula early on in school. It seems pretty straightforward, doesn't it? Except that it's not. Anyone who's ever had a disagreement with a spouse, friend, or coworker knows that the exact opposite is true.

Try to recall a situation in which you were certain you said something, only to learn, to your utter dismay, that the other person had no recollection whatsoever of your saying such a thing. In fact, the person may recall quite the opposite. Communicating well isn't as easy or as simple as it sounds. People devote years of study to earning advanced degrees in learning to share a message with another person—and still we struggle to do it well. Nonetheless, at its core, communication consists of a message, a sender, and a receiver. The question is, who gets to decide what the meaning of the message is—and where do we measure the impact of such a message?

The meaning of a message lies ultimately with the receiver. That's how we decide what happens with what's been communicated. In other words, what matters in communication is what was heard, not what was said. The impact, not the intent, is what truly counts.

So if Chris tells Kyle, "I like creamy peanut butter," Kyle may hear what Chris said, but then he may think, "Chris doesn't like crunchy

---

* Dagbo and Acuna, "Company Culture."

peanut butter." Chris may have meant "I *also* like creamy peanut butter," but Kyle interprets it to mean "I don't like crunchy." Remember, the meaning of the message lies with the receiver. Kyle's interpretation of the message is the correct one, no matter what Chris meant. If he wanted to express his appreciation for both styles of peanut butter, he should have said so.

At any rate, Chris doesn't know how his message was received until he receives feedback. So Kyle needs to ask a clarifying question or give some kind of feedback to show that he heard and understood the message.

As the old joke goes, a wife texts her husband, who is a computer programmer. "Go to the store and buy a loaf of bread. If they have eggs, buy a dozen." So the husband returns home with twelve loaves of bread. It sounds silly, but it's an example of receiver-based communication and a good indication that the sender needs to be aware of the communication style of the receiver.

We all have our own experiences, beliefs, preferences, background, and worldview. All of those give us different lenses through which we experience other people and events. When one person hears a blunt message, they may think they're being yelled at, whereas someone else may think the speaker is simply being clear. Our life experiences affect the way we send and receive messages, so communication is more than just what's said. It includes who says it, who hears it, and what was meant. We must consider the meaning behind any message, the potential meaning a listener may ascribe to it, and the unique styles of communication each person uses. There's more than one way to get your message across, and on a self-led team, we have to adopt many styles of communication depending on the people involved and the context.

Dealing with Different Communication Styles

DiSC is a standardized personality test in which you are asked several questions and allowed to determine whether or not they apply to you. From there, you're given a score in four different personality quadrants, and you get insights into your personality type and preferred communication style. If you know someone else's style, this tool can help you communicate more effectively with them. DiSC stands for "dominance, influence, steadiness, and conscientiousness."*

Here's a simple breakdown of the different letters:

- Those with personalities in the *D* quadrant tend to be more confident and direct. Their emphasis is on bottom-line results. They tend to be political leaders, police officers, or others in positions of authority.

- The *i* types are more open and concerned with relationships and influencing or persuading others. They tend to be writers, artists, marketers, and public relations professionals.

- *S* personalities are usually dependable and prefer cooperation and sincerity. They excel in the medical and therapy fields and in customer service.

- *C* types place more emphasis on quality, accuracy, expertise, and competence. These are typically engineers, scientists, analysts, and programmers.

Typically, in the DiSC profile, a person has one main personality trait and a secondary trait. So you could be a *Di*, an *SC*, a *CD*, an *Si*, and so on. Of course, there aren't hard-and-fast rules as to personality types; there are plenty of exceptions. Instead, they're general patterns of behavior. For example, *D* personality types tend to favor direct communication, as if making their point in bulleted statements. They can be intense in the way they communicate. But an *S* personality type, the one who wants to avoid conflict, may recoil from that communication style.

If two *D*s are talking to each other, they're likely to be direct without causing a problem or hurt feelings. But when communicating with the other three personality types, *D*s will find that 75 percent of their team doesn't communicate in the same way. The *D*s' requests may come

---

* Discprofile.com, "What Is DiSC?"

across as orders to those with different profiles. The *D*s communicate in a way that doesn't speak to their team, which makes them less engaged and confuses them.

For example, say someone with a *D* profile—let's call her Denise—goes to someone with an *S* profile—Steve—and says, "I need the status report by 4:00 today. It was late last time, and that put me in a bind with Bob."

In Denise's mind, she was direct and clear. She made sure Steve knew what she needed, when she needed it, and what the consequences would be for Denise if the report is late. But in Steve's mind, Denise just yelled at him. He's been working hard and has a lot on his plate, including the status report. He's just trying to get stuff done so he won't be yelled at, and he's too intimidated to ask Denise if he can shift a couple of his responsibilities to someone else so he can get the reports done on time.

This difference in communication style illustrates the subjectivity of communication. The meaning lies in the message that's received, not the message that was sent. In other words, it's the impact on Steve, not Denise's intent, that's important here. Why? Because Steve is the one who needs to carry out the action, and if he misunderstands Denise's intent or simply doesn't understand the message, the work does not get done.

Does that mean that Denise was wrong and she actually did yell at Steve? Not at all. Does it mean Steve was right and he deserves an apology? No, not that, either. It means they need to better understand each other's communication styles and learn to work with each other in those nuances and discrepancies. Denise may not have thought she was yelling at Steve; she may not have even raised her voice. But that's not how Steve took it. And if Denise were a wise leader, she would have spent the time to adjust her approach when dealing with Steve.

That doesn't mean a leader has to be a chameleon or walk on eggshells. Denise shouldn't have to change her communication style multiple times per day to match each person she talks to. That would be exhausting. But it would help if she understood how other people receive her message so that she can at least be aware of what she's dealing with. Rather than change their entire DiSC personality type, everyone would be better served if two people could meet in the middle during a discussion. The subjectivity of human experience means you have to put some time into the way you talk with the people on your team. Put some energy into learning one another's communication styles so that you can understand what each person means and hears.

Years ago, Chris—who is a high *D*—had an assistant who we'll call Allison. Allison liked to explain everything and enjoyed receiving a lot of information and details. Chris wanted only bullet points about what needed to be done and didn't need a lot of meetings to go over everything, but Allison did. He also felt that because Allison needed so many details about how to do a project, by the time he gave her all the information, he could have already done it.

So Chris said they needed to meet in the middle. Allison had to understand that he spoke in bullet points, but Chris agreed to provide her with more information than he usually did. Once they both figured that out, they were an amazing team and got a lot more done together by being aware of each other's communication styles and personalities. By meeting in the middle, both people felt heard, felt that they communicated effectively, and were empathetic to each other's style.

Forget the Golden Rule

Leaders often have the mistaken belief that there is only one way to communicate: quickly, directly, and bluntly. Corporate America has bought into this idea and labeled people as good communicators if they fit this model and bad communicators if they don't.

Billions of dollars have been spent trying to get people to communicate more like their leaders (e.g., "You need to be more assertive"), totally ignoring the fact that 75 percent of people in business don't communicate that way.

One reason leaders don't fully engage with their people is that they're projecting. They're following the Golden Rule—do unto others as you would have them do unto you—trying to communicate with people in the way they want to receive communication. But that doesn't work. Many executives and managers tend to score a high *D* on the DiSC profile and therefore prefer to be direct, speak plainly about problems, and hear bottom-line solutions right away. Incidentally, Ds also fear being vulnerable and open. They love to speak to others who are like them because their communication styles match perfectly. But i personality types (the "relationship builders") don't like to talk to Ds because they feel that Ds are cold and impersonal. Rather, i types prefer to ask questions, share stories, and tell those stories as part of the process.

In some offices, we've seen employees post their DiSC profiles on their door so that when you go to them, you know how they communicate and make decisions. You know whether you need to communicate directly with that person and give solutions first or you need to spend a lot of time sharing details and answering their questions. Knowing where someone is at and giving them what they need to best do their job is an important part of building a great culture.

We often misunderstand this principle. If all of us practiced the Golden Rule and did unto others as we would have done unto us, there would be a lot of frustration and irritation. People don't want you to treat them as you want to be treated. They want you to treat them as they want to be treated. When you know a person's communication and decision style, you can interact with that person in a way that is more productive and efficient for you both. When this kind of information is easily accessible, everyone can understand where each person on the team is coming from and at least try to meet them somewhere in the middle. The D will know not to interrupt and to let the other person ask questions. The i will know not to share their entire story, to allow for interruptions, and to get to the point quickly. And so on. Knowledge is power, and when we understand how a person prefers to communicate, we understand a person. The Golden Rule is no longer enough. Don't do unto others as you would have them do unto you; do unto them as *they* would have you do unto them. That's empathy. And it takes a good listener to even know where to start.

Developing Trust

It was spring and heating up in Afghanistan. The incoming special operations task force was going to be the US Marines; Kyle had been working with the US Army until then. It was two months into his 2012 deployment. The Marine Forces Special Operations Command (MARSOC) hadn't been around as long as the SEAL teams had, let alone the Green Berets, and as a result they didn't have as much experience as Kyle's team. They'd been around for only six or seven years, which meant their senior personnel were Marine conventional forces and hadn't been at the shooter level of MARSOC.

As SEALs, Kyle and his crew were less regimented than the Marines. Marines are known for their crisp uniforms and clean-shaven faces, whereas SEALs are wild cards. Kyle had a beard as long as Santa Claus's at the time. At the organizational level, the differences were magnified, so it was a big learning curve to adapt to the Marines' logistics, supply chain, communication style, and the rest. The SEAL team just did things differently; they did everything differently.

Kyle's lead petty officer, Nick, was dealing with a lot of frustration from the incoming command administration as they worked through their assumptions. Nick would come into Kyle's office, which was just a twenty-by-twenty-foot wooden box. There were five or six men in there at the time. The Marines, Nick said, didn't understand how everything worked and were always asking questions that took up his time. Kyle offered to get on a call with the sergeant major to see what was going on.

During the call, Kyle was very professional, but the sergeant major had a lot of preconceived notions about what SEALs were like. He thought they weren't organized enough, certainly not as properly regimented as he and his men were. They were on a video conference call, and within minutes he was making comments that reflected his prejudice, saying things like "I'm surprised you even have a shirt on. All you guys do is walk around without shirts or work out."

Kyle tried to tell him that he was just there to help and ensure the command transition went smoothly. The sergeant major was annoyed and wanted Kyle to work with the go-between instead of directly with him. Of course, the go-betweens were also Marines, new to the battlefield as well, so Kyle was trying to go directly to the sergeant major instead of creating more confusion. "I knew I had nothing to hide from this guy," he recalled, "so I invited the sergeant major down to visit us and stay with us for a week, to come on missions with us to see who we really were. I wanted him to see we were serious and were running a tight ship, despite his preconceived notions about us. I went all out and said, 'I am formally requesting your attendance at my VSP [village stability platform] for one week. Please come down.'"

The sergeant major was blown away by the invitation. Kyle joked with him to remember to bring his gun and said that he could be Kyle's right-hand man on some missions. A command sergeant major, for the record, is about a twenty-five-year service veteran, and those last four to five years would have been spent in a more managerial or executive role. And here was Kyle, this big-bearded SEAL, asking a sergeant major to come on a mission for the first time in years, to which the senior non-commissioned officer responded, "Yeah, maybe I'll make that happen."

Determination Wins the Day

Nothing happened right away, but Kyle and the sergeant major kept having calls every week with some of the other team members. There were eight of them who would go around the virtual room and provide updates. The sergeant major didn't mention Kyle's invitation for a couple of weeks, so Kyle followed up and invited him again. The sergeant major brushed him off and didn't commit. The next week, Kyle followed up again, this time in front of all the other VSP team leads, and asked when he'd come down. The sergeant major said he would. Four weeks later, Kyle invited him again, and once more, he said he was planning on it.

The fifth week, Kyle invited him again. By then, they were comfortable enough to joke about the matter, understanding that it was a bit of a cat-and-mouse game at this point. The sergeant major told Kyle he'd bring his workout clothes, and Kyle shot back that his workout had been only three hours long that day. Just a short one.

Finally, the sergeant major did come down. At first, he was very regimented, wearing his crisp, clean uniform, wanting to sit down individually with all eighty-five people on Kyle's VSP team. Kyle had a female engagement team, a civil affairs team, engineers, Afghan National Army

Special Forces, US Army conventional forces, and his own SEAL platoon. The sergeant major sat down with everyone to see what was going on, determined to maintain his separation from the group. Another two days went by with him in his crisp uniform, but then the uniform blouse came off. Now the sergeant major was working out in his fatigues and tightly laced boots. His belt was perfect, as was his undershirt. He was still prim and proper, just a little unbuttoned now. The next day, the sergeant major caved and put on shorts like the rest of the group. It had been 100 degrees every day, but this was the first time this man had been out of uniform. The day after that, he was in shorts and a T-shirt in the makeshift gym, having fun and joking around with the other men. He was becoming a part of the crew.

Kyle took the sergeant major on a couple of missions and saw that he was having a great time, really coming alive. By the sixth day, the sergeant major had his shirt off and was walking around in shorts and flip-flops. He had fully assimilated. Still professional, of course, but now a part of the brotherhood. By the seventh day, he didn't want to leave. At this point, he knew everyone's stories and all about their families. He was one of the gang.

When it was time for the sergeant major to head back, the colonel himself came to pick him up via helicopter. They all had dinner together, and it was clear to the colonel what had happened. The team's camaraderie was through the roof; and every day thereafter, Kyle could call the sergeant major with anything he needed and get it.

The closest coalition force to that group was about fifteen kilometers (a little more than nine miles) away. It was a VSP, a village stability platform operated by Marines. Kyle had previously gone there to see how their operations were run and had offered feedback on security: how to do it, how to improve it, and so on. The team had turned down Kyle's offer, though. A month and a half went by, and Kyle joked to the command sergeant major on a video conference call about when he was going to visit again. The sergeant major said that he couldn't wait to hang out again.

The very next day, the closest VSP (led by the Marines who came in with the command sergeant major) had an insider shooter. A man with an AK-47 made his way into the compound and moved toward their tactical operations center. Their security wasn't sufficient, as Kyle's team had warned them. The shooter sprayed the entire center, killing the officer in charge, the team chief, the number two in charge, and the number three officer. The very first call the command sergeant major made was to Kyle, asking him to get over there right away.

Kyle got the whole team ready within fifteen minutes, and they were on their way. He got on the phone with the command sergeant major, who told him what was happening. The team established security, and Kyle took over as VSP commander for the next four days because of the trust the colonel and command sergeant major had in that team—all because of a single first visit. They were now commanding two VSPs.

Constant effective communication can build trust, create efficiency, and lead to all kinds of opportunities for increased responsibility. When you communicate effectively and display trustworthiness within your team and someone needs you the most, you're ready to respond.

Not What You Say But How You Say It

Granted, none of this is particularly revolutionary. In many respects, basic communication skills can seem trivial and somewhat basic. But the fact that a thing is simple does not mean that it is being done. In fact, we often overlook the simplest, most important actions in our daily lives *because* they are so simple!

Many people aren't connected to the mission of their organization because even the leaders at the very top aren't embodying what the team is supposed to be about. A self-led team is driven by the team members' values, communicating what's important in the clearest of ways. If you want to get others on board with the culture you're trying to create, you have to pay attention not only to what you say but also to the way you say it.

How can you improve your communication? How do you convey your messages in the most easily understood manner? How do you make sure your communication style meshes appropriately with other people's communication styles without scaring them or irritating them? In our experience, it comes down to six fairly easy practices:

1. Be honest and transparent. Create an environment in which facts are aired without hesitation. This sets an expectation that all communication, both from you and to you, is open and honest. Then when someone comes to you with their problems, they'll tell you when they've messed up, and you can act with empathy and help them find the solution.

2. Work with your teammates to understand their preferred communication styles. It's about understanding their communication styles and meeting them at least halfway between their preferred style and yours. You can't expect them to conform to your preferred style anymore; this isn't the 1950s.

3. Be humble. You don't have all the answers. You don't know everything about the company, each person's job, or even your own job. You may like to pretend that you do, but you don't. And you only look foolish or like a blowhard know-it-all when you act as if you do. Ask for input and ideas. Ask for suggestions. Ask for help. Trust that the people on your team know more than you do—about something.

4. Listen to your team more than you talk. Remember, communication is about listening as much as it is about talking, maybe more so. That means shutting your mouth and listening to your teammates, what they're saying, and how they're saying it.

5. Ask your team for solutions. Stop barking orders and start asking: "What do we need to accomplish together? What do you feel our goals could be? What do you need help with?" And then direct them, guide them, support them. That's a lot different from barking orders.

6. Check in with your team members individually. Ask how they're doing and what's going on in their lives. This is less about digging into their personal lives than letting them know that you care enough about them to ask after them. Remember their family

details and information that's important to them. Write it in a notebook if you have to. Caring about others allows your words to carry greater weight; people will listen more if they know you see them as a person and not just a means to an end.

One technique we like to use is to take an individual for a quick "walk around campus" and spend five or ten minutes just walking with that person: down the hall, on the way to the cafeteria, or even just outside. If you're in your car, you can call someone and ask how they're doing. Just to check in. Not asking for anything or checking on the status of a project. Just seeing how they are. This is healthy and effective communication in action, the kind that gets others to listen to you. You don't have to say a lot for people to listen to you; on the contrary, you have to listen a lot. No agenda, no need for updates. Just connection. The more you engage, and the more deeply you do so, the more people will trust you—whether you carry the title of leader or not.

Your communication style is one of the major contributors to your team's success. It can build up or tear down a culture. It shows a certain amount of empathy or a lack thereof. Communicating, obviously, is how you assign projects, how you offer guidance and coaching when needed, and even how you might enact discipline. If you can't communicate well, nothing else will ever develop. Poor communication skills can destroy everything you've tried to create, so if you have to focus on one thing, focus on becoming a better, more effective communicator.

Whether you're a leader or not, effective communication is the very foundation of a company's success, and those skills are necessary whether you're a CEO, a middle manager, or on your first day of the job. If you can't communicate your ideas to colleagues, those ideas will die a quick death. Such a failure will greatly limit your ability as a team member to accomplish any goals. Do whatever you can to get better at communicating. Walk the talk before you open your mouth. And don't be afraid to step aside when someone who can carry the message better than you can steps onstage. Communication can make or break a team. Your colleagues depend on healthy communication. The mission depends on it. Hell, your entire career depends on it.

11

RITUALS REINFORCE CULTURE

In 1965, the University of Oregon was quietly cultivating some of the best distance runners in the world. Years later, this same running club would become famous for the Olympians it would generate, names that included Steve Prefontaine, the miler who captured the attention of an entire nation and died just as suddenly as his star rose. A few years earlier, this school had graduated a young Phil Knight, who subsequently spent a year traveling the world only to return home and ask his former coach to help him start a shoe company. The coach was Bill Bowerman, the company was Nike, and the rest is history.

Bowerman changed the face of running forever—and he did it using rituals but in ways his athletes often found baffling. One biographer and former student wrote that "Bill loved to bewilder." In the words of Kenny Moore, he was a "difficult, dignified professor of kinesiology" who liked to crack jokes about peeing off bridges and raise funds for classical music festivals.* The man was a paradox. He saw himself as

---

* Moore, *Bowerman and the Men of Oregon.*

an educator but didn't concern himself with the emotional well-being of his students. He wasn't there to be anyone's daddy and would often forget the names of his runners while committing their mile times to memory.

Each young man who made the cut, however, invariably testified to the efficacy of the man's methods, even if they didn't particularly care for him as a person. Bowerman would push his men to their very edge, often concerning himself with who his runners were dating and what they were eating, all in an effort to get the best out of them. No one ever forgot an encounter with Bill Bowerman, but he might not remember you. His runners craved his approval and feared his wrath, all the while wondering what was going through his mind. "When a trucker kept flattening his mailbox," Moore recounted, "he booby-trapped it to puncture the guy's tires."[*]

The track coach was famously hard on his runners and in ways that were often disorienting, cutting one student from the team for having too many extracurriculars while chastising another for spending too much time training. He was structured and unpredictable, as evidenced by one particular rite of passage that he enforced on nearly every new runner.

A Runner's Rite of Passage

Throughout history, men and women have ritualized the passage from childhood to adulthood in myriad ways. In ancient times and in pre-industrial cultures, young men were often sent off on vision quests, whereas young women would celebrate their first menstrual cycle through ritual and ceremony. Each rite of passage is intended to remind the person experiencing the act, as well as those witnessing it, that something significant has transpired. Who this person was before, they are no longer. In some cases, the youth might return from an experience with a new name or title, often with their own mother pretending not to recognize them.

---

[*] Moore, *Bowerman and the Men of Oregon*.

A ritual is a cultural conspiracy, a way of collectively declaring "This is who we are." In such a culture, once you cross a certain threshold, there is no coming back. Your identity is forever altered, and you are now a permanent member of this tribe, understanding that many have gone before you and done the same. When done right, this transaction between community and individual creates a nearly unbreakable bond. In the case of Bill Bowerman's running club, however, the passage from "outsider" to "insider" happened not inside a sweat lodge but within the confines of a sauna—and it was far from consensual.

One year after Bill Bowerman cofounded Nike, a young John Woodward found himself in the sauna with his soon-to-be-famous coach. A mere freshman, Woodward was completely unaware of what was about to transpire. That particular day during cross-country season, Bowerman left the sauna to take a dip in the pool, leaving his towel on the bench. Unbeknownst to Woodward, who had been sitting next to his coach, there was a set of big brass keys underneath the towel. After fifteen minutes, Bowerman returned, picked up the towel containing the keys—which were now as hot as the rest of the room—and pressed them into the top of Woodward's thigh. The young runner was trapped at the end of the bench, struggling in futility to get free but held in place by the firm grip of his coach. Bowerman smiled, completing the ritual before releasing the young man and exiting the sauna without a word. Woodward looked down at the red welt, mystified, as a small crowd of his peers cheered in unison, "Welcome to the team! Welcome to the team!"

Woodward was far from the only one with such an experience. In 1991, Phil Knight invited all the past Men of Oregon, as they came to be called, to a tribute dinner for their old coach. Each man took a photo with Bowerman in front of a half-built sauna with the keys and towel hanging in the background. John Woodward later recalled, "We had what would now be considered a sociopath for a coach." Others are not so quick to judge Bowerman for his less-than-orthodox approach. There was something undeniably powerful about the man and his methods, something his students just couldn't shake, something that led many to call him the greatest running coach of all time.

Radical Thinking Is Required

Rituals protect the culture you've created and codify it. They maintain the sanctity of what previous generations of people have designed and developed. This is how we build on the contributions of those who came before, how we "stand on the shoulders of giants." How else can we see beyond the vision of our predecessors? We need rituals and ceremonies to do this, but great teams are not developed by merely following a list of arbitrary rules. Greatness is the result of radical thinking, not conformity.

It takes imagination and vision, as well as discipline, to develop and sustain world-class cultures. In the case of Bill Bowerman, he was never quite satisfied with what was considered normal for a runner or a running coach. He believed most athletes overtrained, and because of this he encouraged those who had just joined his team to cut down on the miles and step up their intensity. The result was that his runners got fewer injuries and increased their overall speed, a method for distance running that is still popular today.

Running less to run faster may seem contradictory, but this is a metaphor for how Bowerman spent much of his life—breaking tradition to find better, more efficient ways. To be an iconoclast, in some respects, is necessary for any culture creator. As significant as a ritual may be, it is also important to do something new, something bizarre and potentially revolutionary, so long as it serves the mission. After a trip to New Zealand, Bowerman was inspired by the counterintuitive training methods he observed there and ended up writing a book to codify the process. It was called *Jogging* and helped launch a worldwide fitness movement.

Another ritual the misfit running coach insisted upon was making his athletes their own shoes. Convinced that the right track shoe, just like the right training regimen, must be tailored to the runner, Bowerman didn't see any footwear on the market that worked for his guys. "The ordinary track shoe is covered with junk," he told *Sports Illustrated*,[*] commenting on certain flourishes such as leather trim, tongues, and even laces. "All unnecessary," he claimed. Forced to create his own solution,

---

[*] Maule, "Masters of Endurance."

he borrowed his wife's waffle iron and poured melted rubber into it to create the first-ever waffle sole, then carefully stitched together the shoes, which would last for only a race or two before the next competition required a brand-new pair.

This same kind of radical thinking worked its way into the ethos of a little shoe startup that eventually became synonymous with the words "victory" and "winning." Nike took the world by storm, working its way into every major athletic event by the turn of the century, and its success was due in part to the coach who first made the shoes. If you want something done right, the Bowerman mode of thinking went, you are going to have to do it yourself—and you're going to need to do it differently from how everyone else does it. To create a great culture, one that has the potential to not only change an entire organization but affect the whole world, you have to be willing to stand out. You've got to take some risks, going against the grain when required, all for the sake of something extraordinary.

But being radical is not enough. You've got to create something that outlasts, something that outlives, a team that is truly self-led. And this requires the right rituals.

Finding the Right Rituals

In 2018, employees of Ramsey Solutions saw something a little different when they gazed out at the parking lot one December morning. Waiting outside was a fleet of buses ready to take all 750 employees on an all-day Christmas shopping spree, paid for by their employer. Without warning, work for the day came to a halt, and CEO Dave Ramsey announced the surprise to his team. Hundreds of men and women excitedly exited the building and boarded the buses, headed for the Mall at Green Hills, many with over a thousand dollars of cash in hand. They spent the day spending their boss's money on Christmas presents for their families. To this day, this is a Christmastime tradition for every employee of Ramsey Solutions, one that happens in tandem with an extravagant holiday party. For new team members, ending the year like this can be a bit bewildering. How could a boss do such a thing? It is the reverse of

Ebenezer Scrooge, taking the day off to show appreciation to your employees instead of demanding more of them. This, too, is a ritual. And it tends to go over better than a set of 180-degree brass keys forcefully pressed into a young person's skin.

Every successful team has a metaphoric closetful of rhythms and tools they use to remind themselves of who they are and what they're about. These are the little rituals, mantras, and slogans we use in any culture to remind one another of what is important. At a ball game, a celebrity might come out on the field and sing the national anthem, and the crowd almost invariably joins them. A ritual is a practice that we don't even have to think about that reinforces a common ethic and cultural identity. If you go to a gym, you might see people wearing shirts with sayings like "Winning isn't everything; it's the only thing." When such a statement is shared among peers in a like-minded environment, nothing needs to be said. One person nods knowingly to another, and the ritual is complete.

This is how cultures are not only created but cemented. So many norms are hidden, inconspicuously repeated over and over again. The fish doesn't know it's in water, and the "water" is always the experiences we take for granted. Rituals remind us of what is essential as well as what is acceptable. Every time we practice a ritual, whether we are reciting a mantra or following a custom, we are agreeing with the culture and reinforcing it. These practices reduce the unnecessary stress of having to solve a problem one has already encountered. When you complete the ritual, you know that all's "right" with the world, at least for the time being, that you have done your job, that you are still a part of the tribe. Of course, the type of ritual a team engages with matters just as much as having a ritual at all. Not all rituals, obviously, are created equal; and the fact that we've always done things a certain way doesn't mean it ought to continue. After all, it wouldn't do to "burn" our team members at the altar of ambition, would it?

Certainly, as the Bowerman story indicates, the fact that a ritual can be enforced doesn't mean it's worth repeating. And at what cost? It is undeniable that great organizations require rituals, and that such customs and norms are signals to the outside world as to what this culture values. But there is a difficult way to do this and an easy way. The easy way is that of the tyrant, one in which you're burning keys into the thighs of your team members and causing them to live in fear of you. The harder path is that of the self-led team, where a single leader doesn't mandate the ritual for everyone—but he or she may have to go first.

In this case, who you are and what you become as a team is something that is discovered and codified together. This is far from easy but is certainly longer-lasting and ultimately more replicable. It is the difference between an intimidating coach pushing his athletes to their utter limits because they are afraid to defy him and a leader giving his team the day off to buy Christmas gifts with his money. In the case of Bowerman's running club, they certainly got results; but can these rituals be carried out if you remove the head of the organization? Absolutely not. Such an organization is a "spider" in the sense that everything that made it great dies with the leader. Ramsey Solutions, on the other hand, is more of a "starfish" in that at least some of these norms can be carried out without a charismatic leader at the helm. That's what it means to be self-led, and developing the right rituals allows you to protect what makes your culture unique. Just make sure it's something that can happen even without the one who perhaps started the practice in the first place.

We Are What We Repeat

Every culture has its own unique set of rituals. When you are deciding what kind of culture you want to create or maintain, think carefully about the rituals you choose to reinforce it. How do you develop a set of practices that inspire, engage, and transform a team long after the leader has left the room? What does it look like to continue creating rituals in a world where so much about traditional leadership is evolving? If you want your team members to come together and focus, to work as a cohesive unit, you have to help them find the right rituals, the routines and habits and slogans that will pull them together to get the job done.

Rituals can come from anywhere. Someone can have an idea that turns into a practice that gets repeated over and over, often unconsciously, until everyone is doing it. But we have to be careful not to conflate causation and correlation. A baseball player might play an exceptionally good game and connect that to the fact that he didn't wash his socks that day. Now he will superstitiously vow to not wash his socks until the end of the season, when in reality, the socks have nothing to do with the game. A little less trivially, we may find ourselves in situations where we are blindly following what the boss says, not knowing why and too scared to challenge the system. This is not necessarily a bad thing. All human beings copy one another as a way of surviving. Adapting to our surroundings through submission to authority and even cultural norms is often the best way to belong to a group of people, to fit in. A problem, however, arises when we do this without understanding what we are doing.

Humans are a ritualistic species, and though our practices may look different from those of our ancestors, we still find ways to commemorate that which is important to us through everyday rituals. Consider the first-day-of-school photos parents may take of their children. Don't forget graduation ceremonies and weddings, as well as honeymoons, birthdays, and funerals. All of these are forms of ritual, as are the customs for many people of praying before a meal and standing in recognition of their nation's flag being displayed in public. Actors who say "Macbeth" inside a theater are supposed to go outside, turn in a circle three times, and spit. Rituals make us remember what matters most and can even serve to motivate us. The Boston Red Sox third baseman Wade Boggs used to eat chicken liver before every game, took batting practice at precisely 5:17 p.m. every day, and wrote the Hebrew word *Chai* ("living") in the dirt before each at-bat, despite not being Jewish.

Navy SEALs have a set of practices they do before each mission, practices that depend on the team and the individuals. Some men repeat the same phrases over and over; some write goodbye letters to their loved ones in the event that they don't return. Yet others recite their favorite Bible verse or take a cross with them on their tour. We all find our way to sometimes seemingly odd behavior that gets so ingrained in us that we hardly think about it. This is the power of ritual, and naturally we want to harness it for positive change.

Things are not necessarily that different in civilian life. When you sit down to Thanksgiving dinner, does everyone say something before you eat? Do you go to the same place for spring break every year? When someone buys a new car or goes hunting for the first time or graduates from high school, does your family have a special way of celebrating these events? Everything we do over and over is a form of ritual, and these all can be forms of cultural identity.

It has been said that we become what we repeatedly think about, and that may be true. But more than that, we are what we repeatedly do. Action may follow thinking, but application is where we solidify any habit, turning it into a ritual. Pay attention to what you find yourself doing on a daily basis because each choice says something about who you are. How do you take your coffee? How do you eat your meals? Do you have a favorite place to sit during meetings? Some preferences are obviously more significant than others. But every little quirk, every repeated action, contributes to the narrative of our lives. In a way, we become what we ritualize, with each action contributing to the culture we are creating together. Such actions, when repeatedly shared by others, can create a sense of belonging and contribution for almost anyone.

The best rituals are the ones that take rote tasks and turn them into something interesting, even memorable, further cementing a person's identity as part of the greater whole. The marketing agency McCann Manchester, for example, has a company ritual that brings everyone together and has nothing (and everything) to do with work: cheesy playlists. In this ritual, all team members contribute their favorite embarrassing guilty pleasure songs, and then the team blasts the playlist to celebrate the completion of a project. The ritual creates a shared experience, something that breaks employees out of the humdrum monotony of a project that's gone past deadline. It also holds them accountable to a real deadline and gives them something fun to look forward to once the job is complete.

When Kyle was in the SEALs, they had a ritual called New Guy Games, a competition that took place during Unit Level Training when two or three platoons were together, going through a six-month training period in preparation for deployment. Toward the end of each week, they would place little wagers on the new SEALs, saying things like "If the new guy in your platoon loses, you'll be responsible for the range cleanup and picking up all the brass." The losing side might have to buy the first round of drinks or clean all the vehicles or do whatever the opposing side chose. If your platoon was the winner, you might sleep in a little the next day and show up at the range with a cup of coffee just to rub it in.

The games were based on agility and teamwork, rather than just strength or speed, so that even the smallest guy could compete. The stakes were considerable and fair, so everyone wanted in. Imagine how much pride and trash-talking went into preparing for the New Guy Games each Friday night. There was a lot of competition, not just among the new guys but also among the older SEALs whose platoon pride was on the line. It was fun, of course, but there was more to it than mere diversion. The competition involved lots of cheering and hollering and high-fiving as everyone watched the new guys in various games. It brought everyone together as the older guys made sure the new guys were trained well. Their ability to compete in the games meant they were mission-ready: they had been staying in shape, were mentally fit, and still felt prepared for what they needed to do. Of course, this meant not only during the games but after, when it really counted.

The benefit of this ritual was that it wasn't a top-down procedure, relying on a single person to enforce it. Everyone was in on the games, and that positive peer pressure ensured that they were continued. Not to mention, the games were a fun motivator for doing something they already needed to do—stay in top physical and mental shape in preparation for the next mission. This sense of competition among SEALs, however, never goes away. It lives with you for the rest of your life. As a SEAL, you may find yourself still competing in your mind with guys years after you return from a mission. But just as with the games, it all came from a good place. The more competitive the men were, the more elite an organization the Navy SEALs became. SEALs want to stay physically fit, mentally fit, agile, and healthy because the other SEALs are doing the same. The ritual reinforced a cultural ethic of excellence, buoyed by peer-to-peer competition. How do you know, though, whether a ritual that pits team members against one another is good for the organization or ultimately cannibalistic? Simple: if it makes each individual stronger while also strengthening the collective whole—which in turn makes each individual member even better—then that is a winning combination.

The right ritual is the one that, when repeated, makes each individual and the entire organization better, stronger, and more equipped to fulfill the next mission.

How Do You Create Rituals?

We need rituals to build camaraderie and to strengthen the core of our organizations. Focused repetitive actions provide clarity of mission, help define the role of everyone involved, and allow us to understand what each person needs. When structured properly, a ritual can engage people in what matters most to an organization and even require the leader to be more engaged as well.

When Kyle was in Afghanistan, every single night before dinner he would bring the entire camp out to do a huddle and see if anyone had any debrief to share with the group. Sometimes these huddles would last a few minutes; at other times, they'd take the greater part of an hour. It didn't matter. In that huddle, everyone was on the same level. They all had something to share and everyone's input was valuable, from the oldest member on the squad to the nineteen-year-old "kid" who had been on sentry duty that afternoon.

This daily ritual was initiated by Kyle but was soon embraced by everyone. Some rituals begin as mandates by the boss, but only the best ones get carried on by the team without the leader. The daily debrief became something that Kyle's platoon looked forward to; it was something they wanted to participate in. The fact that a leader of the company was willing to let each and every man in the group speak up spoke volumes. His willingness to let every team member share what was on his mind, for as long as he wanted, said something about the culture they were creating. This was not a place where you were barked at and expected to take orders without contributing something of your own to the mission. Each man's voice mattered, and every contribution was valued. This created a sense of trust and buy-in, which was necessary for the mission. It wouldn't have worked to have one leader with a vision and a hundred underlings who were just following orders. Simple rituals like a daily check-in among team members can help a group gel and inspire accountability and buy-in.

Other rituals can happen more organically. You don't always need someone in leadership to say "Let's do this." For example, one ritual Chris's team embraced during his time at Ramsey Solutions was to read the same business books together and then discuss them in a sort of ad hoc book club.

One of the books they read was *QBQ!* (i.e., the question behind the question) by John G. Miller. In the book, Miller tells a story about a waiter at a restaurant who serves a customer a Diet Coke even though the restaurant carries only Pepsi products. When the customer asks a different waiter for a refill, the first waiter admits that he walked around the corner and bought a Diet Coke for the customer, going above and beyond the customer's expectations. One day, someone in Chris's office did something extra special, and one of the team members said, "Way to Diet Coke that."

Since they had all read the same book, everyone laughed, and the phrase became a ritual—a slogan of sorts—to say when someone went above and beyond the call of duty. There was no intention of such a phrase becoming something they repeated ritualistically for years after the fact. It just happened. No one introduced the book to the reading group so that people would start saying "Way to Diet Coke that." Unlike Kyle's before-dinner debriefing ritual, this one happened serendipitously. No one required it, but it caught on because it was something they all had in common. They had read the book, had shared an experience, and all had the same knowledge. The laughter that resulted the first time someone said the phrase made it feel special, like an inside joke of sorts, and so they continued doing it. There's more than one way to create a lasting and effective ritual.

Reinforcing What Matters

Many of your team rituals won't be things that are decided on in a board meeting or originate from a corner office. They'll be practices that occur almost accidentally and then get repeated and cemented as part of the culture. There will, at least at times, be a feeling behind the action, and that feeling should not be boredom or dread. It is important, then, to notice when a ritual is being formed so that you can ensure the practices you codify are the ones making your organization better, not just the ones that are getting repeated. When we robotically do what everyone around us is doing without understanding why or for what value, we reinforce and even create new layers of bureaucracy that only disempower individuals and slow organizational progress. Beware the corporate hair ball; it's lurking around every conceivable corner.

The way not to establish a ritual, then, is to try to force it when there's no need. A ritual is going to feel corporate and contrived if it doesn't come from honest experience. It not only needs to fill an obvious need but also has to be practiced on a regular basis. Rituals must be repeated to reinforce the values they represent. If you put a motivational poster on the wall with a cute quote and a picture of a cat, that's not going to do the trick. If no one talks about the ritual or reinforces it, no one is going to believe in it—and it is therefore merely an aspiration. You can talk about values until you're blue in the face, but if you don't get people to consistently buy into the practices surrounding them, they're going to die quickly.

What do you do when someone doesn't buy into a ritual, though? In a typical hierarchically structured organization, you might simply reinforce it anyway, telling the person to do their job or clean out their desk. On a self-led team, however, you might put the grumbler in charge of the ritual. See if they can come up with something better, something truer and therefore more meaningful to the entire team.

If the ritual, then, is bringing in bagels every Friday morning before the department meeting, and someone is grumbling about not liking the bagels, guess who's now in charge of breakfast? The best way to get someone behind something they're not fond of is to put them in charge of it—and see what they do with it. You'll find out pretty quickly whether they just like to complain or they actually have a better idea. And don't be surprised if it's more often the latter.

Complaining is often a request for empowerment, a sign that some-one does not have enough responsibility. If you can complain about something, you probably need more ownership of it. And if you're the one complaining, how can you take a step toward creating a solution instead of criticizing what you may not even understand?

You Need a Slogan

Not only do rituals need to be repeated with actions; they also need to be repeated with words. Slogans are a verbal reminder of an idea you want to convey, a value you have, or an organizational practice you want repeated. Consider the slogan Steve Jobs coined at the original retreat with the Macintosh team in 1983: "It's better to be a pirate than join the navy."[*] This was one of three sayings he opened the off-site meeting with, even including a pirate flag to represent the ethos of rebellion and independence with which Apple started and that Jobs wanted to reclaim through the Mac. Not entirely surprisingly, on April 1, 2016, Apple flew the pirate flag at its Cupertino headquarters to commemorate its fortieth birthday.[†]

In Afghanistan, when Kyle's platoon was going back to help teach the locals how to fend for themselves, the platoon members knew they would be engaging with women, children, farmers, business developers, agricultural developers, and regional district governments. They knew they couldn't be aggressive. They knew they couldn't be loud. They also knew they couldn't leave things the way they found them. They had a mission, after all, and required a simple saying to remind themselves of what they were about.

As we already shared in chapter 3, the team adopted the slogan "quietly aggressive," which became a mantra for them. Even though they were not always conducting direct action missions, and often would be walking peacefully through the valley, someone could start shooting at any moment, and they had to be ready. But they also had work to do with the local population, and this did not involve fighting. It was challenging at times to switch from one context (there is an enemy who wants to kill you) to another (you are there to do community building). To stay focused on the mission, they would remind one another with their slogan, saying it over and over again, communicating their intent until each and every man internalized it. The power of a slogan is that it can shape a culture, making the aspirational actionable.

---

* Hertzfeld, "Original Macintosh: Pirate Flag."
† Warren, "Why Apple Is Flying a Pirate Flag."

A good slogan comes from who you are—it's not slapped on as a formality. It should illustrate the work you're already doing and represent the best of what you hope to do. Nonetheless, it can be exhausting to communicate the same message over and over again. The process can start to feel a little rote, even mundane. And sometimes the greatest of rituals begin with good intentions but atrophy into routine and monotony. It's important, then, to remember that it's not enough to repeat a slogan. You have to keep defining what it means to your team and why it represents something each member values. If you're not communicating a message with purpose, how will it stick?

Kyle's platoon members reinforced their slogan through regular trainings and debriefs. They talked about it often, even taking time-outs on occasion to pause an exercise and quickly debrief a situation that had escalated. In such a situation, one of the SEALs would speak up and remind the rest of the group that they were to be "quietly aggressive." Because this was not a top-down mandate but a culturally accepted norm and value, whenever the slogan came up, they all fell in line with it.

This is the power of the right ritual. When connected to a clearly stated mission and derived from a shared experience, few will resist it. Why? Because in theory, the team members chose it together, and together they continue to enforce it. The concept of a self-led team is not just leadership lingo meant to get everyone to take on more responsibility. Rather, it means a different way of relating to one another and running our organizations, even a difference in what we expect of ourselves. Rituals and slogans are ways we reinforce a team we are a part of, take responsibility for, and want to see thrive. This is an area where we all can and should contribute.

Slogans bring teams together and reinforce existing rituals that further the values of the organization. Athletic teams have mantras they chant before games to psych themselves up. Businesses develop slogans both internally and externally to clarify their message to themselves and to the world. These sayings create a sense of belonging among team members. They summarize a philosophy or mindset and remind everyone of the goal they're all working toward. Without a slogan, it may be unclear to some what this team is really about.

How to Change the World

All great movements—whether political, commercial, or even religious—require a simple message to support them. That's how ideas spread and movements grow. Nike's slogan—Just Do It—became a battle cry for weekend warriors, fitness enthusiasts, and amateur and professional athletes everywhere. To this day, it means a lot of things to a lot of different people, but the common theme is the same: get to work, move more, do better, keep training, don't stop pushing. Similarly, phrases such as Martin Luther King Jr.'s "I have a dream" or Winston Churchill's "Never give up" rallied millions of people to change the world.

Rituals are built around the same idea. They are reminders of what we're trying to accomplish, what we have always wanted to accomplish. The right ritual helps us get into the mindset of doing what we need to do to accomplish the mission: win the war, finish the campaign, increase our market share, and so forth. A good ritual isn't complicated; it's something simple that keeps us in the flow of why we started on this team in the first place. It guides us toward our purpose and helps us remember it when we get off track. Football players may hit the wall as they leave the locker room. Baseball players may touch their bat to the plate in a certain way. Writers may listen to the same playlist on repeat while working on a book. Someone in an office may not check email first thing in the morning as a way of starting the day focused. We all have our own little rituals and, often, slogans to reinforce them. The ritual is the action we take; the slogan is the language we use to remember it. And when we share these practices with other people, we create and reinforce something greater than the sum of its parts.

Even top organizations need ways to stay ahead of the competition. As Jim Collins famously illustrated in *How the Mighty Fall*, the fact that a team is great doesn't mean it will remain that way. All things are naturally headed toward entropy and chaos, and even excellence fades eventually. We use rituals to keep teams focused on what matters most, and we employ slogans to make the message even clearer. Despite pouring billions of dollars into leadership training, most organizations can't figure out this simple part of building a team. No motivational poster or off-site team-building session is going to do it. You need team-generated norms that are deeply connected to your mission, and then you have to commit to ritualizing these practices and reinforcing them with clear, memorable slogans. If the ritual or the slogan is challenged, it needs to be able to stand up to scrutiny, not be something insecurely foisted upon unwilling participants. If someone has a better idea, do that. If not, reinforce the rituals you do have until something better comes along.

The best rituals and slogans don't belong in a human resources manual. You should see and hear them every single day. They should be clearly visible in the daily activity of any team that understands them. In a previous organization, Chris's teammates adopted a practice of doing the things they were best at and negotiating with coworkers to get help on projects they were struggling with. This allowed everyone the freedom to do what they did best and the ability to avoid the things they didn't do well. Still, certain jobs had to get done, so they all agreed to help out when someone was trying to do something they didn't excel at. Eventually, a mantra emerged from this practice—"Lift each other's weaknesses with our strengths"—as a way of reinforcing these behaviors. They didn't need a complex process or explanation. A simple phrase regularly repeated was enough to ensure it happened and that everyone knew what the team was about.

Teams must find meaningful rituals that allow members to do their best work as efficiently as possible. Then they should develop slogans and sayings to reinforce the reason for the rituals so that people don't lose sight of what's important. If you don't know where to begin, find something you can all agree to focus on, and start a simple new ritual that is easily repeated and reinforced with the right language that anyone on the team can understand. Do that and you won't need a towel full of hot keys to motivate your team members. They'll want to reinforce the mission because they helped create it.

PHASE III

SUSTAIN

———

Once we have defined and begun to develop the change we want to create in an organization, we are far from done. This is where the real work begins. Having a strategy and plan to sustain the culture you create is essential for its long-term success, and such an accomplishment won't happen on its own.

Think back to all those resolutions made in previous years or the planner you just bought. Think of every goal you've set, every audacious dream you've ever considered chasing. Was wanting these things enough to accomplish them? Did doing it once ensure that you kept doing it? Or did you need some strategies and tactics to create and sustain the change you wanted? Having a vision for the culture you want to create does not ensure its existence five years from now. We've got to dedicate ourselves to sustaining a self-led team, ensuring its long-term success.

After their thirty-week BUD/S (Basic Underwater Demolition/SEAL) training, Navy SEALs spend another two years continuing their training. They do many familiar things over and over as a way of reinforcing what they've learned. Before and after every deployment, they do Unit Level Trainings, which are long and arduous opportunities to drill the fundamentals into their brains and bodies. Every SEAL works on staying mindful during even the small tasks because those important details can save their lives someday. New habits aren't easy to create, but once you've set them into motion, they can be relatively easy to maintain. The hardest part of starting something new is that it takes intentional effort and planning to make it a priority. On a daily basis, you have to work to build the muscle memory needed for any new habit to continue.

Just as there aren't that many Navy SEALs in the world, there are not that many well-run organizations. The default is to train more leaders instead of restructuring our very organizations and reconsidering how we do teams in the first place. But this is where your legacy is created or forgotten. Can you keep your team nimble and empowered? Will you fight to protect the values you've established? Are you going to keep looking for ways to give away power so that the team can continue to thrive—or will you begin to coast?

This is why corporate America keeps throwing money at the problem and why most people still hate their jobs. It takes effort and intentionality to develop world-class teams, and it just seems easier (at least in the short run) to focus on leadership. But as we have seen, these are bankrupt ways of thinking and archaic in terms of how to organize a modern team. It's time to do things differently. Leadership conferences are the equivalent of going on a GORUCK adventure weekend and calling yourself a SEAL at the end.* It's not true, and you're not even close. You haven't created a basis of understanding on which to build—all you've had is a taste of a different world. There's no foundation; therefore, whatever you've learned tends to quickly leave without adequate reinforcement.

If you want to be successful in any endeavor, you must dedicate yourself to a disciplined and proven process. It takes time to become great. This is

---

* GORUCK is a twelve-hour endurance event led by current or former members of military special forces such as SEALs or Green Berets.

where culture gets established—in the small daily habits that add up over time. In Phase III, we learn to sustain what we've created so that it can have an impact for the long haul. We have not come this far, as the saying goes, to come only this far. Let's push on to the end, which could be the beginning of everything.

12

FROM RITUAL TO RHYTHM

So far, we've talked about mantras, slogans, and rituals—all ways of developing a culture that can transform an organization and reinforce a new normal that emphasizes the importance of the team over any particular individual.

For example, a ritual of regular stand-up meetings can remind teammates that others are relying on them and therefore challenge them to do their best. Who wants to let their team down? A slogan like "Lift each other's weaknesses with our strengths" allows a group to not waste time and energy on improving what they do worst. A mantra like "quietly aggressive" can harness the strength of a bloodthirsty SEAL team and redirect it toward rebuilding a community.

Without a defined structure or purpose, most rituals and habits devolve into a loosely collected mishmash of motivational quotes and practices. This is why it's important to create a cohesive structure that provides direction for a team. How do we create and maintain our newfound rituals? We do that with what the military calls "battle rhythms."

Battle rhythms, according to the US Department of Defense website, are "a deliberate daily cycle of command, staff, and unit activities intended to synchronize current and future operations." For our purposes, they are regular routines that help us build and reinforce the culture we've created. These routines can be strategic, such as giving status updates or meeting certain productivity goals. Or they can be more lighthearted, with the primary intent of building camaraderie. Rhythms can be motivating as well, as when we repeat certain mantras or slogans as a team. These are all shorthand ways to reinforce specific practices, reminding us of what's important.

These rhythms are not necessarily something you have on your calendar, but you still know they're coming. You know that your favorite newsletter comes out every Wednesday morning or when your favorite podcast drops a new episode. You know when "your" show releases a new season or what the best time is to book your favorite restaurant for dinner. Rhythms are how we live our lives, taking the mundane, sometimes chaotic reality of life and turning all those actions into something routine and consistent. Rhythms create order out of disorder, and they become the lifeblood of any successful organization.

On a self-led team, what develops the culture are all the little things that intentionally add up to something monumental: the daily huddles, monthly huddles, and quarterly retreats. That's your culture. Those are your rituals and rhythms, and when chosen with care and intention, they maintain what you've fought so hard to build. On the other hand, when we continue a list of arbitrary practices no one understands or appreciates, we are left with a lifeless bureaucracy that inspires no one. Intentional rhythms and routines are the way out; we must consciously choose the behaviors and practices we want to reinforce. When we do that, we create something far more extraordinary than any individual could even conceive of—because we do it together.

Your rhythms are yours. No one can create them for you, and every organization has its own. It's the one-word check-in before a daily huddle. The 10:30 a.m. coffee break you take with friends. The tapping of the plaque on the office wall each morning before the day begins. These patterns of behavior reinforce and instill the ideals you want to internalize both individually and collectively.

It's important to not get too rigid in these rhythms. If you make the rhythm the focus, you lose sight of its true purpose, which is to create culture and advance the work of the team. Everything else is a distraction or a rut you've fallen into. Getting your team in sync through regular and intentional communication, sharing your common goals consistently, pushes everyone to do their best and operate according to their strengths.

A battle rhythm is how you keep a team on track and empower each member. If all teammates can learn what they need to do on a regular basis and are trusted to do it, they'll be able to manage their own rhythms without being regularly reminded. And the team will flourish as a result. Ultimately, knowing your rhythms can help everyone understand what needs to be done, which is a mode of self-leadership. On a self-led team, you don't have to wonder what's the next thing for you to do. You know. Because you've developed a rhythm that works and is easy to understand. Because you're empowered. Trusted. Responsible.

If the leader of your team were to suddenly quit, go on a trip, or even die, could your department run without this person? Maybe the leader is you. Could your team members do without you? Would they flourish or suffer? A self-led team can continue to function as it always has, even without the leader, because its members understand their mission and goals. They know what they have to do to meet their objectives every single day. Obviously, the absence of a team member introduces challenges, but no single member is so integral as to be irreplaceable. This is the power of rhythms and rituals and why self-led teams make the difference.

Rhythms Strengthen Culture

Rhythms don't have to be complicated. One of the SEALs' battle rhythms is to huddle up on the morning of a mission, review the objectives of that mission, execute the mission, and then come back to debrief. Then, depending on the length of the mission, they might go out and do it all again the next day. That's a rhythm. It's simple, it's easy to repeat, and it ultimately increases the team's morale and motivation.

But how do you begin creating such rhythms for your team? One of our favorite culture-strengthening practices is texting a team member on the weekend to tell them how much you appreciate them. No talk of work or deadlines or anything related to the job. Just a friendly check-in. You'd be surprised what buying lunch for a colleague or taking that same team member on a walk can do.

When these sorts of engagements happen within the confines of work hours, it's acceptable to reinforce a sense of urgency for upcoming deadlines. You can use these check-ins to hold others accountable to the standards they have set and agreed to meet. Just be clear about your purpose for the meeting ahead of time. If you say it's personal and start talking business, you've lost all credibility. And remember that what makes a rhythm powerful is that it is reinforced and repeated over and over. This is what tells us it's important.

Another rhythm is regular competition, not just with industry peers but also within your own organization, finding ways to improve one another's skills. This could be a friendly wager, a companywide "battle of the bands" competition, or a scoreboard for the sales team to track who's entitled to the highest tier of commissions each month.

When it comes to rituals, you have to find the things that help your team win and then continue to do those things over and over. Pick out something you did right and repeat it. That's a rhythm. Focus on what helps everyone do their best work, and find daily and weekly ways to reinforce that habit. This is what makes organizations excellent and allows teams to excel. You can't get to the good stuff without a willingness to endure the mundane.

This is how little rituals get born. Some may seem like superstitions, but these consistent actions repeated over time become our regular battle rhythms, which end up creating the culture we want. There's a reason why human beings have embraced rhythms and rituals for centuries—they work. This can be as practical as taking someone to lunch or something far deeper. Regardless, when you've found a tactic that works, repeat it. This is how excellence is created. Even if you "know" objectively that listening to "Eye of the Tiger" before a presentation doesn't actually make you a better speaker, there's nothing wrong with a comforting and motivating ritual. If you feel that it works, then it does.

It's important to pay attention to the rhythms your team is creating, whatever they may be. If you are not paying attention to what's happening around you, you're missing a lot. You can't reinforce rhythms you aren't aware of, which will set back the development of your culture. Some organizations' rhythms are so deeply embedded that they bind and unite everyone, becoming the basis for everything that follows. Such rhythms create a sense of camaraderie, the magnetic culture that everyone wants to be a part of.

On the first day of Navy SEAL training, everyone has to shave their head. This is a tradition meant to give the new recruits a uniform look, to immerse them in the culture and make them feel they are part of a larger unit. At this point, there are relatively no differences between anyone. Everyone has the same uniform. Everyone wears the same boots. Everyone has their name stenciled across their chest. It's been that way for decades and will continue for the foreseeable future. Such consistency underlies the integrity of any great organization. You know what to expect from them, and this builds trust and respect both within the organization and outside it. When others see us embodying our own values and sticking to them, that is attractive.

The military is full of such rituals. One of Kyle's favorites happens at the end of First Phase training, after everyone has just been through Hell Week. The SEALs have just spent six days running drills. They are exhausted and proud of what they've accomplished. Running on pure adrenaline, they have sat in the ocean together, arms linked, singing songs to one another to keep from hallucinating. When Friday night rolls around, after a ridiculously trying eight weeks, there is the ritual of a skit. Each BUD/S student has an opportunity to create a theatrical presentation in which they make fun of the instructors who just put them through Hell Week. Everyone laughs; they goof off and bond. The whole experience brings everyone even more closely together. This is a ritual that matters.

Even the rhythm of making your bed with "hospital corners"—which no military person will ever forget after being screamed at about it for months—helps create a culture. Hospital corners may not save a life, but there's something significant about everyone doing the same thing every day in the same way. Rituals reinforce a culture of precision and accuracy; rhythms instill discipline and encourage commitment to the mission, whatever it may be. This enables each SEAL to follow orders and take direction well. Disciplines become rituals, and rituals create rhythms, which give everything we do deeper meaning. What we do on a regular basis in an organization becomes the bedrock of the culture we are creating.

Are Your Rhythms Working?

Battle rhythms will help you make the most strategic and correct decisions possible. They will help your organization reduce waste, boost efficiency, and accomplish goals in less time than you thought possible. But what do you do when they're not working? How do you even know? And what do you do when you discover you've been doing the wrong thing the whole time?

Chris once hired a senior project manager named Michelle for a software company he worked for, and this person was someone who came with a lot of experience. She joined the team and after a few months told the company it was running at 20 percent efficiency.

Every time the team began a new project, Michelle said, they were starting from square one. "We have the same features in most of the apps we build," she claimed, "but we restart building them every single time because we don't categorize them or price them out. The sales team can't do it because they keep coming back wanting to know what the price is."

Leadership kept rescoping the project, the development team kept rebuilding the product, and the quality assurance people kept retesting it. "But," she said, "if we just made it a standard feature, it would increase our efficiency by 80 percent." The team would need fewer developers, would do well with a smaller quality assurance team, and could complete its projects faster, which would mean spending less time meeting about this particular feature. This would not only save money; it would make money for the company.

At this point, the company had a battle rhythm it followed. It had regular scoping meetings and communicated with the whole team on triple-checking everything. It thought it was doing it right.

The company didn't realize how much money it was losing just following the same inefficient rhythm it had subscribed to for years. It took an "outsider" to help with this—and if not for her, the company would have missed it altogether. How, then, do you create effective battle rhythms when none exist, and how do you review the ones you have in place that may, in fact, be inefficient? You start simple and stay simple.

Creating the right rituals and rhythms for your organization is easier than you think. In fact, you likely already have some of them in place and just haven't been paying attention.

When your team meets, do you know ahead of time who speaks first? Do you get a cup of coffee before you start your day? Do coworkers have informal gatherings, like getting together in the lunchroom just to shoot the breeze? Any consistent practice done with a certain amount of intentionality and focus is a ritual; over time, these actions become rhythms.

As you identify your existing practices, you may start to see opportunities to create rhythms—or you may find inefficiencies and redundancies that don't make sense. Regardless, with awareness comes the opportunity to improve. Notice what's been happening on your team without your knowing it, and then look for ways to improve what's already there.

If you can build rhythms and cultivate a magnet culture everyone wants to be a part of, you're on your way to creating a team that wins. Rituals and rhythms are all around us. If we want to affect the culture we are a part of, even if we aren't the formal leader, we have to notice what we take for granted in our environment and then find ways to change it.

No matter who you are, you can help your team establish regular rhythms in what it does, creating your own personal rituals and noticing what the team does collectively. As we become aware of these practices, we can become more intentional about them and search for ways to use them to bring the team together. Great organizations don't reinvent the wheel every day; instead, they invent it once and spend years creating ways to help it spin more easily. This is accomplished through rhythms and rituals.

13

—

KEEP LISTENING

Genghis Khan was one of the greatest conquerors in history, amassing an empire whose size superseded those of Napoleon, Alexander the Great, and Julius Caesar. Once he had triumphed over his enemies, the Mongol lord would offer them a choice: bring water to his soldiers' horses as a sign of their absolute surrender—or be horribly mutilated and killed. The offer was far from democratic, and certainly not the gentlest of choices, but those who accepted it often lived in relative peace and were able to enjoy many freedoms, albeit under Mongol rule.

When the Mongols overtook a new people, they often absorbed aspects of the conquered culture into their own, creating a surprisingly diverse and eclectic empire, one unlike the world had seen before. To this day, Genghis Khan is credited as having ruled the largest land empire ever, much of which has been retained in modern-day China, Afghanistan, and Mongolia. Unlike the Romans, whose rule did not extend nearly as far as that of the Mongols, this collection of nomadic tribes did not impose their way of life on others. As the victors, one might say it was their right to demand absolute conformity and assimilation into their own culture. It certainly wouldn't have been out of the norm.

And yet, in many cases, the opposite occurred.

Genghis Khan was religiously tolerant at a time when the Christians and Muslims were killing each other over the Holy Land. In fact, during his twenty-one-year rule, he often sought counsel from Buddhist and Taoist monks, Muslims, and Christians alike.* When conquering a land, he allowed his new people to retain their native religions and much of their original culture. In fact, he often sought ways to retain the native culture and when entering a new land would go first to the clergy, political leaders, and wealthy lords, befriending them (in his own way). Obviously, this strategy was not without its political advantages; he was clearly looking for inroads between his culture and theirs, knowing that if he reached the powerful first, the rest of a society would more easily follow in obedience to his rule. He was also, relatively speaking, radically open to and accepting of both women and cultural minorities.

At a time when they were not considered citizens, allowed to hold land, or able to testify, women were allowed to stand before Genghis Khan's court, and he would listen to them when their husbands weren't performing their marital duties. This mighty and savage warrior was not just a bloodthirsty tyrant; he was, in his own way, a feminist. Not only that, he was, perhaps most important for our purposes, a great listener—to all types of people, including some of society's most disenfranchised. This led to an incredible amount of influence and an empire that held together better than one built on any single culture's customs.

Now, the Mongol empire was far from a democratic society, nor was Genghis Khan what we might consider an egalitarian leader; but he did know how to assemble large groups of people who could manage themselves and sustain a culture. His willingness to listen was key to building such a large and sprawling empire. He had to allow others to lead themselves and preserve their own traditions, which required a certain sensitivity that many leaders, even today, do not possess. If only we could be as "kind and generous" as Genghis Khan. Maybe then our organizations would have a fighting chance.

---

* Eskildsen, *Teachings and Practices*, 17.

Listening = Leading

To be a great leader is to be more than fearsome. Leadership, as we typically understand it, is overrated because it relegates the job of an influential person to creating a list of arbitrary rules and reinforcing them. But that's not leadership. In this book, we've tried to model a new kind of leader and a different kind of organization for you. On a self-led team, to lead is to listen; and trying to lead without listening is the cruelest kind of tyranny. Even Genghis Khan didn't do that. On the contrary, leading others and effecting real change requires a certain flexibility and openness to the perspectives of others. Influence is the ability to take in the opinions of others as legitimate feedback, flexing with the times and paying attention to one's surroundings, and then moving forward with a vision others can get behind. If you are doing that, regardless of title, you are leading—and it's only a matter of time before others start listening.

In the case of Genghis Khan, it would be inaccurate to say that he bent to the will of his people, but it is also untrue that he was insensitive to the needs of his subjects. For all his reputation as a ruthless conqueror, he was unusually tolerant of other cultures and receptive to new ideas. And this makes sense. If he wanted his empire to work, he would have to be aware of whom he was conquering and what mattered most to them. How else can you influence a person? One of the world's first superpowers was made possible not only by a single leader with an indomitable will but also by the ruler's willingness to allow and cultivate diversity.

Respecting the views of others, even if they run contrary to your own, illustrates an innate understanding of what makes an organization last. The ability to shift and bend with increasingly diverse circumstances makes a leader nimble, not weak. As a culture grows, it inevitably becomes more complex, so allowing space for such complexity is what helps a group of people sustain their cultural norms for a long time. Genghis Khan understood this, and we must as well.

This is where we are: in Phase III of this culture-making process, at the point where we must work to preserve our most sacred rituals and processes. To sustain any movement is difficult, which is why most great leaders eventually recede into mediocrity or irrelevance. That will be true for your own efforts to radically transform your organization. It takes more than a weekend seminar or a stroke of insight to change a culture. To reap the benefits and rewards of such a transformation requires incredible discipline. If you need repetition and reminders to reinforce a mere mantra, how much more is required to build a long-lasting, impactful culture? Sustaining a culture is an ongoing, continuous process, and being humble enough to keep listening and accepting feedback as you go is necessary.

Keep Listening

Communication is key to creating and sustaining change in any organization, and it cannot be faked. When you authentically listen to what other people are sharing, you can go back and make tweaks to old initiatives, improving them as they develop. No matter how good the original plan, you can always make something better—so long as you never stop listening. But when we find ourselves in charge of a team or perhaps an entire organization, it becomes more difficult to take in all the inbound messages and sort through them.

An understandably typical response to this onslaught of information is to just tune it all out. Executives may decide to stop checking email or filter all meeting requests through their assistants. They may insulate themselves from their direct reports by hiring an operations person to oversee all the people. None of these decisions are necessarily bad, but they belie a common mistake we see lots of leaders making, and that is to put themselves into a position where it's hard to hear the voices that count.

In 2000, Kevin Sharer became CEO of Amgen, one of the world's largest biotech companies, and made it his mission to grow the company quickly and at all costs. He put his head down, focused on maximizing profits, and didn't look up for the next seven years. This period, he later reflected, was a season of life in which he found himself in the "ego danger zone." He didn't listen well to anyone, was not open to feedback, and was generally disengaged from the team that was supporting him.

In 2007, Sharer learned that one of the company's products, Epogen, a red blood cell stimulant, was believed to cause a slightly greater risk of heart problems for patients. The US Food and Drug Administration ordered changes in the way the medication was prescribed, which led to significant decreases in profit for Amgen and subsequent layoffs. As CEO, Sharer was forced to let go 14 percent of the company's staff, and the whole thing took him by surprise.

At first, he was indignant. This, he complained, was everyone else's fault. "I had become impatient and arrogant," he later admitted. Then one day while waiting for his family at a restaurant, he had an epiphany. The company's failure was his fault and no one else's. The whole thing was caused, at least in part, by his poor listening skills and could have been avoided.*

Sharer had treated conversations as transactional and would tell others what to do without getting their full input or context. He later confessed that he'd be thinking about eight different things while pretending to listen to someone, get impatient with the person, and blurt out what he thought ought to be done. Realizing that he was responsible for the entire debacle, the Amgen CEO vowed to change his listening habits once and for all. He knew the future health of the company was contingent on his ability to pay attention, and he didn't want to blow it again.

In the workplace, leaders get so focused on what they believe is their primary job—driving profits, driving outreach, driving productivity—that they often forget the people required to make such changes. On occasion, we all need to take a step back and reengage with our team on a personal level, connecting with the people who make our work possible. Regardless of where you may be in the pecking order of your organization, it's good to understand what your peers are feeling, what they think is going on in the organization, and how they feel about their work. The culture can easily take a turn and become something nobody wants if you're not consistently intentional in reinforcing the vision you've all created together. You have to keep listening.

---

* Bryant and Sharer, "Are You Really Listening?"

When you forget to keep listening, you miss things. Things you could be doing. Things others should be doing. Things you could do better. You might miss little nuances that could make somebody's day better or allow your team to really gel. You might forget to check in with someone who shared a vulnerability the other week. These missed things add up, and the tragedy of these losses is that you won't have the team any individual wants to be a part of—because we all want to be heard and acknowledged, not forgotten. You'll also miss the opportunity to praise people when they are doing a great job. You'll miss the chance to thank people for their hard work, encourage them, or simply express your gratitude. Listening is the glue of any successful culture; it's what makes future improvements and innovations possible.

When Kyle was in Baghdad, his SEAL unit would perform routine direct-action missions in the dead of night, and extreme quiet was a necessity as they approached the target. To do otherwise would have meant instant death. Around two or three o'clock in the morning, when the entire world was asleep, the team members would park their vehicles about half a mile away from the target destination and carefully sneak over.

One of the SEALs would creep up to the front or side of the building and place a C-4 explosive charge on the exterior, then scurry back to join the others. Total, utter silence was critical to the success of any mission. If someone accidentally kicked a can or brushed up against a fence and made a noise, that small disturbance could cost the team the entire mission. If they lost the element of surprise, they lost everything. Listening, therefore, was crucial.

Once the charge was placed, there was only one small sound, which was that of a short transmission over the radio: "Placing charge, T-minus one minute." Then there was silence—unmoving, breathless silence—as everyone waited, counting down in their heads: "59 . . . 58 . . . 57 . . ." One team member might softly pull an ear out of their headset to listen to the surrounding sounds, scanning for anything out of the ordinary to see what might not fit. A dog barking in the distance. A truck driving from one town to the next. They were searching for something amiss: a shout or the sound of men walking, even gunfire. "Thirty seconds," someone would say over the radio, again followed by dead silence. Then it was a simple "3 . . . 2 . . . 1" countdown on the radio, followed by a massive explosion.

BOOM!

That was the signal for everyone to execute the mission from wherever they were hiding. Whether they were climbing over a wall or going through a window, as soon as that explosion went off, each SEAL spilled into the building as quickly as possible. They all had to be extra quiet, listening to everything around them, in case of any surprises. All success starts with listening, and sometimes it just might save your life.

Engage Sincerely

How do you engage with your team members in a way that's meaningful for them but still productive for the organization and sustainable for the long haul? Keep engagement as a priority. Recognize that developing a habit of consistent listening and awareness is going to take a lot of emotional capital to pull off, but if you don't engage with people, such negligence will only create bigger issues later. People will get frustrated, productivity will suffer, and your top talent will quit. The only ones left will be those who are too scared to leave.

We once worked with a woman we'll call Sally who was frustrated in her work, complaining that she didn't know where her teammates were half the time. Some days they were in, some days they were out. As a member of this team, Sally was confused by not knowing, and it created a lot of stress for her. She didn't know what people were up to, whether or not they were doing their jobs, and why they weren't telling her. She made up all kinds of stories about where her teammates were and why they weren't including her in their plans, both personal and professional. Dwelling on this made her unhappy. When we dug into the reasons for her situation, we learned a few things.

"How do you know they're not all on a site visit when you think they're out of the office?" we challenged.

"They don't tell me anything!" she huffed.

We discovered, however, that Sally and her three colleagues literally sat in a square cubicle together, working all day. They were the only four people in that pod, so it wouldn't have been hard to overhear plans that were being made. You just would have to pay attention. Sally admitted that she tended to tune them out when the trio was talking but then wondered where they were when suddenly she was sitting in the cubicle all alone.

As it turned out, it was not that these individuals weren't being forthcoming with their plans for an upcoming trip or get-together; rather, Sally wasn't paying attention to what was going on around her. She was sitting right next to them as they planned these trips. She didn't need to just listen more; she needed to pay better attention to the signals around her in the environment of which she was a part.

OODA Loops and Staying Frosty

The Navy SEALs have two tools that are especially useful in listening intently and sincerely. The first is called an OODA loop, which is a four-step decision-making process that SEALs use in mission planning. The acronym stands for "observe, orient, decide, act." It means that you filter the information available to you as it comes in, put it into context, decide on a path of action, then execute that decision as best you can.

To do this, first you need to orient yourself and know where your North Star is. Where are you, and where do you want to be? What's the mission, and where does success lie? Understand the geography and context of your environment, including previous experiences anyone on the team may have had, any new information, and so on.

Then, once you decide on the action you're going to take, make the call.

After you've made your decision, reassess where you are and what's going on, putting this new information into context, making a new decision, then executing.

This is an OODA loop. It's an ongoing process, one that requires you to be constantly listening and observing what's going on around you. You talk with your people and gather information, then compare what you find with information from other sources. And as you make adjustments, you compare your results with ever-changing information and data. And on and on the loop goes.

The second tool is a phrase SEALs often say to one another: "Stay frosty" means be on alert at all times. When you're cold, you're sharp, more physically aware of your surroundings. When you're warm, you're lethargic, relaxed, so you don't move as intently or with as much precision. Usually your senses are a little dull. On a mission, you don't want to lose your vigilance. "Always be cool" is the motto, and that means staying frosty at all costs.

The demise of a culture occurs when the appointed leader and other key stakeholders are losing their edge. They aren't aware of what's going on around them; they're not listening. When that happens, it's only a matter of time before the team experiences a slow descent to the bottom.

Take the time to meet people wherever they are. Don't call people into your office or a meeting room to check in on them; go to them. In their book *In Search of Excellence*, Tom Peters and Robert Waterman advocate a practice called "management by walking around," in which you tap into the culture of your organization and effectively lead it by engaging with the people you are trying to manage.

Walk with your team members for a mile in their shoes; see how they experience each day. Meeting your colleagues like this, watching them, listening to them will teach you things about them you wouldn't otherwise know. It'll help you understand what work is getting done and what isn't. It'll reveal opportunities and challenges faster than just about any other strategy.

What, exactly, do you do to make this connection? It doesn't matter. You can take someone to lunch or walk around the campus together or simply get a cup of coffee. Hanging out with the people you call your coworkers, even for only a few minutes on a regular basis, can change everything about your working dynamic. By doing this, you're showing them that you care because you're investing time in experiences with them. Whether you're the boss or just another peer, they know you're trying to make a connection, and often this is appreciated.

It doesn't take a lot of time to show someone else they matter. You don't have to schedule an hour-long meeting to go and listen to someone. It could be a five-minute walk, a two-minute round of speed Ping-Pong, or a leisurely stop at a friend's cubicle for a few moments. What's nice is that when you go to them, you aren't beholden to someone else's schedule. You can leave and get back to work whenever you need. Your time is your own, so your day isn't hijacked by another person. All it takes is a few minutes out of your day, and you don't even have to postpone any deadlines.

Investing in other people works as do all the best investments: slowly and over a long period of time, and usually trending toward positive results.

Maintaining the Habit of Listening

Self-led teams, like gardens, need to be cultivated, not managed. At times, the fruit from your team will be healthy and vibrant and all will be well. During these times, you need only keep saying yes to the energy coming from the team, perhaps gently guiding on occasion but never overpowering the momentum.

Then, of course, there will be times when things aren't going well, seasons of stagnancy and even struggle. What do we do then, when our garden is not bearing what we want, when it grows weed or attracts pests? Remember that even the healthiest of cultures is not immune to problems. Any great thing, even the most ideal of environments, cannot hold back the forces of chaos forever. Sometimes, as a member of this community we will need to do our part to make sure it's as healthy as possible, that the garden is still growing.

So what do we do with the garden? We water it, tend more carefully to it, feed it whatever it needs. In an organization, the food is always the same: *listening*. When things aren't going well and we don't know why, we listen more. If we are the leader of a team and we have no idea what everyone is doing, we listen more. If we are a low-ranking colleague and have virtually no power on the team, we listen more. If we have a sense of what needs to be done but no one pays attention to our ideas, we listen more. Only a fool rushes in to solve a problem he doesn't understand. Don't just jump in and try to fix things; pay attention. Get curious about the situation before you assume you know what's wrong. The team will tell you.

Your team members will let you know what's missing or what they still need. They'll let you know what you aren't doing or what's not working or even what could be better. When we don't take the time to pause and tune in to the frequency of others, we run the risk of losing the trust of our team. Who, after all, wants to listen to someone who won't hear you out? It takes only a minute, yet most of us don't do it.

If, instead, we listen to others, leaning in more intently and opening ourselves to potential solutions and recommendations, we avail our-selves of a wealth of knowledge. If you ask sincerely and earnestly what's wrong, people will tell you. They'll not only tell you what the problem is; they'll even share their ideas about how to fix it. People, especially members of an organization, are great at this.

There is never a shortage of opinions in a dying organization, and all this information is wonderful data to have. We can take it all in, learn from it, then decide what to do next. We might even try to carry out a plan recommended by one of our team members. If we can make that happen, they'll notice that and perhaps appreciate it. When we do this over and over again, giving people the dignity of being heard, consid-ering their recommendations, and occasionally applying them when we can and it makes sense to do so, we make ourselves an ally to as many of our coworkers as possible.

Fighting Complacency

The most common impediment to this continued habit of listening is busyness. When we get too busy to listen, we start to silo ourselves and create unnecessary dysfunction. Problems arise when people stop listen-ing to one another, when they stop hearing one another out, especially when those not listening are leaders—and often, they are.

When leadership gets busy, it gets complacent. And what follows complacency is sloppiness. We start taking certain things for granted; we lose our edge and don't continue to innovate and experiment in the same daring ways we once did. We stop being frosty, and in our malaise, we end up reverting to old ways of doing things, safer ways. And we inevitably create the organization we previously had, which will only bring in previous results.

This is where you have to be mindful of everything you're doing. You can't run on autopilot, regardless of where you stand in the organizational structure. To sustain a self-led team, you have to approach each day and each conversation as a brand-new, hearing-it-for-the-first-time encounter. It all goes back to listening.

Busyness is not always something we can avoid. Sometimes life sends its storms of urgency and there's nothing we can do about it. But complacency? That's not a given. We can always stay engaged with the work we're doing, who we're doing it with, and why we're doing it. To do all that, you just have to keep caring. It's harder than it sounds; people prefer a new catchphrase to a daily habit. Human beings crave novelty and run away from discomfort (if they can help it). Comfort and complacency are natural human impulses, and without awareness, we are likely to slide into the occasional rut.

Isn't this, after all, why we keep seeing new voices in a certain industry tell us the same old stuff in new ways? After all, how many personal finance experts do we need to finally get the message that you can't spend more than you make forever without going belly-up? Similarly, in how many different ways can you tell people what it takes to lose weight and become healthy? But if all people needed to solve their most challenging problems was the right information, more people would be healthier, there would be fewer chronic diseases, and everyone would be wizards with their money. But do people actually do it? Are they listening?

Well, of course they are—in a sense. They *do* listen. They hear every word, often loud and clear. They may even go home and start meal planning or making a budget. Until they don't. Until they quickly revert to their old habits, to what they are used to. They go back to the junk food, back to the online shopping, back to all those habits that created the problem in the first place. It wasn't that they weren't listening. They were; they just got complacent. They stopped trying, stopped being mindful of their surroundings, and slipped back into old habits, undoing everything they had worked so hard to do.

Having good intentions and falling short of your goal is not uncommon; it's quite normal. Making new habits and following through on them is difficult, which is why most people repeat the same old patterns every single new year. It's easy to start some new habit strong and then get complacent when it gets hard, abandoning the practices you've been trying to follow—especially when real life hits. That happens to teams as well.

Even the best organizations decide on cultural norms and customs that would make them great and commit to them. They may even develop a list of nonnegotiables that become their core values, going so far as to create a mantra and a handful of rituals to reinforce the new normal. And then reality sets in, and all these ideals start getting pressure-tested. This is where the rubber meets the road and your commitment is really challenged.

It's not just that you want to listen; you need to pay close attention to everything that's happening, like a SEAL in the middle of a night mission. Every sound, every gesture, every little movement matters here. To sustain great cultures, we've got to keep listening as intentionally as possible. Otherwise, it'll be unending chaos.

This is your mission: to make a renewed effort every single day to listen to your team, your bosses, your customers. Stop trying to be the superhero. Focus on what your team can accomplish, not what you can accomplish. Stop trying to find the solution to your department's problems. Empower others. Then listen to them. They will tell you when something is wrong. But don't just start listening. Keep doing it, long after you think you should. Watch the ego that will surface at times with thoughts like "I know better." Remember Kevin Sharer and what nearly devastated Amgen—a simple habit of not listening.

Most companies, most *people*, just get tired of listening. We tune out what's being said because we're tired and it takes so much effort to constantly be directing our attention to others. We've got our own things to do, and we just start to tune out the other voices. Someone may begin talking and it sounds like the parents in a Peanuts cartoon: "Wah, wah, waaahhhh . . ."

As humans, we don't spend enough time talking with one another and really, truly listening. Not just waiting for our turn to speak but actually tuning in to the words and emotions of our clients and co-workers, not to mention our friends and family. To truly listen. Doing so could change just about anything. Of course, there's more to it than just listening.

Processing What You've Heard

One of the nice things about reading physical books—a rarity these days, to be sure—is that when you encounter a powerful idea or a powerful statement, you can slip your finger between the pages, close the book, and take a few minutes to process what you've heard. You can contemplate the words you read, considering their meaning and why it matters. But in conversation (or even when listening to an audiobook or podcast), there is no time for processing or pausing. The narrative just keeps going.

The same is true with our minds, which are almost always racing with information and words, ideas and emotion. When listening to someone, we don't allow ourselves time to process what we're hearing from them, and it's hard to tune out all the clutter already clogging our mental air ducts. We're so busy with our current list of responsibilities and worried about the next project or meeting or trip that we don't take time to process what we've just heard. It could be lifesaving, world-changing information, and we just missed it.

Listening is essential, but the second part of this is that we also need to process what we've heard. Taking in content without applying it is the same as trying to catch the wind. We need to somehow harness the energy coming at us and do so in a way that is useful. It's important to take time to chew on what someone has just told you. This may require patience. Allow the other person time to collect their thoughts. Let them think through what they want to say. Give them time to chew on what you've shared, as well.

If needed, take down some notes from your conversation; you might even consider it a brief "report" of sorts. Highlight the important issues and topics you discussed, then take time to ruminate on them and process the information. What lessons can you learn? What can you do better next time? What did this conversation reveal to you about the person you just talked to?

Does this apply only to leaders? Of course not. Anyone can have a conversation, and we all can give each other the gift of listening. This habit applies to anyone who aspires to make their team a little better and wants to be trusted and empowered more. Active listening, ruminating on and processing what you've heard, and just generally paying attention to your surroundings can be practiced at any level of an organization. And the sooner we do it, the better off everyone will be.

After all, Genghis Khan may have started his rule as emperor with a certain level of openness and tolerance toward foreign religions, but it was his grandson Kublai Khan who brought about a more benevolent rule and peacefully encouraged a diversity of culture throughout his empire.

Following the tradition of his grandfather, Kublai Khan was receptive to outsiders and even brought outside emissaries into his court. These emissaries, one of whom was the famous Marco Polo, served as consultants in art, trade, and technology, helping the khan solve whatever his latest problem might be.

Known as the wise khan, Kublai Khan brought in the surrounding external cultures, building connections with their intellectuals and thought leaders, soliciting advice from the world's leading experts. As a result, he helped his people make great advancements into modernity that continue to have ripple effects. How did he do this? He listened. He kept listening. And that makes all the difference.

14

HUMILITY IS A HABIT

In 1901, Thomas Mann published a novel in which he depicted the decline of a wealthy family, not dissimilar to his own, called the Buddenbrooks. In the story, a German family of grain merchants builds a tremendous amount of wealth, consolidates it into a family business, then proceeds to squander nearly all of it within a couple of generations. The novel was Mann's first but eventually helped him win the Nobel Prize in Literature, and it continues to receive widespread critical acclaim. The story represented a phenomenon all too familiar to many Americans, especially at the turn of the twentieth century, a phenomenon that came to be known as the Buddenbrooks syndrome.

The Buddenbrooks syndrome describes the tendency of a family business to decline over the course of three generations. This effect came to describe the destinies of many wealthy families of industry and trade, including the Rockefellers, the Guggenheims, and more. In less than a lifetime, what their family spent generations building was all but completely dismantled.

This is all too common an occurrence. Typically, the pattern is something like this: the first generation builds wealth through struggle and triumph, the second attempts to carry out their parents' legacy but lacks their discipline, the third squanders resources on pursuits such as art and philosophy.

What causes the downfall of such family dynasties? How can a relatively small group of people go from being poor immigrants to one of the richest families in the world, only to lose it all in another generation? The answer is humility, or lack thereof. What makes wealthy families go broke is either a faulty memory or an unwillingness to retain the frugality from their early years. Simply put, they forget where they came from.

This is more common than we realize: the downfall of a leader or an entire family empire comes down to losing their grip on reality. Our organizations suffer when leaders forget that humility is not a privilege but a necessity for building healthy, long-lasting cultures of excellence. This continues to happen because we've had the wrong expectations of the people leading us.

For centuries, we've been taught that our leaders are infallible, that they are at the top of the pecking order and we ought to trust them. Why else would they be leaders? A thousand years ago, kings were believed to be divinely appointed, and by association their nobles were equally inerrant. Such classism has continued well into the twenty-first century, when we celebrate CEOs as saviors of their companies and even of our economy. Political and military leaders act as if they are demigods, believing their orders ought to be followed without question. Meanwhile, we—the masses—flock to speakers and authors and influencers with all our questions, making them millionaires in the process. It's all bullshit.

We've created a model in the corporate world that has spilled into every other facet of our culture. We attract a charismatic visionary—who often possesses narcissistic tendencies—and we ask this person to lead us. These are the people who perpetuate the broken model of leadership we've railed against throughout this whole book, and as we all know, nobody's perfect. Nobody has all the answers. Nobody makes wise decisions all the time. And yet we entrust so many to a handful of individuals who rarely have our best interests at heart. There are too many stories of myopic CEOs who crash and burn, making one bad decision after another for themselves, which ultimately leads to the ruination of a company or an individual—and sometimes, sadly, both. The fact that only a few have emerged unscathed from such a toxic culture says something about our current model of leadership.

Even the greatest luminaries have made poor decisions on occasion, in some cases jeopardizing the health and future of their organization in the process. Steve Jobs, for example, recruited John Sculley, who got Jobs fired two years later and then tried launching the Apple III, Macintosh TV, and Power Mac G4 Cube—all of which were phenomenal failures. Jack Welch put so much energy and money into GE Capital that its 2008 collapse required a $139 billion government bailout, from which General Electric is still struggling to bounce back. Bill Gates had complete misses with the Windows Phone,* in breaking antitrust law in 2000, and in bailing out Apple when it was weeks away from bankruptcy—and, of course, with the Zune. These men are considered some of the greatest CEOs in our lifetimes, but even they made boneheaded moves. Leadership isn't all it's cracked up to be sometimes, and this is not to say these leaders didn't deserve their positions, only that they weren't perfect. And we should all remember that, as the key to long-term success is not perfection but humility.

Be Open

There's an old story about a Zen master in which people would travel from all over to seek the master's help and learn from him. One day, a scholar visited the master and asked, "Can you teach me about Zen?" As the two talked, it became clear that the scholar had his own opinions and knowledge, which he shared at great length. He failed to listen to what the Zen master said and would regularly interrupt him with his own ideas.

Eventually, the master suggested that the two men have tea. The master poured his guest a cup of tea, and when the cup was full, he continued pouring until the tea overflowed onto the table. The scholar exclaimed, "Stop, the cup is already full! Can't you see that?"

"Exactly," said the master. "You are like this cup, so full of ideas that nothing more can be poured in. Come back to me with an empty cup."

---

* Kim, "Gates' Worst Decisions as CEO."

Gone are the days of the leaders with full cups. Those know-it-alls may still, in fact, be around, but their *time* is over. As any good leader will admit, leaders should not be the smartest person in the room; if they are, they're in the wrong room. A self-led team is a roundtable organization, one in which power and influence are more evenly distributed and everyone gets a vote. You don't get to sit at the head of the table, because there is no head, and whatever your position in the organization, you know that you are surrounded by people whose skills in certain areas outweigh yours. It is not timidity that acknowledges such a reality but rather humility. In the wise words of C. S. Lewis, humility is not thinking less of yourself but thinking of yourself less. It's understanding exactly who and what you are and never assuming otherwise. To be humble is to possess a certain groundedness with the way things are. You aren't deluded or given to grand fantasies; you know exactly what's true and have no misgivings about how important you are in the grand scheme of things. Humility concerns itself primarily with others. You always know there's someone better because you have a clear grasp of what you can and cannot do—that's what it means to be humble.

But in a world where arrogance often gets rewarded, such virtue does not necessarily come easily. In most cases, humility is a habit, a practice that must be reinforced with consistency and discipline. Kevin Sharer, former CEO of Amgen, said in his *Harvard Business Review* interview, "My approach was: 'I'm the smartest guy in the room. Just let me prove that here, in the first five minutes.' I would even interrupt people and tell them what they were going to tell me, to save us time so that we could get to the really important stuff, which was me telling them what to do."[*] As he learned, though, this was the wrong approach, an act of negligence and myopia that ended up costing him and his company far more than he ever could have anticipated. Our focus, then, shouldn't be on having all the answers but on opening ourselves to the right answers, wherever they may come from. As Bruce Lee once said, "The usefulness of the cup is in its emptiness." Leadership is overrated because most leaders naturally feel the pull to come across as confident, as if they had all the answers. As a

---

[*] Bryant and Sharer, "Are You Really Listening?"

result, they only end up alienating the individuals who could help them.

When you're not willing to admit your failures, your colleagues and peers are all too willing to admit them for you. So why not go first? Why not beat everyone to the punch and acknowledge what they all already know? Humility doesn't have to be some picture of virtue or pristine morality. It is, essentially, just honesty. To be humble is to not resist or deny what is true about yourself. The more you do this, the more people will trust you because they'll see you are just like them. You will never build a great team if people can't admit to making a mistake. And we all get our cues from one another, so someone has to begin. No one ever built a long-lasting organization on lies. It's time, then, to start telling the truth.

Give Credit, Take Blame

President Dwight Eisenhower once said, "Leadership consists of nothing but taking responsibility for everything that goes wrong and giving your subordinates credit for everything that goes well."* If on a regular basis you give away all the credit for the great work everyone has done, you will be more believable. You'll look better as a result of making others look better. If you're a leader, this will certainly speak volumes, but it will be no less significant if you are a team member who is giving credit to everyone else when, in many cases, people are looking for ways to take undue credit. As basketball coaching legend John Wooden once said, "A strong leader accepts blame and gives the credit. A weak leader gives blame and accepts the credit."†

If you have ever made a mistake and reflexively thrown someone under the bus for it, you know that others immediately lose respect for you when you do this. They see that you have only your own interests at heart, which will cause them to worry about themselves and their interests instead of those of the team. So, you see, selfishness only corrupts the integrity of a team. Humility, then, is not one of the most im-

---

* Puryear, *Nineteen Stars.*
† Wooden and Jamison, *Wooden on Leadership.*

portant qualities for a leader to have; it is *the* most important one. We all have an opportunity to influence any group we are a part of, and to be a member of any team requires a certain amount of self-denial. We have to assimilate into the team of which we are a part and give everything we can in service of the mission. This attitude strengthens the team and earns the trust of our colleagues. If you want to create something greater than the sum of its parts, there is no other way.

When Kyle was in charge of the West Coast tactical special operations urban combat training, held on the navy-controlled San Clemente Island in California, he committed *the number one* mortal sin as a Navy SEAL. West Coast teams getting ready to go overseas go to this island to be trained in urban combat scenarios in a fake city the SEALs have built. In these scenarios, the SEALs use something similar to paintballs, called "simunition" (simulated ammunition), but with real guns. In the training scenarios, different SEALs take turns playing the enemy. This particular time, Kyle was one of the enemies and was supposed to take on his fellow good guy SEALs.

During the exercise, Kyle spotted someone through his night vision goggles and immediately took aim. The figure looked like a SEAL and moved like one, but Kyle's night vision was a little foggy. Eager to make the kill, he didn't take the time to clear his goggles and properly identify the target. He wanted the win and didn't want to waste time questioning something he was certain of. Instead, he confirmed his aim and shot. At that moment, the "enemy" looked up, then back at Kyle, and said, "What the hell, man?" Kyle's heart sank. He had just shot one of his own men. There is nothing worse than a "blue on blue" shooting.

Kyle knew he had been acting a bit lazy, maybe even a little full of himself, and he realized his attitude had the potential to cost someone's life. Granted, this was a simulation, but the feeling and energy of it was real. That's the power of such drills in the military; you aren't allowed to think of them as play. This is real-life stuff, meant to prepare you for real combat, where the circumstances are far less forgiving. That night, Kyle came clean to his unit and told everyone, "I'm so sorry. I shot Scotty during the exercise, and I want you all to know that." He ran through all of his mistakes, all the errors of judgment, and exactly what he did to cost the life of a fellow SEAL.

In his confession, Kyle laid it on the line in front of everyone and made himself vulnerable. He didn't try to hide it, didn't try to blame Scotty for dressing and moving like a SEAL while playing a bad guy. He owned the mistake and explained how he had done it all by himself, and this created a whole new level of trust from the unit. Even though he had earned his teammates' trust and respect in the past, this move raised their opinion of him. If we want to have considerable influence, we will also have to be more vulnerable than we might prefer. Vulnerability and humility are key in earning the respect, trust, and affinity of others. You may think, "I don't need anyone to like me; I need them only to do what I say." But even in the military, that doesn't work anymore. Besides, if you have that attitude, that's exactly what you will get. People will only do what you say; they won't show any initiative and certainly won't help you when you need it the most. If you look out only for number one, others won't look out for you. But if you put them first, if you're humble and own your failures, your teammates will do whatever it takes to help you. It's only natural.

Serve Others

When Jungkiu Choi moved from Singapore to China to become the head of Consumer Banking at Standard Chartered Bank, he learned that one of his obligations was to visit the different branches and pressure branch managers to cut costs. This aspect of the job caused him a lot of stress and didn't actually accomplish what the bank hoped it would. So Choi decided to change the nature of the visits—since they weren't working anyway.

Rather than flex his power and flaunt his position, he would show up at a branch unannounced and serve breakfast to all the employees. After that, he'd hold informal huddles with the teams and ask them how he could improve their branch. In one year, Choi visited eighty branches in twenty-five cities. His huddles revealed a lot of pain points that, when alleviated, helped everyone do their jobs better, such as offering training for the new banking systems and upgrading the branches' computer memory so that it could handle new software. With these and other changes during Choi's two-year tenure, customer satisfaction increased by 54 percent and customer complaints were reduced by 29 percent. The employee attrition ratio, previously the highest of all foreign banks in China, became one of the lowest.*

All of this had nothing to do with paradigm shifts, fancy leadership training, or special strategy sessions. No one held an organizational overhaul or created a blue-ribbon committee to write a new mission statement. What *did* they do? Jungkiu Choi made himself vulnerable by showing up unannounced and serving breakfast. Humbly, he asked people for help and solicited their ideas. When people offered their opinions and insights, he listened and tried to make their suggestions happen. They asked him for something, and he served them however he could.

Humility and service go hand in hand. When you assume a humble attitude, you will easily serve your team; it'll just feel right. In turn, your teammates will see your humility and may want to meet you in that energy, reciprocating however they can. When you adopt a service mindset, generosity will surround you. It might even catch on.

Six Practices of a Humble Leader

We can see how humility can affect the morale of a team and even impact its overall success. But can you really cultivate humility, or is it just a personality trait that you're either born with or not? As it turns out, we can practice being humble, and the more we do this, the more we attract the right kind of people who can help us develop a self-led team. There are six crucial practices of a humble leader, and the more we do each of these, the more we humble ourselves and begin to build trust. Here they are: listen more, talk less; show appreciation; step out of the spotlight; admit when you've made a mistake; don't micromanage; and welcome criticism.

1. Listen More, Talk Less

To be a good leader, you have to be a good listener; humility and listening are inextricably linked. If you are in a position of influence, it doesn't

---

* Cable, "Humble Leadership."

mean you know more than anyone else. Rather, your job is to help your team succeed, and the best way to do that is to listen. The less you jabber, the more you'll be able to hear and the better you'll be able to respond.

2. Show Appreciation

A little goes a long way. In meetings and on group chats, call out people for their successes; publicly celebrate the wins of the team. Send a hand-written thank-you note. Leave a voicemail on Friday night on a team member's work line, thanking them for something small they did that week. Make sure people know how much you appreciate them, whoever they are and regardless of who you might be. When team members are traveling, find a way to send flowers or gift cards to their spouses. Let their partners know how proud you are of them and what a difference they're making on the team.

3. Step Out of the Spotlight

When someone compliments "your" efforts, make sure they know you have a team working with you; point out who else deserves the credit. You may have led the charge, but few successes are solitary in nature. We all need to lean on others on occasion, and greatness is almost always a group effort. When you make other people look good, you're actually solidifying your own reputation and gaining more power and job security.

4. Admit When You've Made a Mistake

Own your mistakes and admit to them quickly. When Kyle inadvertently shot his teammate and then owned his mistake, things turned out better as a result. Kyle's teammates respected and trusted him more, and the experience made him a better, humbler leader in the long run. Yes, it's risky to put yourself in a vulnerable position like that, one in which you admit you're wrong, but if you have ever tried to hide a mistake and it was later found out, you know how awkward that can be. All it does is label you a liar when the truth finally does come to light.

5. Don't Micromanage

To guide a self-led team, you don't need to be the smartest person in the room; you just need to be able to trust people. If you don't want to get stuck in the endless loop of micromanaging everyone around you, find competent people to do their jobs—and then let them. You hired these people presumably because they're good at what they do. If they can't do it without your input, then you hired the wrong people and it's back to the drawing board.

6. Welcome Criticism

This can be hard. Hearing how far you've fallen short or screwed something up doesn't feel good. But it can be useful. No, an annual review can't feel much better, because all your misdeeds may be spelled out for you at once, but that's only because of how shallow most criticism is. To truly change things, we have to go deep, as close to the source of the problem as possible. This is why the SEALs use a 720-degree performance appraisal, which includes a 360-degree review from peers, subordinates, and superiors, and then a second 360-degree review that involves interviews with those same people. It allows the navy to get an in-depth and accurate assessment of an individual from a variety of perspectives, which is tremendously helpful.

We need to be as open to the same kind of honesty and feedback from our own teams. After all, you'd like to give it, wouldn't you—to tell everyone where they need to improve and fix things for you? Isn't that right? But if they all have things to improve upon—and since you're not infallible—then it stands to reason you might have a few things you could work on as well. It can be difficult to take criticism, but it's necessary. You don't magically stop making mistakes once you reach a certain level of experience. If anything, people may start hiding your mistakes from you the more senior you become, at which point honesty is invaluable. If you are willing to listen to others and their recommendations on how you can improve, you're going to learn so much more than any seminar or workshop could ever teach you. That's leadership. And even if you're not a leader by position, this is one area in which you can lead by example, demonstrating an emotional capacity to put others first and not feel the need to hog the attention. Humility is not a gift; it's a habit—and the more we practice it, the better we'll get.

15

STAY AGILE

Enduringly great organizations are not mere behemoths. To be truly great for a long period of time, to establish the kind of legacy that extends beyond a generation or two, you have to be better than big. You have to be agile, willing to flex and grow with the times. You not only need to be ready to respond to whatever the world may throw your way, but you also have to build into the very ecosystem of your organization a value of adaptability. Evolve or die, as the saying goes, and it's especially true in the world of work. Refusing to adapt, especially in business, is like signing your own death warrant. Now more than ever, organizations have to be prepared for anything, with the systems in place needed to react. Self-led teams almost always act with agility—and when they don't, that's a lesson for next time.

When you hear the word "agility," you might first think of people being light on their feet, able to move quickly, pivot, and head in a new direction. You may even remember the image of world-class athletes such as Mikhail Baryshnikov, who could seemingly defy gravity as he leaped and spun onstage, or the slam-dunking magic that was Michael Jordan. The word might even bring to mind thoughts of innovative companies such as Google and Apple. Or maybe it reminds you of your neighbor who works in software and keeps using the word. But chances are, you don't think about little plastic blocks.

In 1932, Ole Kirk Kristiansen founded a toy company in Billund, Denmark. Or, rather, as a result of the financial catastrophe that was the Great Depression, he started making wooden toys in his shop to try to increase sales. If people didn't have the money for an ironing board, he reasoned, they might still be able to afford cheap toys for their children. Two years later, Kristiansen named the company LEGO, after the Danish phrase *leg godt*, which means "play well."

This new endeavor, however, did not play well with the market. It was far from smooth sailing for many years, and this wasn't the first tumultuous period in Kristiansen's life. Before starting LEGO, the young carpenter had started his first business as a woodworker, only to have his children accidentally burn it down—along with their home—while he was traveling for work. He also lived through two world wars, endured Nazi occupation of his country, lost his first wife, and staved off bankruptcy for many years while building what became one of the largest toy companies in the world. For years, LEGO struggled through one set of difficult circumstances after another while the founder's family members offered to bail him out on one condition: *stop making toys.* That was one thing Ole Kirk Kristiansen could not do.

The ambitious Dane had started making toys as a way of keeping his head above water when everyone was tightening their belts, but it had become more than that. An earnest carpenter, he had developed an affinity for this new craft, taking it seriously and making the best toys he could make. Soon, this affinity grew into a passion, and Kristiansen refused to cut corners. Focused intently on each step of the process— from the birchwood he picked out and dried for two years to the three coats of lacquer he applied to each and every toy—he loved his work and took pride in the honesty of it. The company continued to struggle until the man decided to focus exclusively on toy making, and that's when it really started to see some momentum.

In 1947, LEGO bought a plastic injection molding machine that made it possible for the company to start making plastic toys at scale. What came next was finding the right type of plastic that would allow the blocks to stick together. The result, of course, is what is now the world's most famous plastic brick, what many of us colloquially (and incorrectly) call "legos." The design for the world's first plastic building block was patented in 1958 by Godtfred Kirk Christiansen, the founder's son, and after that history truly was made.

Today, the company employs more than fifteen thousand people worldwide and has offices in Denmark, the United States, the United Kingdom, China, and Singapore. It has no plans to stop anytime soon, always pivoting and experimenting in pursuit of its mission to make education fun and play more educational.

Keep What Generates Energy

As any leader of a great organization knows, it takes discipline to stay great, and every entropic force in the universe is working against you. Self-led teams develop a discipline of paying attention to their culture so as to never get too bloated; and if things get off track, they quickly correct the issue. However, even the best of teams face all kinds of unforeseen obstacles. One important value is agility, which is the ability to respond well to surprises.

As Jim Collins wrote in *How the Mighty Fall*: "The signature of the truly great versus the merely successful is not the absence of difficulty, but the ability to come back from setbacks, even cataclysmic catastrophes, stronger than before. Great nations can decline and recover. Great companies can fall and recover. Great social institutions can fall and recover. And great individuals can fall and recover. As long as you never get entirely knocked out of the game, there remains always hope."[*]

Your ability to not "get entirely knocked out of the game" rests almost exclusively on your willingness to change. In 2014, LEGO Digital Solutions implemented the Scaled Agile Framework (SAFe), a set of workflows designed to scale agile practices to an enterprise level. The company's head of project management, Eik Thyrsted Brandsgård,

---

[*] Collins, *How the Mighty Fall*, 120.

helped the small but growing team roll out a set of practices that would improve their collaboration model. What they were working with had been sufficient for a team of five, but now that they were over twenty and growing, they needed a new model.

"Much like creating something from LEGO® bricks," according to one report, "they built their transformation one piece at a time." They began by inviting twenty managers to a two-day class. After that, they started training teams, starting with one at first and repeating the process until they had twenty teams fully trained in the new practices. As the report continued, "They approached every step as a learning journey, allowing for creativity along the way. When something didn't seem like a good fit, they weren't afraid to experiment." They borrowed from other workflow approaches and tweaked their own methodology until all their needs were met with just one simple principle to guide them: "Keep the stuff that generates energy."*

There's not a simpler, clearer definition of an agile approach to any project or task your team may face. Stick with what lights you and your team up. Don't get stuck holding on to customs or habits that no longer serve you and maybe never did. Hold on to what offers more energy than it takes. Agility is about so much more than movement or speed. True agility is a state of mind: a willingness to work with whatever the circumstances may be and take the best action now, even if that means waiting. An agile mindset is an intentional one, and agility is a necessary habit worth cultivating if you want to sustain a long-term culture of self-leadership.

Recently while attending a business conference, we heard some employees of a large organization talk about the lack of agility in their workplace. It took them eighteen months, they explained, to update a piece of hardware or software. They had to field-test it and approve all the required technology, running it through so many points of contact that by the time it got through the system, the technology was outdated. It was maddening. They were always running eighteen months or more behind the standard. The organization was large and successful, but it

---

* Scaled Agile, "Case Study: LEGO Digital Solutions." © Scaled Agile, Inc.

was just not agile enough to innovate in its own field. And that was a problem because the organization they were complaining about was part of the US military. They were frustrated, and any sane person could see why. Most organizations start out fresh and full of energy only to get bogged down with unnecessary layers of bureaucracy that ultimately make them a more miserable place to work. A willingness to shed those redundancies for the sake of greater productivity is the mark of an agile team.

Sadly, it doesn't work that way for most teams. A lot of organizations are in the same place: stuck in their own ruts, falling behind the competition. It's the worst when you know what needs to happen but are completely disempowered to carry it out. You may see a new opportunity arise or a new market to push into, but you can't start quickly enough or get people focused in time to pull it off. It's hard to "mobilize the troops" when you can't get everyone to show up at the same time. Or you may have an expense problem and the company is hemorrhaging $30,000 to $40,000 per month. You need to get it fixed fast or you may not make payroll—and somehow you just can't seem to get the boat moving in the right direction. That is the opposite of agility, and it is the norm for far too many organizations—and as you can see, this will kill a team.

Being agile means you're able to quickly address opportunities and deal with problems as they arise. Of course, there may be a minimum buffer between knowing there's a problem and taking measures to solve it. Every organization has a gap between stimulus and response, even if it's only a few minutes. But the wider that gap, the less agile you are. The trick is to make that space between action and reaction as short as possible.

Every organization has its own bureaucracies and forms of red tape. Your team has its own, even if team members are not aware of them. Agility does not mean rushing into the heat of battle too early. It means allowing the proper time to take in the information of a situation and responding appropriately without unnecessary delay. As an organization gets bigger, things tend to run more slowly; and over time, inefficiencies naturally develop. An agile approach to team management allows you to stay nimble while still providing the necessary structure to get the job done well and in a way that aligns with the core values of your organization.

Agility Is About Execution

Kyle used to have a sign in his office that said, "Ideas are shit, execution is everything." In other words, if you came into Kyle's office with a good idea, you needed to have an executable plan to go with that good idea. The result? It drastically improved the quality (and quantity) of ideas presented to Kyle. It may sound elementary, but when you create an expectation like this, you communicate to your people that they have the freedom and ability to research their ideas and come up with a plan to bring forth a fully thought-out idea.

When Kyle was in Afghanistan in 2012, a member of his support team, an electronic communications tech named Will, came to him with an idea and an executable path for the idea. Back then, in Afghanistan, there were these massive blimps. They were just like hot air balloons that floated above Afghanistan. They had incredible 4K cameras that focused on the entire region, and on a clear day an operator could see for seven or eight miles. The problem, as we said earlier, was that the US military was eighteen months behind technologically, so the only person who could see the camera feed was one guy sitting directly below the blimp. His job was to watch the feed and then inform the rest of the battlespace of what he saw.

Will told Kyle, "I've got an idea for getting that feed to our TOC" (tactical operations center). He described his idea, and Kyle's team built radio frequency (RF) repeaters and tied them into the blimp. Then they bolted the RF repeaters to trees for about a seven-mile string and bounced a 4K camera feed all the way from the blimp to the TOC. They were the first ones in Afghanistan to do anything like this. It took a couple of weeks, but they finally had live, real-time visual intelligence that worked as well as Google Earth. Now all they had to do was radio the operator to redirect a camera to focus on a particular area, rather than waiting for someone to call them and relay the things they were seeing.

But they didn't stop there. They wrote a white paper and disseminated it to all the units in Afghanistan so that they could reproduce the technology. It actually had an impact on all of the US forces in the country. Eventually, one of the big military contractors developed technology based on the idea. That all happened because Kyle had created a culture in which his team could bring in an idea and it wouldn't get crushed and thrown by the wayside. But his team members also knew that if they had an idea, they needed to have a way to execute the idea.

The Power of a Lean Team

One of the many things the SEALs do well is to understand their mission and the footprint they need for such a mission. Their missions could require one or two SEALs or a thousand. Sometimes a mission required only a sniper and a radio communicator. At other times, missions required a fire team, which is four SEALs. Or a squad, which is eight SEALs. SEALs are good at understanding a mission's requirements and keeping their teams agile.

But agile doesn't always mean small. At times, a battalion may be most agile for a mission. Of course, it's easy to bash the big bureaucracies of the world, like the US government and huge corporations, but those massive bodies have their place in the world. We are big believers in the value of a lean team, which has just enough members to reach its goals and no more, and in which each team member is working at full efficacy. When you are lean, you are better able to be agile. Just ask anyone in the lean manufacturing or agile software engineering fields. When we say "agile," we mean able to mobilize quickly, nimble, and empowered to act easily. "Lean," on the other hand, means you're not growing or scaling inefficiently. You can grow, but you do so as needed, not just for the sake of growing.

If you want to develop a lean team, start with your organizational structure and your overall mission. Then look at everyone's roles and responsibilities and start asking questions. How much overlap is there between two people's roles? Is that really two people's worth of workload, or is it only one? Do you really need three graphic designers? You have only four sites, so why would you add a fifth site manager? It's a simple yet difficult process because you're continuously looking for inefficiencies. You have to constantly spend time refining the team, looking at it, and knowing you're getting everything you can out of your team.

You're not a lean organization if each team member is doing the work of three people. Then you're just cheap, and you'll burn out your team members quickly. They'll leave and go somewhere else, and you won't be able to find new people to replace them. Then you'll be overworking your team even more, and as you're congratulating yourself on a lean operation, they're all polishing their résumés and looking for easier jobs. In that sense, Navy SEALs are a naturally agile culture because everything they do is project based. Teams come together as needed for a mission, and leadership shifts according to what's going on.

A business is typically not organized this way. Many organizations, however, have found the value in breaking up their larger departments temporarily, saying, for example, "This is a marketing initiative, but we need three people from operations for a few weeks." Then, when the project is over, those three go back to their regular work. Maybe the human resources department needs to create some internal communications newsletter templates, so it works with a member of the marketing team to create some good-looking templates. These are called tiger teams, and they're used to address issues quickly and efficiently.

A tiger team is a self-led team. Personnel are pulled from different departments on the basis of the skills and knowledge each individual brings to the situation. These teams are lean and agile, and they last only as long as the project or crisis is in play. Once the project is complete or the crisis is over, the team disperses and awaits the next project. In the future, we will take for granted that this is the only way to organize a team.

Leaning Out

Self-led teams thrive in lean environments. They can easily incorporate other people when needed because each person understands the problem and is empowered to do whatever the project requires. When things move quickly in an organization, everything tends to flow better. You don't want to rush, but finding the right pace is essential to getting your whole team to buy into the mission.

A common problem with bloated corporations is that when several people share responsibility, there's no one to blame. Or, rather, no one is willing to take all the blame. We have no problem pointing fingers at others while looking into the camera and saying that "mistakes were made." We may or may not have had something to do with them. When no one is accountable, long-term growth and resiliency in an organization is nearly impossible. When no one takes responsibility, no one grows or learns to do better next time.

In agile work environments, there's less of the blame games and more personal responsibility. And because so many choices are made in real time, it's easy to accept responsibility for a bad outcome because the sooner you catch it, the faster you can solve it. Mistakes are welcome because they help us reach our goal faster.

A self-led team takes agility to another level. Often, if there's an issue on a team, the leader has to call the whole team together, talk about the problem, and start looking for solutions—or, worse, wait for the team to tell the leader what the problem is. By the time the problem reaches the leader, it has festered and become a major issue. A self-led team, on the other hand, seizes on any frustrations and deals with them as quickly and effectively as possible. A lot less ego is involved because the stakes of each action are a lot less than they would be if the team had let it all build. Now taking the blame isn't something to be so scared of.

On a self-led team, every team member is empowered and responsible for the mission of the team; therefore, problems tend to be found sooner and solved faster than if they had to be run up the chain of command. Team members don't report a problem and then sit back and wait for it to get bigger. They fix it. As we've noted, the Navy SEALs, unlike much of the rest of the military, are organized according to the objectives of each mission. When things change in the field, you don't have time to run an idea up the chain of command. You've got to be agile, make a decision, and take the next step *now*. Knowing that your team is enabled to solve problems on the fly and that all members understand their responsibilities is the key to staying lean, focused on the work at hand. When people are trusted fully and held completely accountable, they do their best work, discovering efficiencies and solutions that others would not have seen. All members of the team are capable of leading themselves and stepping into the team's operations to take over.

This is one reason why Navy SEALs keep their teams tight and small; the leaner you are, the fewer complications you're going to have. More people in the room doesn't necessarily mean more success for a mission. When teams are small, made up of competent experts, and encouraged to be agile and self-led, they will naturally innovate, solving problems more quickly than could be done in a hierarchy, and pivoting along the way.

Ultimately, agility leads to trust, and trust leads to empowerment. Most people feel the opposite in their workplaces; they aren't appreciated, much less empowered. Often, they feel as if they are in grade school again, having to ask for permission to go to the bathroom. But good parents teach their children to live independently, to not need mom and dad in order to survive.

This is how you engage people in their own lives: by entrusting more and more to them and allowing them to feel the consequences of their choices. There is no other way to empower people than to let them have more responsibility and, slowly, over time, feel the weight of it. Self-led teams and organizations do this better than most, and by doing so, they create a culture that engages all team members, expecting as much as is reasonable from each person. The more agile you are, the easier this becomes.

THE FUTURE
OF LEADERSHIP

In 2012, Kyle and his Navy SEAL team were leading an unconventional warfare campaign to help the Afghan people retake control of their country and build a police force in the village of Malozai in Helmand Province. That was where they developed the mantra of "quietly aggressive" and learned so many of the strategies and tactics we've explored in this book.

About halfway through their deployment, the secretary of the navy, Ray Mabus, announced that he was planning to visit them. When Kyle heard the news, he told Rob, the officer in command, to keep their report simple. "We're good," he said. "We don't have to get into the weeds in our intelligence reporting or our debriefs on what we're doing over here. We can actually discuss alternative energy solutions for our camp. That noisy generator is really pissing me off lately, and I know the think tanks are working on some great solutions."

The plan was to show Secretary Mabus around the compound, introduce him to the team, and let him address the men himself. At the time, only two US Navy camps in all of Afghanistan were doing what they were doing, so Kyle and Rob figured they had it easy. *Don't do anything to stand out, keep it super simple, and relax.* That was the strategy. The secretary had been mostly a career politician, so a serious debrief would likely go over his head. They wanted to keep it light, have lunch with the boss, and enjoy an easy afternoon answering any questions he might have.

Fast-forward a couple of weeks and in comes the chopper with Secretary Mabus disembarking with his entourage. Immediately, Kyle looked over to Rob and tried to get his attention, seeing that the last person to exit the helicopter was Michael Vickers. "Oh shit, oh shit!" Kyle mouthed to Rob.

In 1980, Charlie Wilson had recruited Vickers because he was the Central Intelligence Agency's foremost subject matter expert on all things Afghanistan, and Wilson needed a better grasp of the situation. In 2012, though, Vickers was undersecretary of defense for the United States, reporting directly to Leon Panetta, who reported directly to President Barack Obama. Vickers was the brains behind the US Department of Defense's strategy in Afghanistan, a strategy that Panetta, the Central Intelligence Agency, and the secretary of defense had all been following. If you've ever seen the movie *Charlie Wilson's War*, Vickers was the nerdy-looking guy playing chess with four people at once. This was a man who was beyond intelligent, and his reputation had preceded him. You didn't want to make a mistake in front of a guy like that, and he had just stepped out of the helicopter.

As they walked to the camp, Kyle was sweating bullets, realizing that he should have prepared better. Walking over to Vickers, he introduced himself, then turned around and told one of his junior officers to run inside, grab the latest update, and ready the debrief. "Let's be prepared to get into the weeds," he said. It was no longer just the secretary of the navy who was visiting; it was also "Mike Freakin' Vickers," the guy who had been on the ground in Afghanistan for forty years. He was not someone you could BS and not someone to whom you'd want to say "I don't know."

As Rob and Kyle launched into their debrief, Vickers sat and listened intently. He didn't ask any questions; he just slowly nodded on occasion. After the meeting, Kyle walked the man around camp, and they chatted for a while before eating lunch together. As the visitors began to leave, Vickers pulled Kyle aside and gestured for him to come close. In the palm of Vickers's hand was a coin: the Undersecretary of Defense challenge coin.

Originally, challenge coins were used as forms of legitimizing an important person's position in the military, proving they had served on a particular tour or were a part of a unit. They were kind of like an old-school business card but not the kind you can print at Office Depot. These days, such coins demonstrate that a person is a member of an elite organization. Here was the guy who had spent the past forty years studying Afghan culture and unconventional warfare theory—he knew it all—and in that moment, he leaned toward Kyle and gave him his coin.

Vickers shook Kyle's hand and said, "Buck, I gotta tell you something. You guys get it. You're doing incredible work. You understand the strategy of what we're trying to do here, and you're leading the effort. You're the tip of the spear. I'm looking forward to going back to Leon Panetta and President Obama and singing your praises. Bravo. Job well done."

As it turned out, they hadn't needed to prepare anything. They hadn't needed to do anything exceptional. They had been doing it all along, building a strong and flexible team that was loosely but carefully organized around a central mission. They had developed a set of values, slogans, and rituals that had become a crucial part of their culture. And there was no replacing that. They had become a self-led team, and everyone could see the impact.

You get it, too. You've seen it not just in the examples in this book but anytime you've been part of a group in which things really came together. A group in which each person had bought into the purpose of the team and what they were all there to do. You know the thrill of taking responsibility for a mission that sounds exciting and meaningful to you, one in which you can see yourself playing a significant part in the execution of the objective. Who doesn't want to be a part of something like that?

Leadership is overrated because we've misunderstood what it is. Effective leadership no longer requires a single person at the helm for the rest of that person's life; in fact, new models for organizing teams of people demonstrate that this is not only no longer necessary—it's harmful. The future of our organizations, and therefore our world, is in looser, nimbler squads of self-led teams. It's not enough to recognize the importance of creating great cultures; we need to understand that without the agility and humility of a self-led team, we stand to repeat the past and build yet another bureaucratic institution that doesn't live up to the potential of what it could contribute.

We all understand how important it is to be part of an environment in which we feel valued and trusted. We can see how defining, developing, and sustaining such norms are important. But what do we do now? We start with the branch we're on. We take the next step, stepping up and out in whatever ways we can. We don't wait to be appointed leader because that's no longer how it works. The future of organizations is self-leadership; we're already seeing it throughout government institutions and in the business world.

The future of leadership is you. It's all of us. Every time we step up, speak up, or call attention to the way things could be better, assuming full responsibility for whatever we can, we contribute to this new model of what it means to lead. We bring a little bit of the future into the present, taking our first real step toward a culture that people will want to be a part of. When you create something like that, people are not tempted to leave and work elsewhere. In organizations in which all individuals are both empowered and rewarded for their contributions, individuals fight tooth and nail to protect that culture and reinforce it wherever they can.

And so it is with us now. We must continue to learn and grow, fighting to protect the cultures we want and looking to improve on what we do not want. We need to listen to our peers, acting with humility and agility, looking for ways to nurture the kind of experience we want to be part of. When we do this, we may without even realizing it be creating an environment in which we all can grow and thrive. No longer do the unsurprising statistics about people hating their jobs need to be true. People will recognize problems before some head honcho has to call attention to them and will rally whoever they need to solve those problems as quickly and as efficiently as possible. When they make mistakes, they will admit them openly and honestly, and the team will only get stronger as a result. They will empathize with one another, and they will regularly reinforce their rituals and rhythms because these remind everyone of their values, which they work hard to protect and preserve. They will have become a self-led team.

And from this team will come other teams when necessary. All team members will take what they've learned and, in turn, become leaders in their own right. Why? Because they've been doing it all along, perhaps without even knowing it. It's not that we don't need leadership; it's just that we've grossly misunderstood and poorly measured its impact. The whole system is being dismantled, ushering in a better way of helping human beings accomplish their goals.

Together, we can be part of the leadership renaissance we're witnessing throughout the world. This is the future of our organizations, and those of us who see it can work to help it spread. The right kind of leadership is the kind that makes everyone a leader, that respects the role of each person and expects significant contributions.

That doesn't mean we won't have managers or bosses will go away entirely. It means we will no longer have anyone to blame for our problems but ourselves. It means that soon there won't be one leader calling all the shots, and the sooner we start acting the part, the sooner we will experience the future. It's your job to change things, and the good news is you've already begun.

Bravo. Job well done. Now, let's keep going . . .

Acknowledgments

From Chris and Kyle

We want to express our most sincere appreciation and gratitude to the following people:

Our writer and editor, Jeff Goins. Jeff, this book would not have been possible without your invaluable contributions and expert guidance. From the very beginning of this project—the book proposal, down to the last citation and footnote—you helped us turn our ideas into a polished, cohesive manuscript that we are all proud of. Your passion for storytelling and dedication inspired us, and we feel so blessed to have had you as our guide and champion. Together, we have created something exceptional with this book that we hope will touch countless readers' hearts and minds. And we know it would not have been possible without your extraordinary talents and excellence. From the bottom of our hearts, thank you.

Our researcher, Michelle Neumayer. Michelle, your incredible ability to dig deep into data and find articles that back up every concept in this book has been invaluable in helping us create an authoritative and creative work. From the beginning of this project, you brought a wealth of experience, knowledge, and expertise to the table. Your dedication to detail, passion for research, and unwavering commitment to excellence helped us uncover critical insights and data we would have otherwise overlooked.

Erik Deckers, for his help with the writing process. Erik, thank you for your writing and research contributions to this book and for your help in taking all our conversations and stories and bringing some structure to them. We couldn't have done it without you!

Dr. Roger and Lori Bingham of Liberty University, thank you so much for helping us throughout this writing experience. Your tough grading and guidance have been instrumental in achieving this goal. Your dedication to helping us get organized and focused on the right things was just what we needed in moments of confusion and uncertainty over these years. Your commitment to excellence inspired us to strive for nothing but the best. Your willingness to lend an ear or support when things got off the rails was always just what we needed.

Our agent, Roger Freet, at Folio Literary Agency, thank you for the hard work, dedication, and guidance you provided throughout the publishing process. Your unwavering commitment and expertise were instrumental in securing a book deal with HarperCollins and ensuring our project was a success. Your willingness to go above and beyond, your keen insights, and your ability to answer all our questions were all essential in navigating the complex publishing landscape, and we could not have done it without you. We are forever grateful for your guidance, encouragement, and support. Thank you again for your insights and your enthusiasm.

And the HarperCollins team. Wow, we did it! And it's especially thanks to our amazing team and two special people we want to give a shout-out to: Mickey Maudlin and Chantal Tom. Mickey, we cannot thank you enough for believing in us from the beginning and taking a chance on our book. Your enthusiasm and support were infectious early on in the process, and we are so grateful for your guidance and advocacy throughout the publishing process. You truly are a publishing legend! Chantal, you were a lifesaver in helping us launch this book. Your tireless efforts, attention to detail, and commitment to making this book a success were simply incredible. And to the entire team at HarperCollins, thank you for your hard work, your creativity, and your passion for books. We are honored to have worked with such a talented group of people, and we cannot wait to see what amazing things we will accomplish together in the future. Here's to many more books, many more laughs, and many more successes. You all rock!

From Chris

I would especially like to take a moment to express my heartfelt gratitude to the following people:

My coauthor, writing partner, and best friend, Kyle Buckett. Kyle, this book would never have been possible without your contributions, insights, and unwavering support. From the very beginning of this project—starting with all those lunches at the Kensington Cafe in San Diego—you brought a wealth of experience, knowledge, and creativity to the table. Your stories and perspectives added depth and richness to our narrative, and your sense of humor and lightness of spirit helped us navigate the inevitable challenges and obstacles that we encountered along the way.

I also want to express my deepest gratitude to a group of individuals who have played an instrumental role in shaping me as a leader: Floyd Tidd, Lyndon Buckingham, Murray Cameron, Andy Brock, Rick and Kathy Norviel, Boyd and Sandi Oliver, my mother Roberta Hardy, Mark Stevens, Bill Hampton, Dave Ramsey, and Suzanne Simms.

Each of these incredible individuals has poured their time, energy, and expertise into my life or my career, and often both, selflessly guiding and mentoring me every step of the way. From the lessons they taught me to the examples they set, they have each had a profound impact on who I am today. I am forever grateful to each of these individuals and feel blessed to have had you in my corner every step of the way. Thank you for your selflessness, your generosity, and your unwavering support. I am honored to have had the opportunity to learn from each of you.

And to my family, Mindy, Cameron, and Bronwyn. Let me express my deep appreciation and gratitude for your unconditional support as I began writing a book. You have sacrificed so much to allow me to pursue my dream, and I cannot thank you enough for your unwavering love and support. Thank you for being my rock, my inspiration, and my everything. I love you all more than words can express.

Finally, I want to dedicate this book to my heavenly Father, who has been my protector and source of love throughout my life. My heartfelt prayer is that my work will be a blessing to You and Your Kingdom. My greatest aspiration is to make You proud and to hear You say, "Well done, my son." May my words inspire others to seek You, to trust You, and to find the peace that only You can give.

From Kyle

I would like to thank the following people and groups:

The SEAL teams. Thank you for all the opportunities I was afforded in my career. I am forever grateful and will never forget all I have learned from each of you along the way. You are all warriors, and I am humbled to have stood amongst you. My family and I are grateful to have men like you "Going Round Taking Names."

The fallen. Thank you for your courage. You were the great ones. Your bravery and commitment will never be forgotten.

Echo platoon. You are the standard. The example that should be measured against. It was an honor to serve you. Your professionalism, expertise, and dedication has been and will always be a great source of pride and inspiration to my family and me.

Rob Sarver. Thank you for your leadership. One of the best officers I have known, always trusting the men to get it done, while focusing on long-term strategy and initiatives. You fostered a culture of collaboration and teamwork that will live through this book. You are one heck of a leader, and it is no surprise that everyone in our platoon has gone on to have very successful careers.

Nick Miller. Thank you for your leadership and setting the example. You made it easy to be a TAC Lead. You are the man. I am still laughing thinking about our pranks. Where are my damn keys!?!

Mike Heltzel, my original skipper. I will never forget your "hardness." You are the GOAT of "hard." Your friendship and support over the years has been a constant source of strength and inspiration. Your ability to make me laugh in all situations, and your willingness to lend an ear and offer advice has been a life's joy and blessing. You have this unbelievable ability to motivate those around you and focus on what matters, no matter how cold it is! I am honored to have served alongside you. Thank you. Love ya bud, you are a dear friend and I'm grateful to have you in my life.

249: the last hard class. Enough said.

Jojo. Your wild spirit and nonconformist attitude have been an inspiration to me throughout my life. Your unique approach to life has taught me to embrace challenges and never give up on my dreams. Your unwavering support and encouragement have been invaluable, and I am grateful to have you as a friend.

Kyle Brant. Wow, we made it, pal. Never forget that day on the mountain. Thank you for your willingness to allow me to share that testimony. Your ability to analyze situations and make informed decisions have taught me to approach challenges with a more nuanced perspective. Your unwavering support and encouragement have been invaluable, and I am grateful to have you as a friend.

Dave Silverman. Thank you for your vision and strategy. Thank you for your work ethic. Thank you for showing me firsthand what a TRP CDR should look like. You have been instrumental in shaping my career. Humbled to work alongside and learn from ya!

Hans Garcia. Your unique approach to problem solving, using humor and proactive intelligence, has been an asset to me in my personal and professional life. Your ability to find creative solutions to difficult challenges has taught me to approach problems with a lighter heart and a more positive mindset. Go feed some Turkeys!

Gary Ryals. Twenty years later, still enjoying our phone calls, bud. Your ability to analyze complex situations and develop effective solutions has taught me to approach challenges with a more calculated and thoughtful approach. Your impact to SOCOM will echo for years to come. Few may know, but I am proud to be part of the few.

Rock 'n' Roll. Your wisdom and sage advice have been a guiding light in my life. Your ability to see the big picture and offer sage counsel has taught me to approach challenges with a more thoughtful and patient attitude. Your unwavering support and friendship have been a constant source of comfort and inspiration, and I am grateful to have you in my life. Thank you, bud, for your service and for always reminding me to stay grounded and focused on what truly matters.

Mike Rice. Your fearless and fierce warrior spirit has been an inspiration to me in every aspect of my life. Your unwavering commitment to excellence and determination to succeed has taught me to always push myself to be the best I can be. Your support and loyalty have been a constant source of strength, and I am grateful to have witnessed you as a leader and to have you as a friend.

Alex West. Thank you for your dedication to our veterans. What you have created with One More Wave is a true inspiration! Thousands of lives have been impacted because of what you started, and it's incredible to watch. Wow!

Walter Dittmar. Your unique approach to problem solving, using humor, and phenomenal stories, has been an asset to me in my personal and professional life. Your ability to find creative solutions to difficult challenges has taught me to approach problems with a lighter heart and a more positive mindset. Keep those dogs safe and watch out for those hawks!

Jesse Houseknecht. The best swim buddy a dude could ever have. A rock star. Very proud of your accomplishments, of course, but more important I am proud of the man you are. I know how much you care and love your family, and what they all mean to you. It is evident to all who come into contact with you and the family. I always beam with pride when I am able to tell a friend about you, and brag about ya. That will never stop.

Dave Swartz. To my ride-or-die, you have been a constant source of inspiration and joy in my life. You have been the man in the arena and have made it out alive. Through thick and thin, you have always been there for me, and your presence in my life has made a difference. Thank you for being you.

Danny Nisbet. Your wild spirit, while also having a parental care to you, has been an inspiration to me throughout my life. Those who truly know you know what I am talking about. Your unique approach to life has taught me to embrace challenges and never give up on my dreams. Your unwavering support and encouragement have been invaluable, and I am grateful to have you as a friend. Now go have a tail!

Brian Beringer. You are missed. Thank you for your discipline and guidance. I will always be grateful. I will see you again. I look forward to that reunion, my friend.

Rob Harless. Rob, your ability to analyze complex situations and develop effective solutions has taught me to approach challenges with a more calculated and thoughtful approach. Your unwavering commitment to excellence and attention to detail have been a guiding force in my life, and I am grateful to have you as a friend. Thank you for your service and for always reminding me to strive for excellence.

Boe Nankivel. You are the epitome of the ABCs. Your calm and collected demeanor in the face of adversity has been a constant source of inspiration and learning for me. Your ability to keep a level head and make sound decisions under pressure has taught me to approach challenges with a more measured and thoughtful approach. Thank you for your service to our country and for being a truly "ABC" leader.

Billy Lyman. We seriously need to surf. Stop working so hard. Your friendship and support over the years has been a constant source of strength and inspiration. Your ability to make me laugh even in the toughest situations, and your willingness to lend an ear and offer advice has been invaluable. You have this unbelievable ability to motivate those around you and it has been instrumental in many personal lives, not just mine. I am honored to have served alongside you. Thank you. Love ya bud, you are a dear friend and I'm grateful to have you in my life.

Jonathan Gumbert. Buddy, thank you. Your commitment to excellence and high standards of performance have taught me to approach challenges with a more disciplined and focused attitude. Though at times it may have been difficult to hear, your constructive criticism and leadership have played an instrumental role in my personal and professional growth. I am grateful for your mentorship and leadership, and I am honored to have served and surfed with you! We need to surf our special spot! BR surfers assemble!

Kevin Corsini. Thank you for your belief in me. Thank you for the honor you bestowed upon me. Being the recipient of a doctorate during such a tumultuous year and being honored with the opportunity to represent the organization then and now is a privilege I do not take lightly. And it was all because of you and your belief in me. Thank you.

The staff at the Department of Defense Office of Prepublication and Security Review. You have a thankless duty, but your efforts are appreciated. Thank you for all you do.

Joe Fischer. Thank you for your dedication to your teams. You truly cared, and it was visible to all around you. Thank you for your work ethic. You have been instrumental in shaping my career. Appreciate you, Joe.

Joe Musselman. Thank you for your dedication to special forces' next season of life. You have helped many lives through www.honor.org and I am proud to be a small part of it. Well done.

Jimmy Langley. Love you, buddy! Thanks for always being there for me. Seriously, you will never know what it means to me to have you as a friend.

Mickey and Marie Stonier. You continue to be a shining star example of marriage, love, and Christ. Candice and I love you both and are continually blessed by the example you set in our lives and those around you. Thank you for your love for our military and first responders, and for your dedication to providing emotional, mental, and spiritual support to those who serve our nation. You all rock.

Larry McIntosh. Larry, you are an inspiration of faith in the marketplace, and I will continue to be proud to call you one of my life's great mentors.

Miles McPherson. Thank you for showing me in my younger years how to follow the Lord's calling on your life. Staying true to Him and watching your gift of evangelism has always been an inspiration and encouragement in difficult times. Thank you.

Mike Levitt. I have learned so much from you. I appreciate your trust in me. I thank you for all your hard work, connections, and advice. Your intuition brought me tremendous value. I have found your mentorship to be invaluable, and I only hope this book inspires many, just as you have inspired me.

Michael Vickers. You will never know what that conversation meant to me. Appreciate all you have done for our nation. Thank you.

Rob Garnett. Habibi! I would like to extend a heartfelt note of gratitude to you, my dear friend and mentor. Your unwavering support, guidance, and friendship have been a constant source of inspiration and motivation in my life. As my sea daddy, your service to our country has been a testament to your courage and dedication. But your continued work in serving veterans after your career is what truly sets you apart. Your commitment to helping others has taught me to approach life with a more selfless and compassionate attitude. I am honored to call you my mentor and blessed to have you as my best friend. Thank you, buddy, for your service to our country and for always being there for me. You are my brother and my best friend. I love ya.

Mindy Mefford. Thank you for your love and support for me. I know it has taken countless hours over many years to pull this off. You are a saint. God has a special mansion ready for you.

Charlotte, Madeline, and Victor. Thank you for being my support, my inspiration, and my everything. I love you all more than words can express.

Kelsey and Des. I thank the Lord for the "FAB FOUR" all the time. You have always been there for Candice and me and make the process of life fun and easy. Our lives have paralleled in so many ways, and we are forever grateful to the parents and the aunt and uncle you have become to our children and yours.

Eddie and Jen. Thank you for raising an amazing woman. Wow, you did good. I pray that Candice and I do as well with our daughters. God bless you.

Chris Mefford. I would like to take a moment to express my heartfelt gratitude to my coauthor, writing partner, and one of my best friends, Chris. You were there offering your support, encouragement, and wisdom whenever I needed it. Your generosity of spirit and kindness of heart has inspired me, and I feel so blessed to have you as my writing partner and friend.

Mom and Dad. I would like to express a special note of gratitude to my parents, Bill and Connie, for their unwavering love, support, and guidance throughout my life. Their commitment to each other and to God has been a shining example of what a great marriage and parenting looks like. Their dedication to our family and their tireless efforts to provide for us have been a constant source of inspiration and motivation in my life. They have taught me the value of hard work, perseverance, and unconditional love, and for that, I am forever grateful. Thank you, Mom and Dad.

Candice Buckett. Your love, encouragement, and patience have been a constant source of strength and inspiration for me throughout this process. I know it has taken countless hours over many years to pull this off, and I am truly grateful for your understanding and support. You have sacrificed so much to allow me to pursue many of my dreams, not just this one. I cannot thank you enough for your unwavering love and support. Thank you for being my rock, my inspiration, and my everything. I love you all more than words can express. You are truly my Proverbs 31 woman. I love you with everything I have. Thank you.

God. To my heavenly Father, who has loved me and protected me my entire life. My prayer is that I would be a blessing to You, to Your Kingdom, and that You would be proud to call me Your son. I love You.

Bibliography

Adkins, Amy. "Only 35% of U.S. Managers Are Engaged in Their Jobs." Gallup, April 2, 2015. https://www.gallup.com/workplace/236552/managers-engaged-jobs.aspx.

"Arnar Bill Gunnarsson (KSÍ): How to Produce a Golden Generation." *Duke*, accessed March 29, 2023. https://www.duke.lu/ksi.

Arnason, Arnar. Interview in "The Secret Strength of Iceland Football." Urban Soccer Park, accessed March 29, 2023. https://www.urbansoccerpark.com/iceland.

Bahcall, Safi. *Loonshots: How to Nurture the Crazy Ideas That Win Wars, Cure Diseases, and Transform Industries*. New York: St. Martin's Press, 2019.

Bryant, Adam, and Kevin Sharer. "Are You Really Listening?" *Harvard Business Review*, March–April 2021. https://hbr.org/2021/03/are-you-really-listening.

Businessolver. "2017 Workplace Empathy Monitor." 2017. https://info.businessolver.com/hubfs/businessolver-2017-empathy-monitor.pdf.

Cable, Daniel M. "Humble Leadership and Employees' Seeking Systems." Chap. 7 in *Alive at Work: The Neuroscience of Helping Your People Love What They Do*. Boston: Harvard Business Review Press, 2019. http://dan-cable.com/wp-content/uploads/2019/03/Alive-at-Work-chapter-7.pdf.

Campbell, Jeff. "Pushing Forward with Jeff Campbell." Interview by Kyle Buckett and Chris Mefford. *CultureForce*, September 2020. Audio, https://open.spotify.com/episode/7j8FajVNkSvcQBTCJejR5t?si=837750ef0a9b4ab4&nd=1.

Catmull, Ed, and Amy Wallace. *Creativity, Inc.: Overcoming the Unseen Forces That Stand in the Way of True Inspiration*. New York: Random House, 2014.

Clear, James. *Atomic Habits: Tiny Changes, Remarkable Results; An Easy & Proven Way to Build Good Habits & Break Bad Ones*. New York: Avery, 2018.

Clifton, Jim. "Why We Hate Our Jobs—and How We Can Learn to Love Work Again." Op-ed. *Fiscal Times*, June 15, 2017. https://www.thefiscaltimes.com/Columns/2017/06/15/Why-We-Hate-Our-Jobs-And-How-We-Can-Learn-Love-Work-Again.

Clifton, Jim. "The World's Broken Workplace." Gallup, June 13, 2017. https://news.gallup.com/opinion/chairman/212045/world-broken-workplace.aspx.

Cody, Jim. "Self-Directed Work Teams Are More Productive." LinkedIn, February 24, 2016. https://www.linkedin.com/pulse/self-directed-work-teams-more-productive-jim-cody.

Collins, Jim. *How the Mighty Fall: And Why Some Companies Never Give In*. New York: HarperCollins, 2009.

Cook, Frederick A. *Through the First Antarctic Night, 1898–1899: A Narrative of the Voyage of the "Belgica" Among Newly Discovered Lands and over an Unknown Sea About the South Pole*. Cambridge: Cambridge University Press, 2015.

Cool Antarctica. "Adrien de Gerlache—Belgica Belgian Antarctic Expedition 1897–1899." https://www.coolantarctica.com/Antarctica%20fact%20file/History/antarctic_whos _who_belgica.php.

Curtin, Melanie B. "Employees Who Feel Heard Are 4.6x More Likely to Feel Empowered to Do Their Best Work." *Inc.*, September 5, 2019. https://www.inc.com /melanie-curtin/employees-who-feel-heard-are-46x-more-likely-to-feel-empowered -to-do-their-best-work.html.

Dagbo, Jeff, and Sam Acuna. "Company Culture: Private Equity's Intangible Value Creation Lever." Gallup, August 13, 2020. https://www.gallup.com/workplace/316883 /company-culture-private-equity-intangible-value-creation-lever.aspx.

Dalio, Ray. *Principles: Life and Work*. New York: Simon & Schuster, 2017.

Dees, Jared. "How a Series of Blog Posts Turned into a Multi-million Dollar Bestseller." Medium, January 2, 2017. https://medium.com/artist-life/andy-weir-martian-3fde 9447f763.

de Haaff, Brian. "It Costs $3,000 to Onboard New Employees—Here Is Why It Is Worth It." LinkedIn, February 14, 2019. https://www.linkedin.com/pulse/costs-3000-on board-new-employees-here-why-worth-brian-de-haaff.

Deloitte. "2020 Deloitte Global Human Capital Trends for Tech, Media, and Telecom." https://www2.deloitte.com/us/en/insights/focus/human-capital-trends/2020.html.

Deloitte. "2021 Global Human Capital Trends." https://www2.deloitte.com/content /dam/insights/us/articles/6935_2021-HC-Trends/di_human-capital-trends.pdf.

Discprofile.com. "What Is DiSC?" Accessed March 29, 2023. https://www.discprofile .com/what-is-disc.

Duffy, Kate. "An Amazon Driver Was Told She Would Be Fired If She Stopped Delivering Packages During Tornado Warnings: Report." *Business Insider*, December 17, 2021. https://www.businessinsider.com/amazon-driver-illinois-tornado-keep-delivering-lose -job-return-warehouse-2021-12.

Edmondson, Amy C. *Teaming: How Organizations Learn, Innovate, and Compete in the Knowledge Economy*. San Francisco: Jossey-Bass, 2012.

Eskildsen, Stephen. *The Teachings and Practices of the Early Quanzhen Taoist Masters*. Albany: State University of New York Press, 2004.

Eyre, Hermione. "James Daunt: The Man Who Saved Waterstones." *ES Magazine*, December 11, 2014. https://www.standard.co.uk/esmagazine/james-daunt-the-man-who -saved-waterstones-9913047.html.

Fahey, Sean. "The Real Cost of Bad Hiring Decisions (and How to Avoid Making Them)." *Forbes*, March 10, 2022. https://www.forbes.com/sites/forbeshumanresources council/2022/03/10/the-real-cost-of-bad-hiring-decisions-and-how-to-avoid -making-them/?sh=1a5686c25dac.

Ferguson, Donna. "The Secret of How Amundsen Beat Scott in Race to South Pole? A Diet of Raw Penguin." *The Guardian*, May 16, 2021. https://www.theguardian.com /environment/2021/may/16/the-secret-of-how-amundsen-beat-scott-in-race-to -south-pole-a-diet-of-raw-penguin.

Fortune. "Six Teams That Changed the World." CNN Money, May 31, 2006. https://money .cnn.com/2006/05/31/magazines/fortune/sixteams_greatteams_fortune_061206 /index.htm.

Gallup. "State of the American Manager." https://www.gallup.com/services/182138/state-american-manager.aspx.

Gatollari, Mustafa. "Jeff Bliss Went Viral for Telling off a 'Lazy' Teacher, Here's What He's Doing Now." Distractify, April 2, 2023. https://www.distractify.com/p/what-happened-to-jeff-bliss.

Gentry, William A., Todd J. Weber, and Golnaz Sadri. "Empathy in the Workplace: A Tool for Effective Leadership." Center for Creative Leadership. White paper, November 2011, reprinted February 2016. https://cclinnovation.org/wp-content/uploads/2020/03/empathyintheworkplace.pdf.

Godin, Seth. *Tribes: We Need You to Lead Us.* New York: Portfolio, 2008.

Hall, Rick. *The Man from Muscle Shoals: My Journey from Shame to Fame.* Monterey, CA: Heritage Builders, 2015.

Halldorsson, Vidar. *Sport in Iceland: How Small Nations Achieve International Success.* London: Routledge, 2017.

Harvard Business Review Analytic Services. "The Impact of Employee Engagement on Performance." September 13, 2013. https://hbr.org/resources/pdfs/comm/achievers/hbr_achievers_report_sep13.pdf.

Hertzfeld, Andy. "The Original Macintosh: Pirate Flag." Folklore.org, August 1983. https://www.folklore.org/StoryView.py?story=Pirate_Flag.txt.

Hyken, Shep. "A $600 Billion Employee Engagement Problem Solved: Empathy." *Forbes*, February 25, 2018. https://www.forbes.com/sites/shephyken/2018/02/25/a-600-billion-employee-engagement-problem-solved-empathy/?sh=5c65f153b1a3.

Ipsos. "Public Survey Findings and Methodology: Workers Agree, a Sense of Belonging at Work Boosts Productivity." January 24, 2022. https://www.ipsos.com/sites/default/files/ct/news/documents/2022-01/Belonging2022topline_writeup_FINAL_v2_012022.pdf.

"Jeff Bliss, a High School Student, Gives a Lesson to His Teacher at Duncanville." May 9, 2013. YouTube video, 1:26. https://www.youtube.com/watch?v=8jsUj4DqWfU.

Kantor, Jodi, and David Streitfeld. "Inside Amazon: Wrestling Big Ideas in a Bruising Workplace." *New York Times*, August 15, 2015. https://www.nytimes.com/2015/08/16/technology/inside-amazon-wrestling-big-ideas-in-a-bruising-workplace.html.

Kaplan, Marc, Ben Dollar, Yves Van Durme, and 王大威. "Shape Culture: Drive Strategy." *Deloitte Insights*, February 29, 2016. https://www2.deloitte.com/us/en/insights/focus/human-capital-trends/2016/impact-of-culture-on-business-strategy.html/#endnote-8.

Kim, Eugene. "Bill Gates' Worst Decisions as CEO, According to a Longtime Microsoft Exec." *Business Insider*, April 23, 2016. https://www.businessinsider.com/bill-gates-worst-decisions-as-ceo-2016-4.

Le Phan, Linda. "25 Business Leaders Share Their Own Definition for 'Company Culture' (and Why It Matters)." Medium, March 31, 2017. https://medium.com/@linda.lephan/25-business-leaders-share-their-own-definition-for-company-culture-and-why-it-matters-13fa282e5b.

Maule, Tex. "Masters of Endurance." *Sports Illustrated*, February 22, 1960. https://vault.si.com/vault/1960/02/22/masters-of-endurance.

McChrystal, Stanley, Tantum Collins, David Silverman, and Chris Fussell. *Team of Teams: New Rules of Engagement for a Complex World.* New York: Portfolio/Penguin, 2015.

McDowell, Tiffany, Don Miller, Tsutomu Okamoto, and Trevor Page. "Organizational Design: The Rise of Teams." *Deloitte Insights*, March 1, 2016. https://www2.deloitte.com/us/en/insights/focus/human-capital-trends/2016/organizational-models-network-of-teams.html.

Medici, Andy. "There's a Cost to Keeping Bad Bosses Around—and It's Rising." *Dallas Business Journal*, February 22, 2022. https://www.bizjournals.com/dallas/news/2022/02/22/workers-hate-boss-price-retention-recruitment.html.

Miller, John G. *QBQ! The Question Behind the Question: Practicing Personal Accountability in Work and in Life*. New York: TarcherPerigee, 2016.

Moore, Kenny. *Bowerman and the Men of Oregon: The Story of Oregon's Legendary Coach and Nike's Cofounder*. Emmaus, PA: Rodale, 2006.

Morantz, Alan. "The Trouble with Self-Managing Teams." Smith School of Business, Queen's University, January 30, 2020. https://smith.queensu.ca/insight/content/the-trouble-with-self-managing-teams.php.

Muggeridge, Malcolm. *Something Beautiful for God*. New York: Harper & Row, 1971.

Nink, Marco. "Many Employees Don't Know What's Expected of Them at Work." *Gallup Business Journal*, October 13, 2015. https://news.gallup.com/businessjournal/186164/employees-don-know-expected-work.aspx.

Novak, David. "Recognizing Employees Is the Simplest Way to Improve Morale." *Harvard Business Review*, May 9, 2016. https://hbr.org/2016/05/recognizing-employees-is-the-simplest-way-to-improve-morale?zd_source=hrt&zd_campaign=5503&zd_term=chiradeepbasumallick.

O'Reilly, Charles A. III, Bernadette Doerr, David F. Caldwell, and Jennifer A. Chatman. "Narcissistic CEOs and Executive Compensation." *Leadership Quarterly* 25, no. 2 (April 2014): 218–231. https://doi.org/10.1016/j.leaqua.2013.08.002.

Pendell, Ryan. "Tomorrow Half Your Company Is Quitting (So Win Them Back)." Gallup, December 4, 2017. https://www.gallup.com/workplace/236216/tomorrow-half-company-quitting-win-back.aspx.

Pendell, Ryan. "The World's $7.8 Trillion Workplace Problem." Gallup, June 14, 2022. https://www.gallup.com/workplace/393497/world-trillion-workplace-problem.aspx.

Peters, Thomas J., and Robert H. Waterman Jr. *In Search of Excellence: Lessons from America's Best-Run Companies*. New York: Warner Books, 1982.

Puryear, Edgar F. Jr. *Nineteen Stars: A Study in Military Character and Leadership*. Orange, VA: Green, 1971.

Ronay, Barney. "Football, Fire and Ice: The Inside Story of Iceland's Remarkable Rise." *The Guardian*, June 8, 2016. https://www.theguardian.com/football/2016/jun/08/iceland-stunning-rise-euro-2016-gylfi-sigurdsson-lars-lagerback.

Sancton, Julian. *Madhouse at the End of the Earth: The Belgica's Journey into the Dark Antarctic Night*. New York: Crown, 2021.

Satell, Greg. "This Famous General Says We Need to Redefine Leadership." *Inc.*, November 18, 2018. https://www.inc.com/greg-satell/general-stanley-mcchrystals-new-book-explodes-myths-of-leadership.html.

Scaled Agile. "Case Study: LEGO Digital Solutions." © 2010–2013 Scaled Agile, Inc. Updated January 2017. https://www.scaledagileframework.com/lego-case-study/.

Schawbel, Dan. "Richard Branson's Three Most Important Leadership Principles." *Forbes*, September 23, 2014. https://www.forbes.com/sites/danschawbel/2014/09/23/richard-branson-his-3-most-important-leadership-principles/?sh=2f79ed553d50.

Shanahan, Rae. "One Word Is the Solution to America's $600 Billion Productivity Drain." *Businessolver Blog*, May 18, 2017. https://blog.businessolver.com/1-word-is-the-solution-to-americas-600-billion-productivity-drain.

Spink, Kathryn. *Mother Teresa: An Authorized Biography*. Revised and updated. New York: HarperOne, 2011.

Sull, Donald, Charles Sull, and Ben Zweig. "Toxic Culture Is Driving the Great Resignation." *MIT Sloan Management Review*, January 11, 2022. https://sloanreview.mit.edu/article/toxic-culture-is-driving-the-great-resignation/.

Surowiecki, James. *The Wisdom of Crowds: Why the Many Are Smarter than the Few and How Collective Wisdom Shapes Business, Economies, Societies, and Nations*. New York: Doubleday, 2004.

Taylor, Bill. "Why Zappos Pays New Employees to Quit—and You Should Too." *Harvard Business Review*, May 19, 2008. https://hbr.org/2008/05/why-zappos-pays-new-employees.

Taylor, David. "The Day Aretha Franklin Found Her Sound—and a Bunch of Men Nearly Killed It." *The Guardian*, August 19, 2018. https://www.theguardian.com/music/2018/aug/19/aretha-franklin-fame-studios-muscle-shoals-1967-rick-hall.

Thomas, Ron. "$24 Billion Worth of Leadership Training and What Do We Get?" TLNT, December 12, 2017. https://www.tlnt.com/24-billion-worth-of-leadership-training-and-what-do-we-get/.

Trickle. "What's the Link Between Empathy and Productivity?" Blog post, July 15, 2021. https://trickle.works/blog/whats-the-link-between-empathy-and-productivity/.

"Tryouts for USA Team." May 25, 2010. YouTube video, 2:20. https://www.youtube.com/watch?v=J0nZh9o65nE.

Warren, Christina. "Here's Why Apple Is Flying a Pirate Flag to Celebrate Its 40th Anniversary." Mashable, April 1, 2016. https://mashable.com/article/apple-pirate-flag-40th-anniversary.

Well, The. "The Cost of Replacing an Employee and the Role of Financial Wellness." January 15, 2023. https://www.enrich.org/blog/The-true-cost-of-employee-turnover-financial-wellness-enrich.

"What Happened to Jeff Bliss?" Reddit post, 2018. https://www.reddit.com/r/whicharetheynow/comments/9vgxx0/what_happened_to_jeff_bliss/.

Wooden, John, and Steve Jamison. *Wooden on Leadership: How to Create a Winning Organization*. New York: McGraw-Hill, 2005.